"Too often, bad policy or procedure continu[...] following the rules. In *Cage-Busting Leaders[...]* beyond what's always been done and to go fc[...] until proven otherwise. He offers concrete examples of successfully challenging the status quo in service to student learning."

—**Maddie Fennell, 2007 Nebraska Teacher of the Year**

"If you believe that changing America's schools requires not just a new way of thinking, but a new way of doing, then this is the book for you. Hess illuminates how we often—and unwittingly—tie our own hands in the course of attempting to make reform, thereby perpetuating a 'culture of can't.' Then, with straight talk and pithy examples, he shows how school, system, and state leaders can take the kinds of creative action essential to bringing about fierce change. This is a book that leaders and reformers need to read, reread, and then keep, dog-eared and readily at hand."

—**Monica Higgins, professor,**
Harvard Graduate School of Education

"Rick Hess could not be more spot-on in his characterization of education leaders (and by this I mean any practitioner choosing to lead) as 'caged.' But the key insight is not that cages are created by regulations, laws, contracts, policies, or certification rules; rather, it's that educators 'cage' themselves. This realization is the essence of the book and its examples—and it is the essence of understanding leadership and change."

—**Robert C. Pianta, Novartis Professor of Education, and dean,**
Curry School of Education, University of Virginia, and director,
Center for Advanced Study of Teaching and Learning

"Large organizations exhibit tremendous inertia toward the comfortable. Rick Hess argues in forthright and bold fashion that transformative leaders are not 'cage dwellers': they don't build their own prisons. Instead, they fight the inertia through clear thinking, solid execution, and bold goals. Cage-busting leaders can easily and quickly move from 30,000 feet to the granular, and they don't spend time staring at their feet. *Cage-Busting Leadership* is a great tool for urban school superintendents who are often weighed and overburdened by massive bureaucracies and oppressive regulations that stifle creativity. Let's do what it takes to break out of these cages."

—**Jean-Claude Brizard, former CEO, Chicago Public Schools**

THE EDUCATIONAL INNOVATIONS SERIES

The Educational Innovations series explores a wide range of current school reform efforts. Individual volumes examine entrepreneurial efforts and unorthodox approaches, highlighting reforms that have met with success and strategies that have attracted widespread attention. The series aims to disrupt the status quo and inject new ideas into contemporary education debates.

Series edited by Frederick M. Hess

Other books in this series:

The Strategic Management of Charter Schools
by Peter Frumkin, Bruno V. Manno, and Nell Edgington

Customized Schooling
Edited by Frederick M. Hess and Bruno V. Manno

Bringing School Reform to Scale
by Heather Zavadsky

What Next?
Edited by Mary Cullinane and Frederick M. Hess

Between Public and Private
Edited by Katrina E. Bulkley, Jeffrey R. Henig, and Henry M. Levin

Stretching the School Dollar
Edited by Frederick M. Hess and Eric Osberg

School Turnarounds: The Essential Role of Districts
by Heather Zavadsky

Praise for *Cage-Busting Leadership*

"Impassioned leaders throughout our education system are frustrated by routine and a lack of support. In many cases they are ill-equipped for their crucial work. Rick Hess is a trailblazing scholar who explores a path forward to help leaders break the status quo."

—Michael F. Bennet, Colorado senator, and former superintendent, Denver Public Schools

"This is not just a how-to manual—it is a why-not manifesto. If you can't lead by fighting for the rights of youth, then you should not lead. This book both affirms this credo and indicates many ways in which to achieve this obligation."

—John E. Deasy, superintendent, Los Angeles Unified School District

"Rick Hess raises the bar by challenging leaders to aim for specific education reforms, and he eliminates the most common excuses for mediocre systems by proving that most barriers can and have been overcome already."

—Elizabeth Celania-Fagen, superintendent, Douglas County School District

"When someone decides that it is time to bust out of his or her cage, that person discovers that the bars around the cage are those things that resist real reform. In guiding us out of our cages, Rick Hess indicates how not to RTB (roll the boulder) or fall into TMT (the MacGyver Trap). Once out of the cage, be sure to GGD (get going downhill) and always ask WPAYS (what problem are you solving)? Sound like a great read? It is!"

—Janet Barresi, state superintendent of public instruction, Oklahoma

"In *Cage-Busting Leadership*, Rick Hess outlines a practical, no-excuses guide to problem solving and leadership. Hess tells stories from current education leaders, movies, history, and other authors to give flavor and substance to what is possible when cage-busting leaders push past the limits of 'past practice' and compliance-normed behavior to renew their organizations. In the REEP leadership programs, we find that when a leader can identify where the bars are, he or she will not be content to dwell in the cage."

—Andrea Hodge, executive director, Rice University Education Entrepreneurship Program (REEP)

"Public school and district leaders are mired in rules, regulations, and red tape, and Rick Hess doesn't like it. But rather than complain, he's hell-bent on helping leaders get done the things they need to do despite the challenges. This book provides valuable, concrete suggestions for accomplishing precisely that. Leaders should read it and start to breathe again."

—Joel Klein, former chancellor of the New York City Department of Education, and executive vice president, News Corporation

"We in education are master cage builders. The feds build cages for the states, the states do it to districts, and the school boards do it in turn to their principals. At each level linger bureaucrats, advocates, union leaders, and vendors, each figuring out how to build a perfect cage to suit their needs. The problem is that the cage of pro forma rules and regulations won't do if we're to help children and families—especially those with the greatest and most complex needs—solve the complicated problem of equipping themselves for a productive life in today's economy. Rick Hess tells it like it is: if we're serious about educating kids, we'd be more serious about busting down the cage door."

—John White, superintendent, Louisiana Department of Education

"With *Cage-Busting Leadership*, Hess pulls the subject of educational leadership out of the ivory tower and drags it through the reality of leading school systems, teachers, parents, and children. Hess makes a strong case that an educational leader's success will be in large part determined by the effective deployment of talent, tools, time, and money. But what is most striking is Hess's argument that education leaders have much more freedom in these areas than most imagined. The cage-busting leaders that Hess chronicles combine noble visions with ferocious tactics, and they set the bar for what the next generation of leaders will need to achieve if we are serious about radically improving our nation's educational system. For educational leaders looking for real-world advice on how to best fight for students, this is your book."

—Neerav Kingsland, CEO, New Schools for New Orleans

"It's easy to underestimate the effort it takes to overcome inertia. In *Cage-Busting Leadership*, Rick has illustrated the tools and skills that are essential for transforming the status quo. Leaders who hope to improve low-performing schools and districts will value the insights this volume provides."

—Mitchell Chester, commissioner of elementary and secondary education, Massachusetts, and president, Council of Chief State School Officers

Cage-Busting Leadership

Frederick M. Hess

HARVARD EDUCATION PRESS
CAMBRIDGE, MASSACHUSETTS

Second Printing, 2013

Library of Congress Control Number 2012947126

Paperback ISBN 978-1-61250-506-0
Library Edition ISBN 978-1-61250-507-7

Published by Harvard Education Press,
an imprint of the Harvard Education Publishing Group

Harvard Education Press
8 Story Street
Cambridge, MA 02138

Cover Design: Sarah Henderson

The typefaces used in this book are Minion Pro and Helvetica Neue.

For my grandma, Edythe Rosenzwog,
a natural-born cage-buster if ever there was one,
and for Joleen, who proves an attorney can be
soft-spoken, sweet, and still a lethal consigliere.

Contents

PREFACE

Before We Get Started

THE PREMISE OF *Cage-Busting Leadership* is simple. I believe that two things are true. It is true, as would-be reformers often argue, that statutes, policies, rules, regulations, contracts, and case law make it tougher than it should be for school and system leaders to drive improvement and, well, lead. However, it is also the case that leaders have far more freedom to transform, reimagine, and invigorate teaching, learning, and schooling than is widely believed.

The problem is that in selecting, training, socializing, and mentoring leaders, we have unwittingly encouraged *caged* leadership. You need only to talk to school and system leaders or school board members, observe education leadership courses, or read texts by education leadership icons to understand that leaders are expected to succeed via culture, capacity building, coaching, and consensus—no matter the obstacles in their path. Indeed, talking about how to address or trample those obstacles is typically dismissed by leading thinkers on ed leadership as a distraction.

Now, let me be really clear: instructional leadership, strong cultures, stakeholder buy-in, and professional practice are all good things. The mistake is to imagine that leaders can foster these things successfully or sustainably without addressing the obstacles posed by regulations, rules, and routines.

Meanwhile, the sloganeering and anti-union broadsides launched by impassioned reformers too often blame unions and contracts for all manner of ills, even as they excuse timid, lethargic leadership. This can lead would-be reformers to talk, and to act, as if changes to contracts and policy are self-executing and to underinvest in helping leaders take advantage of reforms. The result: progress is expensive, grudging, and uneven; and when heroic leaders move on, much of their personality-infused success evaporates.

Consider today's efforts to boost teacher quality. We hear a lot about what leaders can't do when it comes to staffing, incentive pay, dismissals, and so on. Much of this is valid. But it's also the case that leaders can do a lot more than is sometimes thought. For example, when John Deasy, now superintendent of Los Angeles's public school system, was superintendent of Prince George's County, Maryland, he transferred hundreds of teachers to new schools and initiated a pay-for-performance system despite the assumption that these moves weren't possible under the collective bargaining agreement (CBA). When asked how he managed this, Deasy's answer was simple: "Nothing prohibited any of this."

Deasy is the exception, not the rule. Indeed, after studying Massachusetts collective bargaining agreements, Vanderbilt professor Dale Ballou observed, "On virtually every issue of personnel policy, there are contracts that grant administrators the managerial prerogatives they are commonly thought to lack. When more flexible language is negotiated, administrators do not take advantage of it [but still] blame the contract for their own inaction."[1] Even charter schools, supposedly besotted with autonomy, frequently choose to dwell in the cage. Legal analyst Mitch Price, of the Center on Reinventing Public Education, has concluded that, given their freedom to craft new "agreements from scratch," charters are "not as innovative as they might be" when it comes to areas like evaluation, staffing, and compensation.[2]

Across the country, I inevitably encounter folks who have cage-dwelling horror stories about getting penned in by rules, regulations, policies, and statutes; and others who have cage-busting stories about finding ways to escape or explode those constraints. This is a book that draws from all of those stories to help current and aspiring leaders understand what the cage looks like, how to bust it, and how to help cultivate and sustain powerful cultures of teaching and learning that are equal to their ambitions.

A few years back, former Columbia University Teachers College president Arthur Levine sketched a sprawling but fairly accurate job description for today's K–12 leaders:

> Principals and superintendents no longer serve primarily as supervisors. They are being called on to lead in the redesign of their schools and school systems. In an outcome-based and accountability-driven era, administrators have to lead their schools in the rethinking of goals, priorities, finances, staffing, curriculum, pedagogies, learning resources, assessment methods, technology, and use of time and space. They have to recruit and retain top staff members and educate newcomers and veterans alike to understand and become comfortable with an education system undergoing dramatic and continuing change . . . Few of today's 250,000 school leaders are prepared to carry out this agenda.[3]

We have done a poor job of equipping leaders to address these challenges; squeeze the most value out of scarce funds; or to make the fullest use of twenty-first-century talent, tools, and technology. *Cage-Busting Leadership* is one modest attempt to help us do better.

WHY ME?

Why am I writing this book? After all, let's be clear: I've never been a school leader, district official, school board member, or state chief, and I've spent relatively little time working in schools or school systems. Instead, I'm an academic who has visited, studied, and supported a raft of school improvement efforts across the nation.

The funny thing is that those who have spent their career immersed in the rhythms of any profession come to regard its policies, practices, culture, and routines as givens. In K–12, where most leaders started as classroom teachers and have spent their professional lives in schools and school systems, there's a natural insularity. That worldview is reflected in the writing on education leadership and how we train leaders.

Now, I've spent a lot of time in and around education schools, school systems, and leadership preparation programs. I've taught aspiring leaders at the University of Pennsylvania and Rice University and education policy at Harvard, Georgetown, and the University of Virginia. I've advised and addressed school and system leaders, teachers, policymakers, turn-around teams, business leaders, and philanthropists. I've consulted with district leaders and new providers. I've studied the content of education leadership. And from it all, I've concluded that much of the blame for the caged state of education leadership is what leaders do and don't learn from the experts who teach, mentor, and train them.

These experts offer much that is of value. But they also leave out much of equal import, and can unwittingly encourage a limiting, caged version of leadership. This is a book intended to complement the more familiar advice. It focuses on subjects, like regulations and contracts, that get short shrift in most ed leadership preparation. It argues that culture and in-structional expertise are critical, but that these are things that follow from hard-nosed decisions and a willingness to bust the cage.

My arm's-length remove from K–12 imposes certain limitations, but also affords me the opportunity to view the forest differently than those more immersed in the trees. This allows me to challenge norms that K–12 veterans may take for granted, ask harsh-sounding questions that tradi-tional ed leadership scholars are disinclined to raise, and draw comfort-ably on comparisons and illustrations from outside K–12 that are anath-ema to most in the space.

WHO *CAGE-BUSTING LEADERSHIP* IS FOR AND HOW IT SHOULD BE READ

Before we get started, let me just say a final word about who this book is for and how it should be read.

While I penned this book with school and system leaders in mind, my experience is that most of what follows will prove useful not just for current and aspiring school and system leaders, but also for school board members, state leaders, those aiding school systems with HR or IT or instruction or accounting or operations, foundation officials, and many others.

Readers will note that the first half of the book is mostly about the basic tenets of cage-busting: why it's necessary, how to think about it, and what the cage looks like. These chapters tend to explain the cage and how to think like a cage-buster.

Starting with chapter 5, we flip the script. The second half is really about how leaders can start to think differently about using talent, tools, time, and money. The chapters offer strategies for slipping through, whittling, or blasting many of the bars that stand in their way and suggestions for handling the practical and political challenges that result. These chapters are about finding ways to serve students to the very best of your ability. That's not just good for our kids and our nation, it's also the secret to schools and systems that are fun, empowering, and energizing. With that, let's get started.

1

It Doesn't Have to Be This Hard

"So I was sitting in my cubicle today, and I realized, ever since I started working, every single day of my life has been worse than the day before it. So that means that every single day that you see me, that's on the worst day of my life."

—PETER GIBBONS, *Office Space*[1]

"Never doubt that a small group of thoughtful, committed citizens can change the world. Indeed, it is the only thing that ever has."

—MARGARET MEAD

IN GREEK MYTH, Sisyphus was a villainous king who murdered travelers and guests. The gods were not amused. As punishment, they condemned him to spend eternity rolling a boulder up a mountain. The nasty twist: every time he got halfway up, the boulder would slide down . . . and he'd begin again.

For those struggling to improve schools, Sisyphus's tale holds an uncanny resonance. It's long struck me that Sisyphus—with his promising starts and recurring disappointments—could be the poster child for a half-century of school reform.

I've often thought that if educational experts and reformers were gathered at the base of the mountain, watching Sisyphus climb, we wouldn't lack advice. We'd yell, "Widen your grip a little!" "Try a different pair of hiking boots!" "Stop for a rest every twenty feet!" Well, we wouldn't use exactly those words. Instead, we'd advise him to use "differentiated instruction," "formative assessment," "data-based decision-making," "extended learning time," or any number of ideas every bit as good and sensible as better boots and a firmer grip.

However useful, all this advice would suffer a common flaw. If the past is prologue, I've a strong suspicion that we wouldn't bother to mention our hero's primary dilemma—that he's trying to roll a boulder *up a mountain!*

In schooling, we've had exquisite success finding ways to talk around the mountain. We offer technical advice. We call for consensus. We devise jargon-laden strategies. What we rarely do is observe that we're asking educators to roll a boulder up a mountain or ask what might be done about it.

What "mountain" do I have in mind?

Ann Bonitatibus, associate superintendent of Maryland's Frederick County Public Schools, relates that "in March or April, our individual schools have anywhere from a quarter to a third of their budget remaining. They consequently go on a spending spree, buying paper, Post-it Notes, copier machines, and other items not critical to instruction. They have a fear—'If I give the money back, I'll never get money in the future.' And I try to tell them, 'No, if you give your money back, that's end-of-year money we could use for systemic needs.' But they continue to make wishlist purchases for the adults, which have no connection to student needs." *That's the mountain*—having to plead with school leaders to spend scarce dollars responsibly.

While serving as chancellor in Washington, DC, Michelle Rhee was a polarizing presence. One of her less controversial moves, however, involved making it easier for parents to know if their children were actually showing up for school. When Rhee became chancellor, the paper chain and balky routines meant that it took more than a week for a parent to know whether his or her child had attended school on a given day. Seeking to speed things up, Rhee's staff figured teachers could start taking attendance on laptops. This would permit the data to be processed and posted the same day. The problem: the Washington Teachers Union (WTU) acknowledged that taking attendance was a permissible work duty, but protested that the collective bargaining agreement prohibited the district from requiring teachers to do "data entry." Ultimately it took months of negotiations to launch a pilot effort in a handful of schools. *That's the mountain*—spending time and energy winning permission to make minor tweaks to established routines.

Former Detroit Public Schools emergency financial manager Robert Bobb thought it important to shift resources into boosting early elementary literacy. Yet when he tried to use Title I dollars for early literacy assessment and instruction, the Michigan Department of Education told him: "No way." The problem? The state said that Bobb's plan violated federal Title I guidelines around "supplement, not supplant." When the district reached out to the US Department of Education, they said that the plan seemed fine. But it's the state agency that makes these decisions. *That's the mountain*—long-established routines that smother creative problem solving.

In Clark County, Nevada, a principal sought to contract out custodial duties and steer more dollars to instruction. The district, however, tracked staff performance by calculating number of custodians employed per square foot. The result: there was no way to opt for any alternative arrangement—or even to gauge whether a school was clean or custodial dollars were being spent efficiently. Frustrated, the principal gave up. Clark County academic manager Jeremy Hauser wryly observes, "That kind of thing has been fairly common in my experience." *That's the mountain*—rigid practices and input-driven metrics that make it tough to spend dollars more wisely.

The mountain is federal program requirements that make it hard to reassign staff or redesign schools, and state regulations that supersize federal rules around Title I or IDEA. It's rigid schedules that prevent teacher leaders from holding team meetings. It's contract provisions that dictate school start times. It's professional development arrangements that tie the hands of principals who want to provide training or support to the teachers who need it, when they need it. It's paperwork that forces staff to spend hundreds of hours a year filling out forms and mandates that require districts to file the same data multiple times in order to qualify for education funds,

Workforce Investment Act funds, or Medicaid reimbursements. In short, it's the accumulated rules and regulations, policies and practices, contracts and cultures that exhaust educators and leaders.

Yet, when it comes to school reform, we have a remarkable ability to look past the mountain. Instead, we wax enthusiastic about new interventions—block scheduling or site-based management, peer mentoring or extended learning time—which work in a few locations but don't "scale." Disappointed, we scratch our heads, agonize about what we did wrong, and then chalk it up to "flawed implementation."

The mountain means that leaders are constantly sweating their way uphill. Sometimes they succeed, for a day or a season, but when they tire, the boulder rolls back. The mountain requires educational leaders to spend most their time asking permission or battling to change old routines—leaving them to tackle the important work, the transformative work, with only the dregs of their attention and energy.

Sisyphus's grip may well be too narrow and his footwear poorly chosen. But forget the grip and the footwear. It's the mountain. Is there any way to deal with—flatten, bypass, dynamite, chip away at—*that*? That's the question that ought to be front and center in every discussion of educational leadership.

STOP ROLLING THE BOULDER

This is a book for superintendents, principals, school board members, teacher leaders, and district and state staff who have been rolling that boulder too long, and are drained, frustrated, and puzzled at why their good work and furious effort is yielding such limited results.

Is it possible to keep that boulder moving uphill? Sure, but only for a while. Think of Deborah Meier's renowned Central Park East Secondary School, hailed as a terrific example of a student-centered model. All was good, until Meier left. Absent her star power and inspiring leadership, the school soon came apart, to the point where Meier observed, "I stopped visiting. It was too painful."[2] Education veterans can tell similar tales of big personalities using charm, charisma, and connections to great effect.

The problem: things tend to roll back down the mountain pretty quickly once that hero moves on.

Maybe Sisyphus couldn't escape his fate. But I'd like to think we can do better. This is a book for people ready to do just that.

Now, you may be wondering: Where are the paeans to children, best practices, and the grandeur of teaching? After all, most tomes on education leadership emphasize heart, culture, and instruction, and here I am talking about bureaucracy and mountains. Sounds like a distraction for someone passionate about teaching, learning, and kids, no?

CAGED LEADERSHIP

Maybe. But let me put it to you another way.

Let's change metaphors. When I talk about transformational leadership, I start with Sisyphus and the mountain because it's a familiar tale and an easy image. The problem: it's hard to imagine what you're supposed to do about that implacable peak.

So let's try another visual. Rather than think about school and district leaders pushing that boulder up a mountain, think of them living in a cage. That cage restricts what they can do and how they can do it. But what if that cage isn't as solid or confining as it seems? What if some of the bars are illusory or frail enough to topple with a hard shove? What if the cage is as much a product of habit and belief as concrete and steel? If that's the case—and I'd argue that it is—leaders can do more than they think. They need to make sure that they're not hunched in cages of their own design.

Leadership always entails two complementary roles. One is coaching, mentoring, nurturing, and inspiring others to forge dynamic, professional cultures. This half absorbs almost the whole attention of those who tackle educational leadership. Lost in K–12 is the second half of the leadership equation—the *cage-busting* half that makes it easier for successful and professional cultures to thrive. You don't do cage-busting *instead* of mentoring, coaching, and inspiring, but so that you can do these things *better*. Cage-busting helps make it possible for you to be the leader you aspire to be.

Cage-*dwellers* spend most of their energy stamping out fires or getting permission to lead, and most of their time wooing recalcitrant staff, remediating ineffective team members, or begging for resources. Cage-*busters* wake up every morning focused on identifying big challenges, dreaming up solutions, and blasting their way forward. I don't know about you, but that sounds like a *helluva* lot more fun to me.

Now, one way to free leaders is by removing the bars that cage them in. District contracts and procurement processes, rules and regulations, state statutes and board policies hinder leaders in all kinds of ways, making it harder to repair a fence, hire talented staff, or schedule grade-level team meetings. I've spent a lot of time addressing these barriers in books like *Common Sense School Reform* and *Education Unbound*.[3]

However, that's not what *this* book is about. While educational leaders are indeed hindered in real ways—and time after time, in place after place, I've had superintendents, school leaders, district administrators, and school board members tell me that they'd like to do something but aren't allowed—it's become clear to me that much of what leaders say they can't do, think they can't do, or just don't do is stuff that they are already able to do. Let me say that again: contracts, rules, regulations, statutes, and policies present real problems, but *smart leaders can frequently find ways to bust them*—with enough persistence, knowledge, or ingenuity.

The problem is they don't know they can. Or don't know how to get started. Or are too nervous to try. Or have never been taught they are supposed to push. This book is for readers tired of dwelling in that cage.

CAGE-BUSTING IS NOT ABOUT PICKING FIGHTS

Because we don't usually talk about educational leadership like this, it's easy for the point to be misconstrued. So, let's get a couple of things straight. Cage-busting is not about picking fights, attacking unions, or firing people, and it does not give cage-busters license to wantonly alienate educators or community members. It is nothing more (or less) than thinking ambitiously about how to create great schools and then doing what it takes to make them real. It empowers leaders, frees them from the iron grip of bureaucracy and routine, and helps them become savvy leaders of a public enterprise.

I'll go further. Not only is cage-busting not an assault on unions or educators, but it holds that leaders need to stop blaming unions, contracts, tight budgets, and the rest for their own failure to lead. Yes, some employees or families will inevitably take issue with some measures that a cage-buster thinks necessary. And any cage-buster worth her salt will stand fast rather than back off from doing what she thinks is best for her students. But conflict is not the goal.

Mike Feinberg, cofounder of the KIPP Academies, eloquently captures the cage-buster's approach to doing what he thinks is right, responsibly and without acrimony:

> At KIPP, we honor teachers. But if teachers are not good, if they're not performing, they need to leave . . . We can't compromise on doing right by the students. Now, before they remove that teacher, our leaders need to look in the mirror. Is there any part of this teacher's failure that's really on you, as the leader? Have you done what was necessary to communicate expectations, give them a mentor, observe them, and support improvement? Can you look in the mirror and say, "I've set this teacher up for success, and they're not succeeding?"[4]

Like Feinberg, cage-busters ask whether they've done everything they can to put educators in a position to succeed. They don't just coach teachers in how to differentiate instruction, they rethink the design of the school and instructional day to make differentiation more manageable. They don't just tell teachers to tutor students who need extra help, they find ways to tap mentors, peers, community assets, or online resources to provide added support. They ask teachers what wastes their time; what disrupts instruction; and how limited time, tools, and resources might be better used. In tackling such questions, leaders help make it clear that they are not blaming teachers but empowering them.

THINKING LIKE A CAGE-BUSTER

Steve Jobs biographer Walter Isaacson has written of Jobs's "reality distortion field"—how the founder of Apple and entrepreneurial icon would embellish, cajole, manipulate, and rage in order to advance his vision. One colleague explained, "In [Jobs's] presence, reality is malleable . . . It was dangerous to get caught in Steve's distortion field, but it was what led him to actually be able to change reality."[5] Having spent hundreds of pages documenting Jobs's often-boorish nature, Isaacson takes pains to note that "dozens of the colleagues whom Jobs most abused ended their litany of horror stories by saying that he got them to do things they never dreamed possible."[6]

That's the cage-busting mind-set. It's not about dreaming, seeming innovative, or picking fights—it's about "distorting reality" to change what's possible. And that can involve some bruises.

Distorting reality may be as simple as principal Adrian Manuel's response to teachers who were consistently late at Accion Academy in the Bronx. Tired of pleading futilely for cooperation, Manuel started docking their personal time—a tactic entirely consistent with the city's collective bargaining contract. He told probationary teachers he could let them go if they didn't get it together; he fired six. Other teachers got the message. With that problem resolved, Manuel could turn to more important matters. "It goes back to principals understanding policy," he says. "The union contract is two hundred pages long. I've read it, and few principals do. I've gone through six or seven appeals and I've never lost because I know the letter of the contract." Under Manuel's leadership, Accion Academy rose in three years from the bottom 5 percent of New York City middle schools to the upper one-fifth.[7]

In taking charge of the turnaround effort at Houston's Alief Taylor High School, principal Walter Jackson faced a common challenge: many students were reading way behind grade level. Meanwhile, his high school teachers had little expertise in teaching reading. This is a familiar challenge. Jackson opted for an unfamiliar solution. "I asked myself, 'Why couldn't an elementary teacher, who approaches instruction using a phonetic standpoint instead of whole language, teach high school kids how to read?' So I experimented and filled every reading vacancy I had with someone who had experience teaching elementary reading." Jackson's move helped drive big reading gains, to the point where 90 percent of his students were proficient on Texas's reading assessment.

As executive director of Colorado GEAR UP, a state program to help prepare low-income students for college, Scott Mendelsberg serves a large number of Spanish-speaking Latino students: "Now, in every walk of life, being bilingual is a benefit—except in K–12 education . . . Unfortunately," he recalls, "The only way I knew to reward these students was through an AP Spanish course," a semester-long course that these students don't need and many schools don't offer. Then he had an idea:

> One day on a plane I'm reading about the College Level Examination Program exam, a College Board test that is basically a placement exam. I called the College Board and told them I wanted to offer that exam to all the kids I work with in GEAR UP. And the executive vice president said, "Scott, that's not what the test is designed to do. We have AP Spanish for those kids." I said, "The kids I work with aren't taking AP classes. Most of the time, the schools that they're in aren't offering those courses." I asked what they had to lose, since we were going to pay for the test. Last year, we offered that exam to 585 kids in Colorado. Eighty-eight percent of them got college credit on that seventy-five-minute exam. I had ninth-graders and tenth-graders who essentially had a minor in college Spanish from that one test.

Cage-busters devise new solutions to escape familiar frustrations. (See "Finding a Way to Get It Done.") They wonder how they might use subsidized AmeriCorps volunteers or work-study students from local colleges to provide cheap, additional support staff. They ask, à la Boston-based Citizen Schools, how they might use educated professionals in the community to provide extended learning time. They explore how "hybrid" school models might allow technology to augment, complement, or extend classroom instruction.

HOW EXPERTS HAVE ENCOURAGED CAGED LEADERSHIP

Many factors contribute to caged leadership. But one of the most influential and most readily addressed is the shared conviction among experts that the cage isn't a problem. Educational leadership authorities suggest that talk of structures and the cage reflects a "corporate" mind-set and is inappropriate for K–12 schooling. Experts in educational leadership tend

Finding a Way to Get It Done

Cage-busting is about doing everything possible to promote your vision of great teaching and learning—no matter what. New York City's deputy chancellor of education David Weiner recalls when, as a newbie principal at San Francisco's Alvarado Elementary School, he found his inner cage-buster when forced to protect a classroom of vulnerable kids.

"There was a third-grade teacher who was just absolutely unsatisfactory. I'm not joking: she bolted the classroom door to prevent any students who she said 'did not respect her' from entering into the classroom," Weiner says. "The only children [who] were inside the classroom were not African American. The students outside the classroom were all African American males. And these were third-graders!"

Weiner told the teacher that the practice was unacceptable, to no avail. "I called Human Resources to see if we could try to move her out immediately. They said it wasn't possible because she had not received any unsatisfactory ratings." Weiner was left "trying to figure out what the hell to do."

Weiner's solution? "I got myself a laptop and told the secretary I was moving my office to this teacher's classroom. I decided I was going to prevent her from doing this, and that I'd write her up when warranted."

Weiner worked from the teacher's classroom for six weeks. "I'd walk in and put my things down. I ate lunch in there with the students. I set up a desk outside the door so I could have meetings with other teachers and staff. Being in an ineffective teacher's classroom nonstop yields a lot of information. I gave her four or five unsats [unsatisfactory ratings] in the course of three weeks. In two months, she chose to resign. And I moved back to my office."

Weiner tells this story to remind leaders that there are things they have to be willing to stand for: "Maybe I was young and naive, but I'm glad I did it. I mean, there are tough rules that govern state law and union contracts to prevent districts and leaders from doing these types of things. But there are ways to say, 'All right, well these are the rules, and I'm going to play within the rules but I'm going to stretch the limit to where I'm as close to that line as possible.'"

to echo Trinity University professor Thomas Sergiovanni's declaration, in *Leadership for the Schoolhouse*, that "corporate" models of leadership don't work in education and that "We [must] accept the reality that leadership for the schoolhouse should be different."[8] Sergiovanni's charge: "We [need to] begin to invent our own practice," has informed a generation of thinking on educational leadership.[9]

Cage-busters don't believe that school leadership is unique. They agree that it certainly has unique elements and challenges. But they think that inspiring adults, connecting with communities, serving children, leading teams, managing public budgets, and all the rest are roles that have a lot in common with leadership at YMCAs, hospitals, universities, and parks . . . as well as software firms, transit agencies, and charities. In fact, as the dean of one elite business school muses, "I don't know where educators got this idea that business schools do one kind of leadership and they do another. We train students planning to be energy traders, financiers, health-care executives, and nonprofit CEOs side by side. Believe me, they all have very different interests and issues. But the core skills of leading an organization, motivating a team, managing resources, and negotiating an environment are similar across a range of fields."

Readers are likely acquainted with the shelf of influential works by prominent education leadership authorities like Michael Fullan, special adviser to the Minister of Education in Ontario; University of Toronto professor Ben Levin; Boston College professor Andy Hargreaves; Harvard University professor Richard Elmore; University of Toronto professor Kenneth Leithwood; University of Southern California professor Terrence Deal; and University of Missouri-Kansas City professor Lee Bolman. Their advice comes in different flavors, but all emphasize the primacy of curriculum, instruction, coaching, and culture.

Such advice is good and useful. Nobody is arguing otherwise. Cage-busters, too, embrace rich content, rigorous standards, a vibrant school culture, smart use of formative assessment, terrific teaching, and engaged learners.

That said, these experts routinely make two mistakes. First, they have erected a notion of *instructional leadership* that reifies consensus, deifies stakeholder buy-in, and insists on the "specialness" of education—while dismissing or ignoring the half of the leadership equation that deals with statutory, bureaucratic, contractual, or organizational obstacles. The result: swell ideas that work fine under optimal conditions, but that inevitably disappoint when leaders try to roll them up the mountain.

Second, these experts sometimes wow would-be reformers with bold talk. Upon closer inspection, however, they're not all that interested in the art or the science of exploding (or even acknowledging) the cage. Rather, seemingly brash strategies add up to little more than recipes for boulder rolling.

An easy way to see this is by flipping through the pages of the education magazines that school and system leaders peruse for guidance and advice. It quickly becomes clear that these are suffused with the "five Cs" of the leadership canon—*collaboration, consensus, capacity, coaching,* and *culture*—while cage-busting concerns are largely ignored. In *Educational Leadership*, for instance, between January 2009 and September 2012, *collaboration* was mentioned 142 times, *professional development* 180, and *culture* 214. *Collaboration*, the least frequently mentioned of these, tallied more appearances than the combined mentions of *regulation, licensure, compliance, maintenance of effort, supplement not supplant, inept, mediocre, productivity, collective bargaining, layoff, arbitration, grievance, due process, labor agreement,* and *negotiation.* Indeed, during a period of fierce budget cuts and tumultuous debate about teacher evaluation and tenure, the terms *layoff, labor agreement, arbitration, due process, negotiation, maintenance of effort, regulation,* and *ineptitude* appeared a grand total of twenty-eight times in the course of nearly four years.

Over the same time frame, *Phi Delta Kappan* mentioned *collaboration* 151 times, *culture* 245, and *professional development* 256. Again, *collaboration*, the least common of those three, outpaced the combined mentions of the other fifteen terms.

The point is not that the authorities ought to stop paying attention to the five Cs—it's that they need to start paying attention to the cage.

Even some conventional authorities agree that something is amiss. Harvard's Richard Elmore has observed, "Relying on leaders to solve the problem of systemic reform in schools is, to put it bluntly, asking people to do something they don't know how to do and have had no occasion to learn in the course of their careers."[10] In their 2011 book *At a Cross-roads*, Donald Hackmann and Martha McCarthy make clear that the ed leadership professoriate lacks experts equipped to teach the stuff of cage-busting. They report, for instance, on a national survey that shows zero percent of ed leadership faculty claim a primary scholarly emphasis on collective bargaining or school business management, and that just 1 or 2 percent say that it's in school/community relations, personnel management, or technology.[11]

I want to be clear about two things. First, *yes*, I'm suggesting that almost the entire education leadership canon suffers from a giant blind spot. Second, I *am not* in any way, shape, or form dismissing this work. It has valuable things to say, but it only speaks to *one half* of the leadership equation. In ignoring the cage, leaders trap themselves within it.

Ignoring the Cage

As I've noted, most ed leadership authorities devote the whole of their attention to culture, coaching, and collaboration, while implicitly (or explicitly) dismissing challenges like contracts and policy. Richard Elmore suggests that, because "the administrative structure of schools exists to buffer the instructional core" and "teaching is isolated work," improvement is the product "of purely voluntary acts."[12] He thus concludes that "the skills and knowledge that matter" for leaders are those directly tied to "instruction and student performance."[13] In practice, this has too often been taken as advice to focus on instruction and ignore the cage. I'll say it again: instruction and culture *are* key, but this work can be made easier or harder by the way leaders deal with rules, regulations, contracts, policies, and entrenched routines.

Indeed, the canon can seem to encourage timid, plaintive leadership. In *Educational Administration*, Ohio State University professor Wayne Hoy and former University of Michigan dean Cecil Miskel conclude that school leaders "should focus on helping, not directing, teachers to improve their teaching."[14] They suggest that leaders use "special favors, services, and support [to] create social obligations and build goodwill among subordinates. The result should be enhanced development of subordinate loyalty and informal authority."[15]

Such advice suggests that leaders rely almost entirely on warm feelings and good vibes to foster great teaching and learning, and that effective leaders can ignore that inconvenient cage. The result is a pleasantly amorphous vision of school improvement, as when Andy Hargreaves and Dean Fink opine in *Sustainable Leadership*, "Like an excellent meal, deep, sustaining learning requires wholesome ingredients, a rich and varied menu, caring preparation, and pleasing presentation."[16] They go on to state, "Sustainable leadership does no harm to and actively improves the surrounding environment. It does not raid the best resources of outstanding students and teachers from neighboring institutions. It does not prosper at other schools' expense. It does no harm to and actively finds ways to share knowledge and resources with neighboring schools and the local community. Sustainable leadership is not self-centered; it is socially just."[17]

Hargreaves and Fink offer a long list of things that principals ought not do (e.g., harm the surrounding environment, raid outstanding teachers, prosper at others' expense, or be self-centered). What they don't do is help a principal figure out how to act on their advice.

Even thinkers who acknowledge the cage seem to quickly dismiss its import. In *Resourceful Leadership*, Harvard's Elizabeth City touches on the cage just long enough to tell leaders they should focus elsewhere. She writes that, in studying leadership, she has found, "People, time, and money mattered, but there were other elements not on my list of quantifiable indicators that kept cropping up. Those elements were vision, hope, trust, ideas, and energy, and they seemed to matter at least as much as people, time, and money."[18] Such advice is not wrong, per se. But it does encourage leaders to give short shrift to questions of talent, tools, time, and money, and to presume that worrying about rolling the boulder is unnecessary, or even a waste of time.

Deceptively Bold

Some ed leadership thinkers call for forceful, unwavering action leadership in ringing, cage-busterish tones; yet it quickly becomes clear that they are repackaging the familiar five Cs in edgier language.

Take Michael Fullan's *What's Worth Fighting for in the Principalship*, in which leadership, he explains, "is about taking relentless action in the face of an amalgam of intersecting barriers and creating powerful levers for catapulting the system forward."[19] Fullan writes, "Changing cultures is the principal's hardest job because there is so much previous structure and culture to overcome."[20] This all sounds rather cage-bustery. But that impression dissipates almost immediately upon a closer reading.

Fullan presents six "core guidelines" for "principals who fight": deprivatize teaching; model instructional leadership; build capacity first; grow other leaders; divert the distractors; and be a system leader.[21] Yet those seeking to act on this agenda will find little guidance on how to overcome the barriers he has cited, beyond encouragement to emphasize culture and capacity-building. For example, Fullan acknowledges that "there are individual cases of unacceptable abuse or gross incompetence that must be acted on immediately."[22] However, he then offers not one concrete tip or caution to help deal with that lousy teacher.

In fact, many of the practical barriers that frustrate school and system leaders go unaddressed by Fullan and other ed leadership experts. An Amazon in-text search of *What's Worth Fighting for in the Principalship* produces not one mention of *union contract, union agreement, dismissal, layoff, fire,* or even *Title I.* The same goes for *School Leadership That Works* by instructional guru Robert Marzano. The same is true of Sergiovanni's *Rethinking Leadership,* aside from one mention of *fire* in the context of "putting out fires." Kent Peterson and Terrence Deal's *The Shaping School Culture Fieldbook* contains no mention of *union agreement, Title I, dismissal,* or *layoffs.* They mention *fire* once—again, in the context of "putting out fires."[23]

By ignoring contracts and district policies, these authors—and there are plenty more—seem to suggest that the ability of leaders to observe classes, schedule team meetings, or remove lousy teachers is peripheral to culture building or mentoring. Indeed, one can peruse the ed leadership canon without learning that leaders charged with turning around a failing school or making painful budget cuts may have to wade into treacherous, rule-laden waters.

In *How to Change 5000 Schools,* Ben Levin writes that structural reforms are "necessary to foster and support good teaching and learning practices and therefore requisite to any real and lasting change."[24] Yet Levin then makes it clear that by "structures" he's actually referring to culture, collegiality, and consensus building, and to things like "engagement and commitment by adults" and "appropriate allocation of resources."[25] But all of these good things are significantly shaped by crude organizational realities, to which Levin has given short shrift.

Indeed, when it comes to addressing these realities, Levin balks: "One of the big mistakes many organizations make when they embark on reforms is to combine reform with major changes in the structure of the organization . . . That is almost always a mistake, as structural reorganizations take a great deal of time, engender a great deal of uncertainty among staff, and rarely result in significant improvements in the way the organization works."[26]

How to Change 5000 Schools equips leaders with little beyond prescriptions for culture building. Strong cultures are critical. But telling a leader to build a cohesive culture solely through will or skill is like telling a youth soccer coach to focus on building a winning team culture—no matter that the assistant coach is a bully, the practice field is closed for safety reasons, or the team only has nine players. Tackling these "structural" problems would give the coach a better chance to build a successful culture. Sure, there are superheroes who might succeed anyway, but it's probably not the way to bet.

What About Instructional Leadership?

Some readers may think it's hard to reconcile cage-busting with instructional leadership. They shouldn't. The two are complements, not substitutes. Cage-busting creates the conditions for culture building, coaching, and instructional leadership.

Just 10 percent of principals say they are satisfied with the amount of time they devote to instructional leadership. Public Agenda polling expert Jean Johnson notes, "Fighting for time for instructional leadership appears to be one of the main frustrations of being a principal today."[27] The Urban Institute reports that principals spend only 13 percent of their time on "day-to-day" instructional tasks and programs and over 50 percent on administration and management.[28] Cage-busting can help make other roles more manageable, giving leaders more time to attend to what matters most.

Yet champions of instructional leadership often denounce efforts to address the cage as a distraction. Thelbert Drake and William Roe argue in *The Principalship* that "running a tight ship" is a "distortion of the goal of educating children."[29] When it's suggested that schools and systems need to do a better job of tapping talent or spending dollars smarter, experts snap that kids aren't widgets.

It may seem bizarre to suggest that using time and money wisely is a distraction, yet that notion recurs with startling consistency. Take the unavoidable issue of ineffective teachers. Champions of instructional leadership often imply that responsible leaders should accept the staff they have and then cajole, coach, and collaborate their way to great instruction. Fullan and Hargreaves assert in *What's Worth Fighting for in Your School?* that principals should "find something to value in all the school's teachers. Even poor or mediocre teachers have good points that can present opportunities to give praise and raise self-esteem . . . The worst thing to do is to write off apparently poor or mediocre teachers as dead wood, and seek easy administrative solutions in transfers or retirements . . . Try doing the hard thing, the right thing, the ethical thing, and explore ways of bringing these teachers back instead."[30]

Coaching and cajoling mediocre teachers is important and essential work—Fullan and Hargreaves get that right. Where they go wrong is to suggest that good leaders should do this ad infinitum. This is a ludicrous use of time and energy, and a disservice to the kids involved. Cage-busters coach and cajole *as long as they think it makes sense for the school, system, and students*—and work to briskly replace teachers when that is no longer the case. (See "Oh, Yeah, *That* Stuff.")

Cage-busters seek a world in which, rather than begging or enticing mediocre teachers to improve, school leaders have reliable ways to evaluate teachers and to dismiss them when necessary. Cage-busters seek collective bargaining agreements that expedite the process and quickly resolve disputes. They believe this will permit principals to spend more time working with effective educators and forging a collaborative culture on a staff not peppered with malcontents.

Oh, Yeah, *That* Stuff

I recall one visit to Fairfax County, Virginia. The superintendent had taken me to visit a middle school that had been "turned around" and was now piloting some terrific team-teaching models. We met with the principal and about a dozen faculty for a friendly conversation. The principal enthusiastically told us about the culture they'd established. She explained how the teaching teams collaborated and used data. Teachers avidly shared techniques and experiences.

Near the end of the visit, the superintendent and I once again asked the principal to explain how she'd gotten a troubled school onto this dynamic trajectory. She once again credited teamwork, collaboration, and buy-in. This time, I interrupted and asked, "Okay, but how'd you get all the teachers in a dysfunctional school to suddenly change their behavior? *How* did you get everyone to buy in?"

She looked startled. "Well, not all of them did. We had to change a few teachers."

"Oh," I said. "How many?"

The principal looked quizzically at one of her veteran teachers, as if trying to remember. She looked at the superintendent, as if making sure it was okay to discuss this. Then she said, "Probably about 40 or 50 percent didn't return that first year, and another dozen probably left that following year."

That might've merited a mention, don't you think?

That was an important bit of information. It didn't lessen the school's accomplishment. But it suggests that even this acclaimed principal needed personnel changes to set the table for everything else. It's a problem that this is the last thing the principal would think to mention. And it's an even bigger problem that the experts on educational leadership are uninterested in such things.

HOW WE GOT HERE

The case for cage-busting can sometimes feel like a blame-the-victim exercise, as if we're blaming school and system leaders for their burdens. It shouldn't. Cage-dwelling leadership is the product of professional norms, training, and circumstances that date back nearly a century.

In the early 1900s, influenced by education psychologist Edward Thorndike and scientific management guru Frederick Taylor, proponents of *progressive education* worked to bring the same standardization and routine to education that they admired in industry and business.[31] The problem, explained Ellwood Cubberley, dean of the School of Education at Stanford University from 1917–1933 and, in many ways, the father of modern school administration, had been that, before 1900, schools had been like "a manufacturing establishment running at a low grade of efficiency."[32]

In short, progressives worked hard to import the best practices of private industry to American education.[33] (This is why the familiar school model bears such an uncanny resemblance to the early-twentieth-century factory.) That model made some sense at the time, helping to manage a massive expansion of schooling in a world lacking modern data tools and communications technology.

Since that era, though, K–12's routines and rules have been largely preserved, as if in amber. Intrusive regulation, petty bureaucracy, and balky decision making have bizarrely come to be treated as part of the schoolhouse culture.

In the private sector, meanwhile, old giants like Univac, TWA, and Xerox have given way to Google, JetBlue, and Apple. These new ventures had the freedom to build brand new cultures, staffing models, evaluation systems, and delivery models that took full advantage of evolving talent, tools, and technology.

In schooling, this passing of the baton is absent. Instead, leaders inherit long-standing schools or school systems. As successive generations of entrepreneurs and thinkers in other sectors have revisited basic assumptions and built wholly new organizations, educational leadership preparation has clung to aged norms. Indeed, those championing more flexible, creative, and quality- and cost-conscious leadership have been pilloried for pursuing "corporate-style school reform" or labeled "enemies" of public education.[34] As I noted in *The Same Thing Over and Over*, "The debate over the sanctity of 'schoolhouse leadership,' then, is really a debate between the defenders of early-twentieth-century management practices and those championing the management practices [favored] by leading public and private organizations in recent decades."[35]

The stale party line leaves leaders ill-equipped to negotiate a profoundly changed world of schooling—where changes in our expectations, the labor market, and the state of tools and technology create new challenges and vast new opportunities to answer them. Indeed, there's little reason to expect that century-old assumptions about how to organize and deliver schooling are necessarily the smartest way forward. It's time to swap out factory-style, early-twentieth-century management for more dynamic, creative, and agile leadership.

Yet, today, few school or system leaders have much experience outside the confines of K–12 or exposure to other ways of thinking about how to best use talent, tools, time, and money.[36] Educational leaders typically start as teachers and receive all of their leadership training in schools of education.[37] More than 99 percent of superintendents have been teachers; as the American Association of School Administrators has noted, the traditional career path for superintendents "involves moving through organizational hierarchy of a public school district."[38] Half of all superintendents obtained their first administrative position before age thirty, meaning they've never had even a brief chance to venture outside of K–12.[39] It's good that our school systems are led by committed, veteran educators. It means, though, that most leaders have little opportunity to see how budgeting, accountability, personnel evaluation, or compensation are tackled in other, more dynamic sectors.

What Educational Leaders Are Taught

School and system leaders recognize there's a problem with leadership preparation. According to polling by Public Agenda, 72 percent of superintendents and 67 percent of principals report that "typical leadership programs in graduate schools of education are out of touch with the realities of what it takes to run today's school districts."[40]

Principal preparation programs devote little or no attention to concerns like removing mediocre employees or seeking out cost efficiencies. Courses emphasize compliance with regulations while giving short shrift to helping leaders learn to utilize data or technology.[41] Indeed, education law scholar Perry Zirkel has suggested that a lack of knowledge and understanding by administrators leads them to overestimate legal requirements and fosters excessive caution.[42]

K–12 leaders are rarely exposed to alternative ways of thinking about management and leadership. In 2007, Andrew Kelly and I reported on a national examination of principal preparation courses. We found "little attention to teaching new principals to hire, evaluate, reward, or terminate employees" and noted that courses were more likely to dismiss such questions as distractions from the real work of culture building. One personal favorite: the week on personnel management titled, "The symbolism of attempting to fire an incompetent teacher." Barely 5 percent of the course weeks devoted to personnel management addressed employee compensation or termination. Readings in preparation courses consisted almost entirely of authors like Sergiovanni, Fullan, Bolman, and Linda Darling-Hammond, who focus on the "unique" challenges of school leadership. Almost absent were iconic leadership and management authorities like Michael Porter, Jim Collins, Clayton Christensen, and Tom Peters.[43]

Organizations in most other fields embrace intellectual and experiential diversity when training and selecting leaders, by hiring or promoting managers from a variety of sectors, roles, and organizations. In MBA programs, students hoping to work in nonprofits and for-profits, in fields from energy to publishing, learn side by side. Not so in education leadership programs, where preparation consists almost uniformly of career educators studying alongside one another.

This state of affairs has drawn concern, even from supporters of traditional educational administration training. In their 2011 survey of the educational leadership professoriate, Donald Hackmann and Martha McCarthy observed, "If leadership preparation programs are to engage in substantive reforms, there must be divergent viewpoints and a willingness to examine departmental norms and practices." Yet they find a lack of "different perspectives within the educational leadership professoriate" and conclude that "educational leadership faculty members seem to remain complacent about issues and problems in the field."[44]

Professional Incentives and Mind-Set

Given their background and preparation, it's hardly surprising that few leaders are inclined to be cage-busters. While leaders in most sectors take for granted the value of rewarding effective employees and removing ineffective ones, such views are more controversial in schooling. Public Agenda has reported that only one in five superintendents deem linking consequences to student learning a "very effective" way to improve teacher quality.[45] Principals were even more skeptical, and most believe that teacher quality can be boosted "very effectively" by increasing professional development or decreasing class size.[46] That same lack of enthusiasm for strategies that promise discomfort or controversy is echoed by school board members.[47]

Leaders also evince little appetite for proposals to streamline operations or improve efficiency. Though 84 percent of district leaders described their district as "inadequately funded" in 2010, 24 percent said they "never considered" freezing outside professional service contracts; 73 percent never considered reducing employee benefits; 70 percent never considered outsourcing custodial or maintenance work; 48 percent never considered finding new transportation efficiencies; and 75 percent never considered closing or consolidating schools.[48] Perhaps this is why, as scholars Rick Ginsberg and Karen Multon have observed, school leaders believe "that all cuts, no matter where they're focused," hurt classrooms, and that anyone who thinks otherwise "doesn't really understand the culture of schools."[49]

The cage-dwelling mind-set even permeates operations and system management. For instance, the Association of School Business Officials reported in 2011 that just 41 percent of its members have a background in business and that only about half hold a degree beyond the BA. While 84 percent of members polled say—sensibly—that managing day-to-day finances and budgeting is one of their top three responsibilities, just one-third say the same about evaluating the effective allocation and use of resources. Understandably, nearly three-fourths report that making cuts to their district budget "keeps them up nights." More surprising is that just 48 percent say the same about demonstrating that tax dollars are spent optimally. In short, operational staff are attentive to system routines, but show less interest in ensuring that dollars are used wisely or well.[50] Let's be clear: the point here is not to criticize school business officials but to suggest how immersive the cage-dwelling culture really is.

In a field where laws, regulations, and contracts color every decision, leaders place surprisingly little stock in understanding legal constraints. In fact, just 3 percent of big-district (twenty-five thousand or more students) superintendents deem legal questions a relevant subject for professional development.[51] Most leaders prefer to ignore the mountain—even as they exhaust themselves rolling the boulder.

Finally, K–12 is rife with estimations of leadership performance that are alternately euphoric and ill-founded. A 2010 survey found that 84 percent of school boards rated their superintendents as good or excellent, and fewer than 1 percent rated them below average.[52] At the same time, New Leaders for New Schools reported in 2010 that principal evaluation systems focus on "the wrong things, lack clear performance standards, and lack rigor in both their design and attention to implementation."[53]

BOULDER ROLLING AND REPLICATION

The five Cs are so appealing, in part, because they feel intimately linked to things we can see in classrooms, hallways, and lunchrooms. The problem with all those terrific models for professional development and differentiated instruction is that they're basically a set of boulder-rolling techniques. Less immediately evident is that all of these things are subject to the accumulated rules, routines, regulations, contracts, and policies that may go unnoticed but shape everything else. Whether promising models work as intended will depend as much upon the shape of the mountain as on the technical merit of the advice.

Even seemingly successful pilot programs depend on much more than the model. When replication disappoints, we tend to blame "implementation" or the program itself. But success often has less to do with the particular practices than with circumstance. Upon closer inspection, many successful pilot programs benefit because implementation is more akin to chasing a boulder downhill than to rolling it uphill. Why is that? A variety of reasons, including:

Philanthropic support: Dollars are often available to fund new initiatives. Such funding allows pilot programs to offer services and opportunities that prove unsustainable when the program expands to new sites.

Expertise: Pilot efforts are, by design, supported by the experts who have conceived of the model (or intervention). They benefit from intense, sustained, loving attention by those who are most invested in the idea. Later sites have less access to that talent.

Enthusiasm: Pilot efforts are launched where the leaders or staff in question are enthusiastic enough to be the pioneers. That passion and sense of ownership are enormously helpful in making early iterations successful.

Accommodations: Pilot efforts are frequently launched in sites where the local leadership has the wherewithal to provide helpful waivers, leeway, or support. For instance, a new academic program benefits from flexibility with regards to staffing rules. When the same models are implemented in less accommodating settings, they frequently fail to deliver.

The truth is we've been able to identify the elements of "effective schools" for four decades, going back to Ron Edmonds's seminal work in the 1970s, but we've struggled, through the whole of that period, to scale up scattered successes. This history illustrates the problem with focusing on instructional and improvement strategies without attending to the statutory, regulatory, contractual, or organizational obstacles. The problem is that we fixate on the climb and turn a blind eye to the terrain. The result is a constant chase for new miracle solutions that never quite pan out.

IS CAGE-BUSTING JUST FOR MARTYRS?

Even when successful, cage-busting principals, superintendents, school board members, teacher leaders, and state chiefs can encounter brutal blowback. Critics have screamed "Controversial!" at a raft of cage-busting leaders, regardless of the merits of the charge. The truth is, leaders can work hard to play nice and woo stakeholders, but those determined to address the cage can still expect aggrieved parties to blast them regardless of the merits.

Leaders deemed "divisive" have become lightning rods, been sued, had their agendas thwarted by diehard opponents, and turned into combatants in larger political debates. For those more interested in leading great schools than in policy debate, this can be a frustrating turn. Moreover, for all the headaches, even successful cage-busters are able to push only so far. They're never able to bust all the bars they might want or need to.

The upshot is that even unflinching readers may say, "Great. You can and should do these things, but will you live to see them come to fruition? And once you've been labeled controversial, won't the school board or community leaders opt for a successor who'll roll everything back?" Even if you think cage-busting is right and necessary, how can you be confident it'll yield anything more than martyrdom?

The cage-buster's response? For starters, as Gene Wilhoit, executive director of the Council of Chief State School Officers (CCSSO), soberly observes, "I don't think you take a state superintendent's job today assuming you're going to retire in it. Most chiefs today understand that, if you are going to take on an aggressive agenda, you have a life span. If you step back and play it safe, you aren't going to make any change, anyway."

It's true that school boards, business leaders, parents, editorial boards, and civic leaders in many communities have long prized tranquility above performance. Leaders who keep the waters calm, avoid harsh cuts, and say the right things tend to earn good reputations and laudatory press.

But things can change. In the past decade, state-level and national advocacy has shifted the center of gravity in K–12, generating more tolerance and enthusiasm for cage-busting than was once the case. Charter schooling, virtual delivery, value-added systems, and new providers offer leaders new tools. Accountability systems, increased transparency, and tight budgets have made it easier to justify tough-minded changes. An increasing number of cage-busters, backed by forceful advocacy and enthusiastic foundations and public officials, means there's some safety in numbers.

And cage-busters can boost the odds they'll be more than martyrs. The pages that follow relay strategies that can help leaders take full advantage of existing laws and regulations, reduce friction, frame the public debate, mobilize allies, and fortify their political position. Smart cage-busters operate strategically, move and speak deliberately, and avoid reckless posturing—building credibility and political capital. And we'll discuss why would-be cage-busters may wish to gravitate toward schools and communities that are ready and willing to support their work, and how to recruit and cultivate local allies to help.

In the end, there are no guarantees. Cage-busting can prove a challenging course. That's why advocates, public officials, and would-be reformers are right to attack the constraints that dissuade many from the cage-buster's path. And it's why so many leaders have chosen the safe, familiar course of the five Cs rather than the perilous promise of cage-busting.

THE BOOK AHEAD

There is a way out of the cage. But it requires that we stop talking about just getting more great teachers or "fixing" schools, and start thinking expansively about how to maximize the amount of great learning, teaching, and schooling. After all, the world of schooling has changed powerfully, in ways that can leave today's schools and teachers ill-equipped for new challenges. Our nation is more diverse and technologically advanced than it was a century ago, while the import of education has grown exponentially.

A century ago, barely one American in ten finished high school; today, we believe it's critical that every citizen ought to have a meaningful high school degree. New technologies and data systems have made possible approaches to diagnosis, intervention, and instructional delivery that were once the province of fiction. We need leaders who can leverage these developments, escape old strictures, and bring our schools into the twenty-first century. Yet even would-be reformers tend to assume the factory-model classroom and its rigid bell schedules, credit requirements, age-based grade levels, job classifications, and physical specifications when talking about school improvement.

I believe that most leaders recognize the frustrations of the cage and are eager to lead more boldly, but are uncertain how to do so. That's a matter of training, intentions, and socialization. But also of ideas and seeing what's possible. That's where this book comes in. It's intended to equip leaders—in schools, systems, and states—with the tools that can help them avoid Sisyphus's dismal fate.

Cage-busting is not a program or pedagogy. It's a mind-set. It's not a substitute for coaching, instructional rounds, mentoring, culture building, or instructional leadership—it makes it possible to do these things better. Once you've embraced the cage-busting mind-set—once you're questioning routines, challenging obstacles, and seeking new possibilities and solutions—transformative leadership becomes more manageable and less exhausting.

Here's how the book will unfold: In chapter 2, we'll discuss some bad habits and how to shake them off. Chapter 3 sketches out how cage-busters tackle problems. Chapter 4 delves into understanding the bars of the cage. Chapter 5 explores how to go after those bars. Chapter 6 discusses how to tap talent, tools, and dollars in smarter ways. Chapter 7 addresses the practical and political side of all this. Finally, chapter 8 offers some lessons and advice for those ready to unleash their inner cage-buster.

What follows can sometimes seem like a lot. To help keep things straight, I'd refer you to the convenient cheat sheet version of each chapter you'll find in appendix A. Without further ado, let's get to it.

2

Seeing Differently

"What is the Matrix? It is the world that has been pulled
over your eyes to blind you from the truth. What truth? Like
everyone else you were born into bondage, born into a prison
that you cannot smell or taste or touch. A prison for your
mind . . . Unfortunately, no one can be told what the Matrix
is. You have to see it for yourself. This is your last chance.
After this there is no turning back. You take the blue pill, the
story ends, you wake up in your bed and believe whatever you
want to believe. You take the red pill, you stay in Wonderland,
and I show you how deep the rabbit hole goes."

—MORPHEUS, *The Matrix*

READERS MAY RECALL the scene. Morpheus, the wily rebel is struggling to open the eyes of Neo, the credulous office drone. Neo must choose
between drowsy comfort and seeing the world anew. Neo chooses the red
pill, and his eyes are opened. That is the path of the cage-buster.

As superintendent of Prince George's County, Maryland, John Deasy
won national acclaim for achievement gains in low-performing schools.
Part of his strategy involved getting terrific teachers to want to work in
those schools. Whereas most district leaders grouse that their hands are
tied, Deasy found a path despite a restrictive collective bargaining agreement (CBA) and the familiar constraints on teacher pay. Deasy seized
upon a little-noticed CBA provision providing eleven-month salaries for
teachers working on curriculum development. He simply announced that

teachers in hard-to-staff schools were also obviously doing curriculum development. This permitted him to pay them as eleven-month employees and offer a 22 percent pay boost. How did he manage this? That's the wrong question: "Nothing prohibited any of this," he says. "Why does it not happen? [Because] most people see the contract as a steel box. It's not. It's a steel floor with no boundaries around it. You've just got to push and push and push."[1]

Matt Malone made a school closure work *for* him while running the school system in Swampscott, Massachusetts, a small suburban district fifteen miles up the coast from Boston: "We closed one elementary school due to budget cuts at the start of the recession. We didn't have enough seats for all of the fifth-graders at the three remaining elementary schools, so I decided that we were going to open up seventy-five seats at the middle school. It was extremely controversial at the time. So I decided to call it a 'pilot model' and sell it that way . . . When all was said and done, we had 130 fifth-graders who wanted in, and held a lottery for one hundred seats. We had tears and heartbreak from parents of children who *didn't* get in." The "pilot" was so successful the district moved all fifth-graders to the middle school the next year.

Yzvetta Macon, a veteran Cincinnati principal, recalls that a key piece of her redesign effort at South Avondale elementary required overhauling the school's established partnerships—even when that meant bruised feelings:

> I decided which partners would stay and who would be released. We hired a new mental health agency and let go of the old one. We told the new one they needed to make some adaptations. They'd need to service the students and their families during school hours and to provide needed medication, resources, therapy, and counseling. The mental health staff needed to make home visits, provide transportation, and schedule meetings with parents during the times parents were in the building dropping off or picking up students. If school started at 8, they needed to be here. And they had to be aware that instruction was the priority, even though our kids had so many health needs. Whatever we needed to do, we needed to make sure that we did not interrupt instruction.

Partnership became a tool for getting kids ready to learn; it was no longer a pleasant, siloed add-on.

Educators routinely complain about duplicative and wasteful paper-work, only to be told, "There's nothing we can do. The federal programs office requires it all." Kim Wooden, chief student services officer in Clark County, Nevada, tells how her staff managed to reduce this duplication for principals in Title I schools:

> Principals were completing the paperwork for the school improvement plan. Then, the Title I office would ask many of the same leaders for the Title I plan [which covered much of the same ground]. So the new Title I director said, "Why can't we combine the plans?" We worked with the school improvement division to combine the templates. Principals can better align the two plans and get all their questions answered at once. They probably spent, and this is a conservative estimate, three hours per school on the Title I plan alone. So we saved 210 school leaders at least three hours apiece through this one change. That's at least six hundred hours of administrative time handily saved.

Cage-busters live by W.L. Bateman's wry admonition, "If you keep on doing what you've always done, you'll keep on getting what you've always got." Doing better requires finding ways to slip through that cage, and smarter ways to scale that mountain. That requires seeing the world in fresh ways and setting aside shopworn assumptions.

THE "CULTURE OF CAN'T"

When it comes to improving schools, we hear a lot about what educational leaders *can't* do. Corinne Gregory, author of *Education Reform and Other Myths*, says, "Working with schools, it seems to me that there is a great deal of 'can't'-ism going on. And what I have found this to mean is that it is much easier [for leaders] to place blame on 'outside factors' and claim they are helpless to change anything as a result, than it is to actually take the initiative to make their own changes. 'We don't have time.' 'We can't afford it.' 'There's a policy' . . . all those phrases are excuses for why change can't happen."[2]

Contracts, laws, and regulations are a real headache. But those who must abide by them also have an unfortunate habit of turning frustrations into all-purpose scapegoats and blaming them for all manner of inaction.

Ariela Rozman, CEO of TNTP (formerly The New Teacher Project), says she's seen this often: "We went into [one troubled Midwestern district] expecting to find a very restrictive contract that kept them from allowing freedoms like mutual consent for all teachers and schools." Instead, Rozman recalls, "We found a very limited, small contract that covered only a few specific topics. And the reason the district was doing a ton of forced placement was because that's just the way [Human Resources] had operated for years. But the superintendent believed it was better to be out there lambasting the union than to be cleaning up his house internally." School and system leaders can do much that they often complain they can't, given enough persistence, know-how, ingenuity, and desire.

One common excuse for moving gingerly on teacher quality is collective bargaining. However, in a 2008 analysis of CBA work rules, teacher compensation, and personnel policies in the fifty largest US school districts, policy analyst Coby Loup and I found that the majority included much room to maneuver. While one-third of the contract provisions examined were clearly restrictive, half were ambiguous or silent when it came to key questions—and 15 percent offered explicit flexibility to school and system leaders.[3] Vanderbilt University professor Dale Ballou studied Massachusetts and found that, on virtually every issue of personnel policy, contracts granted administrators managerial prerogatives they commonly thought they lacked; when more flexible language was negotiated, administrators did not take advantage but continued to blame the CBA for their inaction.[4] Mitch Price, a legal analyst with the Center on Reinventing Public Education, noted in a 2009 study of teacher contracts that, "a lot of these contractual issues are 'smokescreens for those people who don't want to do something.'"[5]

A second common complaint concerns the heavy hand of state and federal regulations. Yet Columbia University Teachers College professor Hank Levin recounts that when the California legislature allowed districts to apply for waivers if they could demonstrate that laws or rules were hampering school improvement, fewer than one hundred waiver requests were made in the first year in a state with more than a thousand districts.[6] More telling, notes Levin, "The vast majority of all requests for waivers were unnecessary."[7] Why were they unnecessary? Nearly all the proposed measures *were permissible under existing law*. Superintendents and boards mistakenly thought their hands were tied or, as Levin observed, were using laws and regulations "as a scapegoat . . . to justify maintaining existing practices."[8] Terry Grier recalls a similar story from his time as superintendent in Akron, Ohio: "In the early 1990s, state superintendent Ted Sanders got tired of all the superintendents complaining about how state regulation and laws were getting in the way of reform efforts. He offered to waive any that did. As I recall, he only had one taker—us." In 2011, the Obama administration's Office of Management and Budget (OMB) launched a major effort to help states identify opportunities to reduce the paperwork burden. Given years of griping from state and local officials, OMB officials were astonished at how little interest they drew. As one administration official drily remarked, "You can say that we were disappointed in the response."

A third excuse is, "We don't have the money to do that." Yet districts rarely prune staff or programs, even when a new product or service might enable nine employees to accomplish what once took ten. The result: labor-saving technologies or services rarely appear cost-effective. Tim Daly, president of TNTP, which helps districts recruit teachers, has related that districts frequently say, "They loved our work [but] we are too expensive . . . that our teachers were $5,000 to $6,000 per head and that their human resources department could recruit teachers for $100 or $150 per head." In fact, Daly explains, "This calculation was based solely on two expenses: fees paid to attend job fairs and ads placed in newspapers. It didn't include any of the costs for staff salaries or benefits, or office space used by the recruiters, or technology infrastructure, or placement costs, or mentoring. They just added up the most readily tallied costs and divided by the number of teachers hired." Managing this way means that reform proceeds only as fast as new resources are layered atop the old.

We see these dynamics play out time and again. One Ohio high school principal hoped to entice two career-changing Procter & Gamble scientists to join his faculty as science teachers, confident that they had the temperament, knowledge, and skills to be effective in the classroom. They had twenty years as practicing scientists and extensive teaching experience from their time at P&G. But their lack of K–12 experience meant they would start at the bottom step on the district salary schedule, making it tougher to recruit them. The principal asked HR whether there was any wiggle room. The answer: "Nope." Well, upon reviewing the CBA, a seasoned education attorney opined that their experience could qualify the pair for several steps, making possible a salary offer nearly $10,000 higher. The obstacle wasn't the contract, it was HR.

Sheara Krvaric, cofounder of the Federal Education Group law firm, frequently works with superintendents who want to use Title I funds to improve curriculum but think the law prevents them from doing so. Yet, Krvaric says, "If they've done an assessment that said their curriculum isn't good and that's contributing to why kids are struggling, they're OK. And place after place will say, 'No, we think the state wouldn't like that,' or, 'No, we think an auditor is going to ding us.' They feel like the whole system has become so bureaucratic it's not even worth the energy to try and fix it . . . There's a million examples, but they all come down to inertia. People just think it's not worth the effort."

There are four self-imposed traps that ensnare many leaders, making it even harder to escape the "culture of can't." We'll touch on each in turn.

THE PLATITUDES TRAP

Cage-busting leadership requires clarifying your values, aims, and vision. In practice, too many leaders resort to vapid generalities that foster muddled thinking.

Leaders are smothered with genial, general advice. For instance, they are told to value "consensus," "collegiality," "relational trust," "coherence making," "child-centered learning," and "professional growth." And well they should. But high expectations, competition, decisive leadership, and discipline are also important. And these values can conflict in messy ways that shrink-wrapped platitudes won't sort out.

Leaders are also constantly being pitched pat solutions. They're told to "leave no child behind," "close achievement gaps," "ensure that all students are college- or career-ready," and "employ data-driven decision-making."

These banalities can too easily stand in for disciplined thought, while stifling hard questions about what they mean in practice. I recall one leader
who, when challenged on some of No Child Left Behind's design flaws,
would snap: "Whose child are *you* willing to leave behind?" Not a great
way to solicit honest feedback or nurture smart problem-solving.

LeAnn Buntrock, executive director of the University of Virginia's Partnership for Leaders in Education, says that learning to parrot platitudes
can hide confusion: "We've been pretty focused on data, assuming that
district and school leaders would understand that you need to analyze this
information to get to the root cause of problems. But last year we realized
that we weren't really sure leaders were making that connection. They've
learned the language but . . . Thinking analytically is not something that,
as far as we can tell, most leaders are learning how to do."

THE "SUCKS LESS" TRAP

When you're scrambling to hit proficiency targets, it's easy to get caught
up in what New Orleans–based 4.0 Schools founder Matt Candler has
aptly labeled the "sucks less" trap. Candler got started with KIPP in the
late 1990s and has spent most of the years since opening and supporting
high-performing charter schools or shutting down lousy ones. Yet he realized along the way that many "high-performing" charters weren't great
schools, they just "sucked less." Candler says, "I didn't get into this to create schools that aren't as bad as the alternatives." (See "Charter Schooling
Is Instructive: For Better . . . and Worse.")

Today, we routinely hail "exemplary" schools for getting low-income kids
to read at grade level. We give a pass to suburban schools that manage to
get their affluent students on to college at high rates. In doing so, we define
excellence as surpassing the minimal bars we've set for reading and math
achievement, high school graduation, and college enrollment. Yet when we
look at these schools, there's a tendency to mimic them rather than try to
build on their successes. As Thomas B. Fordham Institute policy fellow and
former director of professional development at Achievement First Kathleen Porter-Magee explains, "It ends up more like an old-fashioned Xerox,

Charter Schooling Is Instructive:
For Better . . . and Worse

Charter schooling provides an opportunity for schools to escape many, though not all, of the policies, rules, regulations, and contract provisions that apply to district schools. For those unfamiliar with charter schooling, this is because charters are freed from many statutes and regulations, and because they start with a clean slate—with no inherited policies or collective bargaining agreement. At the same time, charter schools are still subject to a raft of constraints related to accountability, special education, federal funds, and whatever else states choose to impose. Put another way, charter school leaders inhabit a bigger cage.

But keep in mind that the autonomy of charter schools is less absolute than many observers may imagine. David Hardy, CEO of Boys' Latin of Philadelphia Charter School, says, "Charters can get caught up in the same regulations [as district schools]. When you start talking about highly qualified teachers, for example, art teachers and drama teachers are included. So we could get Peter Nero from the Philly Pops to come in here and teach a music class, but he's not certified—so we're not allowed." Charters have to fight and claw to ensure their freedom.

Moreover, the reality is that most charters haven't done all that much with their newfound autonomy. The National Center on School Choice at Vanderbilt University reported in 2011 that the role of charter school principals "was not significantly different" from that of district principals.[9] As a whole, the nation's five thousand charter schools have done a modest job of leveraging the ability to hire, pay, and use teachers in smarter ways or to rethink the school day. In a 2011 study of charter school CBAs, the Center on Reinventing Public Education's Mitch Price noted that, despite the chance "to craft agreements from scratch . . . charter school contracts look quite similar to their district counterparts. The new contracts make only modest revisions to traditional compensation models, and tend not to factor student performance into teacher evaluations."[10] Public Impact researchers Dana Brinson and Jacob Rosch note that most charters hire and pay staff much as local districts do.[11] Charter leaders can be trapped by mind-set, even when rules or requirements are relaxed.

More promisingly, a smaller number of charter schools are showing what skilled leaders can do when given the opportunity. Such leaders have created "no excuses" schools like KIPP Academies, YES Prep Public Schools, or Achievement First, where the ability to hire, instill strict discipline, and extend the school year and school day has been used to forge powerful cultures. They have launched hybrid school models like Carpe Diem or Rocketship Education, which use technology and tutors to supplement classroom teachers. The result: a cost-effective, promising overhaul of the familiar model. They have launched academically rigorous schools like BASIS or Match Schools, which boast a degree of curricular rigor hard to sustain outside of private schools or selective exam schools.

Charter schooling does not magically collapse the cage. It does illustrate how smart policy and determined leadership can start to strip out bars and make it easier to create great schools.

where each new copy is a little worse than the one that came before."[12] (In part, this is fueled by overeager philanthropists who reward influential districts for adopting new fads or models in cookie-cutter fashion.) The reflexive search for "best practices" suffers from the same limitations that we discussed in chapter 1. Leaders enthusiastically embrace this particular turnaround model or that instructional strategy, while giving little heed to whether promising results are likely to travel.

Because of the "sucks less" trap, we often fail to aim high enough. We talk about "exemplary" schools where just thirty seniors out of six hundred are getting 4s or 5s on the AP BC Calculus exam. We talk about schools that are "outstanding" because 96 percent of kids are proficient in basic reading and math—without asking how many are fluent in a second language or advanced in science. The emphasis on reading and math scores and graduation rates has made it too easy for us to dumb down our definition of excellence. Cage-busters resist that temptation, and fight like hell to make sure those around them do as well. They ask what excellence looks like, and don't settle for doing well by today's minimalist yardsticks.

When Candler launched 4.0 Schools in 2010, he decided he would no longer settle for "sucks less"; he wanted to cultivate schools that would be profoundly better. While such a course is littered with obstacles, his ambition is a powerful North Star for the cage-buster. The cage-buster begins each and every day asking, "Am I dreaming big enough, thinking bold enough, and being imaginative enough?" Cage-busters seek not models to mimic but new tools they can wield in ever-smarter ways.

THE "MORE, BETTER" TRAP

Perhaps the signature mark of cage-dwelling leadership is the belief that improvement is only possible with additional dollars. The University of Toronto's Ben Levin perfectly encapsulates this mind-set when he opines, "Reformers who think that they can change a system for the better without any new money are probably deluding themselves."[13] The fact is, the most innovative organizations tend to be cash-poor start-ups that rely on moxie, creativity, and elbow grease. Amazon founder Jeff Bezos or Facebook founder Mark Zuckerberg would be puzzled to hear that success requires new resources—given that each led a scrappy, nimble start-up past huge, deep-pocketed, established competitors.

K–12 has long been the province of "more, better" reform. "Innovation" has typically meant layering new dollars and programs upon everything that came before. Superintendents fund new initiatives not by redirecting dollars, but by sprinkling new philanthropic or federal funds atop what's in place. The problem is that this means old routines are rarely challenged and improvement depends on landing ever more resources.

The "more, better" mind-set is also evident at many acclaimed charter schools, where talent and tools are used much as they've always been, and improvement depends primarily on talented people working really hard for long hours with lots of passion. This is swell, as far as it goes. The problem is that it just doesn't go as far as we'd like—especially when the talent well starts to run thin or educators with children and families balk at working twelve-hour days.

Does more money, time, or staff usually help? Of course. But what matters most is what you do with it. And all too often, those extra dollars inspire false confidence and allow schools or systems to avoid seeking a new path. Those who can't see beyond the familiar ensure that they will trudge back up the same path they've trodden before. This is a recipe that Sisyphus would know all too well.

THE MACGYVER TRAP

Readers of a certain age may remember the 1980s TV show *MacGyver*. Each week, MacGyver would find himself in impossibly tight jams, only to escape by inventing some ingenious contraption. Trapped in a Bolivian jail cell with a pillow, a paperclip, and a toothbrush, he'd construct a diesel-powered bulldozer. It was uncanny. MacGyver is the patron saint of today's K–12 leader. Great leaders use a similarly ingenious bag of tricks. They have a buddy in procurement who helps get the instructional materials they need. They're old pals with the deputy superintendent who gets them extra funds for this program or somehow transfers out that teacher.

So where's the trap? First, MacGyverism creates a distorted sense of what's possible. If we've got a hundred thousand principals and fourteen thousand superintendents, there'll be a few MacGyvers able to build a flamethrower out of a Q-tip and a can of bug spray. But most people can't do that. Yet when mere mortals try to draw attention to the bars of the cage—rules, regulations, and policies—they are told by the associate superintendent for instruction or the coordinator of federal grants that they're "making excuses" and should just note how well school X is doing. In this way, MacGyvers can be used to justify boulder-rolling leadership.

Moreover, their own problem solved, MacGyvers see little value in riling state or local officials by pointing out the bars of the cage or trying to dismantle them. In fact, MacGyvers can settle into cozy "see no evil, speak no evil" relationships with state or district officials. New York City principal Anthony Lombardi found ways to empty his school of mediocre educators by pushing them until they opted to transfer elsewhere. But, as Lombardi observes, "I told [the superintendent] one night that what I did was good for my team but bad for his league." That's the dilemma. Lombardi did the right thing for his kids, but cage-busters aspire to more.[14]

At its best, cage-busting pioneers solutions and opens up new opportunities. Vince Bertram, president of PLTW (Project Lead the Way), recalls,

"[When I was superintendent in Evansville-Vanderburgh, Indiana] we were getting principals from schools of education where they were taught by people we had fired. It just wasn't adequate. So we developed our own leadership program with Brown University. We found people who we thought would be great leaders and hired and trained them . . . To make it work, we needed a state waiver from the licensure process. It was really the first alternative principal licensure program in the state." Bertram didn't just figure out how to cultivate new leaders, but blazed a trail that others could follow. *That's* cage-busting.

BRING A BEGINNER'S MIND

It's tough to cultivate the cage-busting mind-set. For one thing, leaders are surrounded by colleagues used to the cage. For another, they're besieged by experts who claim to already know just what needs to be done. A telling example: many leadership authorities continue to tout a 2003 publication by the Mid-continent Research for Education and Learning (McREL), which identified *twenty-one* leadership responsibilities thought to be associated with student achievement. These included: celebrating "school accomplishments," being "directly involved" in designing curriculum and assessment, having "quality contact" with teachers and students, challenging the "status quo," leading "new and challenging innovations," being aware of "undercurrents in the running of the school," and ensuring that staff are "aware of the most current theories and practices."[15] Leaders can get so intent on all of this that they get overwhelmed.

Unfortunately, this can make it hard to see with fresh eyes. Doing so requires stepping back and cultivating what the Zen Buddhists refer to as *shoshin*, or "beginner's mind"—approaching subjects with curiosity and an open mind, even when you think you already know it all. In *Zen Mind, Beginner's Mind*, Shunryu Suzuki puts it aptly: "In the beginner's mind there are many possibilities, in the expert's mind there are few."[16]

Rhode Island commissioner of education Deborah Gist says, "Being the new person means you can say, 'I don't understand, could you explain this?' even though you probably have a sense for what's actually happening. You're able to see things in new ways that folks that have been there a long time just accept as, 'We've always done it that way.'"

Gist recalls that when approving the cut scores for applicants to state teacher prep programs, "I asked questions like, 'How did we arrive at these numbers?' 'How do we compare to other states?' and 'Who has the authority to set the standards?' In that conversation I learned so much. As commissioner, I had the authority to set the cut scores, and I learned our cut score was tied with Guam and North Dakota for the lowest in the country. It had been a pro forma kind of decision for many years. I said 'We aren't going to do it that way anymore' . . . So I raised the scores, and sent a message that things were going to be different."

Chris Barbic, founder of the nationally renowned YES Prep charter schools, left that role to take the helm as the first superintendent of the Achievement School District (ASD) in Nashville, Tennessee, a statewide district created to help turn around low-performing schools. Early in his tenure, he observed, "I'm still trying to figure out what's real and what's not. The best way to do that is just kind of attack it with a beginner's mind, by just constantly asking, 'Why?' The challenge is you've got to build relationships and to have people in your corner who want to help you win. And if you're just walking around right out of the gate pissing everybody off, that becomes tricky. So the art of it is asking 'Why?' enough but knowing when to shut up."

In his 1974 bestseller *Zen and the Art of Motorcycle Maintenance*, Robert Pirsig offers a neat take on the value of beginner's mind.[17] He relates the example of a motorcyclist who has a stuck screw, can't find directions in the manual, and then strips the screw while trying to get it out. Pirsig writes, "You're stuck." And the worst thing, he notes, is that neither the technical guidance nor your familiar routine can provide the "creativity, originality, inventiveness, intuition, imagination—'unstuckness'" you need to solve the problem. But, Pirsig says, cheer up—this "stuckness" is actually "the best possible situation you could be in . . . It's exactly this stuckness that Zen Buddhists go through so much trouble to induce . . . Your mind is empty, you have a 'hollow-flexible' attitude of 'beginner's mind.'"

Pirsig goes on to explain, "If you concentrate on it, think about it, stay stuck on it for a long enough time," you'll eventually "see that the screw is less and less an object typical of a class and more an object unique in itself. Then with more concentration you will begin to see the screw as not even an object at all but as a collection of functions." This helps you find new ways to think about and understand the screw. As Pirsig says, before, "You couldn't think of how to get unstuck because you couldn't think of anything new, because you couldn't *see* anything new."

ONE MORE THING ON MY PLATE

Under boulder-rolling leadership, the usual reward for good work is . . . more work. Think of the terrific third-grade teacher whose reward is that his principal throws an arm around his shoulder and says, "We've got three kids moving up from second grade who are a real handful. You know you're the best I've got, so I need you to take them, okay?" Think of the stellar principal whose reward is the area superintendent saying, "We need a turnaround leader for Johnson Middle School. You're the best I've got, so I need you to take that on, okay?"

Now, it would be one thing if these requests came with recognition, compensation, or opportunity for growth, but they rarely do. Instead, leaders tend to rely on little more than personal pleas and assertions that it's the right thing to do.

Such leadership effectively punishes excellence while encouraging all but the foolhardy to duck and keep their heads down—since the reward for competence is to have higher-ups pile *one more thing on my plate*. This makes it tough to lead and makes leadership unduly exhausting. Happily, cage-busters have tools that can help combat this predicament in a number of ways.

Create Communities of the Willing

The fact that people have chosen to be part of a school, system, or program can make it a lot easier to win cooperation. For instance, asking teachers at a floundering school to do additional tutoring or family outreach may be met with fierce resistance. However, the response of teachers pursuing a position at a new (or rebooted) school may be very different. School improvement models, for instance, can allow leaders to remove or reject staff unwilling to commit to the program. Savvy leaders use that opportunity to establish new expectations and shape a new culture.

Cage-busters can achieve a similar result by enlisting their team to find a way to achieve a common end. When Adrian Manuel led Accion Academy in the Bronx, he wanted to give teachers a full day a week to plan as teams without sacrificing instructional time. That meant he'd need some teachers to teach more than three periods in a row—a violation of the CBA. Manuel says, "So I went to the teachers and said, 'I only want you guys teaching four days a week, but based on your contract, I don't see how you can do this.'" If they wanted the planning time, they'd have to figure it out. He recalls:

> I said, "I'm going to let you all come up with a schedule." And they realized that there was no way they could give their colleagues one day a week without asking people to teach four periods in a row. So they made a schedule and presented it to the staff, and . . . everyone agreed to it . . . Now, if I had made a schedule where we violated the contract, people would have [filed a grievance against] it just because it came from us. But there's a different level of pressure from colleagues saying, "Look, if we do this, we'll get this."

Harness the Notion of Promotion

When the reward for a job well done is just more work, it's not a reward at all. Yet that kind of "reward" is par for the course in much of K–12. Marry new responsibilities to more recognition, opportunity, and pay, though, and now you're talking about this nifty thing called a *promotion*. You want that great third-grade teacher to take those three tough-to-serve students or coordinate tutoring for at-risk kids? Okay. Can you offer recognition, additional compensation, a shift in responsibilities, or a reduction in other burdens to make this appealing?

A weird thing about the merit pay discussion in K–12 is how divorced it is from how we usually discuss professional success. In most professions, the reward for doing great work is not a one-time cash bonus for last year's results; it's a promotion. In other words, employees are rewarded with the expectation they'll do even more good next year. People tend to appreciate the opportunity, while getting recognition as well as pay. Funny thing about promotions: most people don't turn them down, even with the new responsibilities.

Get Creative About Opportunities

Leaders struggle with the inability to reward or recognize staff. As one principal says, "I'd love to make these assignments attractive. Thing is, I can't vary duties or pay, and I don't have anything to offer." On a closer look, he did have things to offer, and you do too—stipended positions, grade-level leadership, coaching roles, and so forth. Yet he wasn't thinking about them as opportunities for staff—they were just things that had to get done. That's a big mistake.

Cage-busters find ways to create new, hybrid roles that permit good educators to take on new responsibilities, assist more kids, or impact students more deeply—and to be recognized or rewarded accordingly. I recall one principal who had teachers clamoring to take on extra duties for no extra pay—because it would help them get into a districtwide leadership development program (which also didn't pay). People are often more motivated by opportunity, recognition, or excitement than a couple of bucks. That's why the notion of promotion is so powerful.

A LITTLE HELP FROM MY FRIENDS

We often hear that only veteran educators can be trusted to run schools or school systems because they understand the culture, have pedagogical and instructional expertise, and carry instant credibility. Fair enough. The flip side is, though, that career educators are . . . career educators, which means they are mostly acquainted with how things are done in K–12. Their expertise ought to be honored and valued, but also complemented by those who can bring other ways of seeing and thinking. Cage-busters avoid getting caught up in pointless, ideological debates about the relative merits of "traditional" or "nontraditional" individuals; what matters is assembling a team that's got the diverse skills and thinking that can help solve problems and best serve their students.

Veteran educators can tap fresh perspectives by seeking advisers, mentors, or team members from both inside and outside of K–12. At 4.0 Schools, Matt Candler brings together educators with entrepreneurs from technology, social work, and other sectors. He notes, "We find that the mix delivers terrific energy and creativity. But we've found that when the mix of educators gets over 65 percent, that goes out the window and everyone settles back into convention. Stirring in people with other views and expertise turns out to be essential." Los Angeles superintendent John Deasy says that, when it comes to pushing the boundaries of what's permissible, his "most formative experiences have developed almost entirely in relationships and mentorships with noneducators."[18]

Those from outside K–12 may find it easier to see that the emperor has no clothes or challenge orthodoxy by asking, "Why do we do it this way?" This is why Lillian Lowery, when she was Delaware's secretary of education, brought in talent from outside K–12 to help implement the state's Race to the Top agenda: "All the folks in our delivery unit came with backgrounds outside education. What we needed were thinkers who didn't have ways of already doing the work we needed to do, but had creative visions about how we could do it more effectively."

How does this work? One tiny illustration. There's been remarkably little attention to how many teachers a given principal can productively supervise. In many schools, principals are expected to supervise and evaluate dozens of teachers. In other fields, that figure would be deemed laughable. Barbara Davison, director of the Saratoga Institute, has reported in the *Journal of Business Strategy*, for instance, that the average span of control across business sectors is one manager overseeing nine employees.[19] The Saratoga Institute has found that companies with about a half-dozen employees per manager outperformed their peers with larger ratios.[20] Such insights, which may be unfamiliar to those inside K–12, can flag blind spots. In this case, the data might raise questions about the number of teachers a principal ought to observe or the number of direct reports that a student services manager should have; and might point to the value of peer review as a creative way to address some of the challenges.

Those with experience outside schooling may question routines that are casually accepted and taken for granted by K–12 veterans. In Austin,

Texas, for example, a group of elite CEOs and financial officers meets regularly with the CFO of the Austin school district to discuss budgeting challenges. Ellen Wood, president of the professional-services firm vCFO and a participant in those sessions says, "It became real clear, real quick, that there are useful strategies and approaches in an industry that even a talented district CFO may not be familiar with."[21]

Cordell Carter joined Seattle Public Schools as a director of school support services after working in the private sector. He says, "Because I wasn't part of the system and was used to asking questions of clients in [my] past lives as an attorney and consultant, I questioned everything. I also knew that any process, no matter how arcane or full of jargon, could be measured and improved." Carter helped design performance indicators for nonacademic departments: "The metrics were things that any business would measure, like cost per invoice processed or time to fill a vacancy . . . The superintendent liked it and ordered all central office departments to create scorecards. [They] changed central office culture; there's no place to hide when you're standing in front of your peers with last quarter's results in hand."

Now, you'll hear some cage-dwellers suggest that outsiders can't possibly provide assistance in K–12 because they lack an appreciation for the uniqueness of schoolhouse culture. And it's true that there are things about schooling that are unique. Of course, the same is true for medicine, engineering, law, agriculture, the armed forces, and manufacturing. It's important to respect the expertise of educators, but educators also need to respect the expertise of those with other experiences and skills. Cage-busters believe that dramatically improving recruitment, information technology, personnel evaluation, budgeting, motivation, and human resources in K–12 has a lot in common with tackling such challenges in other fields.

GET GOING DOWNHILL

Culture matters—a lot. Schooling is about adults working together to inspire, instruct, and mentor kids. Culture is the glue that binds this community of teachers and learners together. But culture is not purely a product of purpose and personality, of hope and hand-holding. It is also a product of that mountain of rules and regulations, policies and practices, contracts and case law. Rather than fight all of that, you want to find a way to make the mountain work for you, so that you're no longer rolling the boulder uphill but are chasing the boulder as you *get going downhill.*

A useful rule of thumb here is the *80-20 rule*, which states that, in any organization, 20 percent of the employees are responsible for 80 percent of the work that gets done. An equally useful rule is that leaders typically spend 80 percent of their time monitoring, mentoring, and dealing with the least effective 20 percent of their team. Heck, principals can spend 10 percent of their time addressing and documenting the failings of a single lousy teacher. Superintendents can devote huge swaths of time to the academic and public relations disasters caused by their worst handful of principals.

It takes a lot of time and energy to monitor, improve, and support low performers. And it's downright exhausting when they're not on board and all you can do is appeal to their better angels.

The roadblocks thrown in the way of removing weak teachers, for instance, make it easier to shuffle such teachers around the district than to remove them. Idaho state superintendent Tom Luna recalls this practice from his time as a local board member, noting, "It was so burdensome to even identify ineffective teachers or get them into any formal PD, that quite often you'd end up buying out a contract and agreeing not to put anything negative in their employee file if they left." Veteran principals know this as "the dance of the lemons." They agree not to give a teacher negative evaluations so long as the teacher agrees to transfer the next year—shifting the problem onto another principal and another class of students.

The Frustrating Case of Mr. Baron

Imagine you're a principal dealing with a teacher who consistently shows up at the last required minute and leaves as soon as the contract permits, does a poor job of keeping students on task, never assigns writing assignments of more than a few paragraphs, doesn't mentor kids—he just isn't getting the job done. You sit down with Mr. Baron to have a firm, supportive talk.

You ask Mr. Baron how he thinks he's doing, what's been successful, and what challenges he sees. You remind him to take full advantage of his colleagues, resources, and data, and ask what else he needs. He tells you that the kids are tough but that things are good. After a half-hour, you feel like you've made zero headway. Finally, you say, "Mr. Baron, we're just not on the same page here. I've observed you eight times this year and last, looked at the student outcomes and, like we've discussed before, we really need to do better."

He says, "I'm doing what you asked. I read the articles and checked out the videos you suggested. I've revised my lesson plans. I'm using the formative assessments and looking at the results. We're good."

You say, "Maybe you think you've made changes, but I'm not seeing the results. We need to get an action plan in place. Like we've discussed, I'd like to see you start assigning writing assignments that require something more substantial from our students. I'd like to see you finding time to tutor your kids when they need it, like some of your colleagues do. And it might require that you find a way to get here earlier or leave later."

He folds his arms and says, "It's like a witch hunt with you. You asked me to use formative assessments; I did. You asked me to use fewer ditto sheets, and I have. But I have a family and other responsibilities. I work the hours I'm paid for. These twenty-something teachers don't have children; I have obligations. I eat lunch during lunch and I grade and plan during my planning time. So, I'm sorry if I can't provide all the extra free tutoring you want—that's not in the contract."

You can say, "It's not just about assigning essays, it's about giving useful feedback." You can say, "But think about your kids," or "I'll have to consider formal action if your attitude doesn't change," but the truth is, you're working uphill. The instructional leadership mantra presumes Mr. Baron will respond to your feedback, at least if you do it right. If he doesn't, you're stuck.

Such naysayers and heel-draggers consume a *lot* of a leader's time and energy. If Mr. Baron won't willingly change, dealing with him requires an exhausting course of formal observations, discussion, documentation, paperwork, and hearings. That's not counting the psychic drain, the negativity in the teachers' lounge, and the rest. A principal with a half-dozen staff members like Mr. Baron can easily spend half of her time just on this handful of teachers. This is soul-sucking work, consuming time and energy that could instead be spent supporting faculty and students, improving curriculum and instruction, or reaching out to families.

Full stop. Let's change the scenario. Now, imagine you have in place policies where Mr. Baron knows that student performance has already put him on a watch list, an observer can enter his room without warning, and three negative evaluations this semester would cost him his job. If he knows these tools are routinely employed, the tone of the conversation is likely to be very different. You can now begin your chat by skipping to, "Mr. Baron, you know I like you and think you've got lots of potential. I want you on our team. But you're just not getting it done, and I won't be able to protect you unless you step it up."

You're no longer pleading for Mr. Baron's cooperation. Now, the unpleasantness is *depersonalized*—it's between him and the system. You're just reporting the news. You've gone from a scold to his lifeline. The consequence for failure is no longer dependent on personal relationships; it's baked into the system.

The story of Mr. Baron reflects a larger truth. In any line of work, some employees will resist changing familiar routines. Such resistance will always call for coaching and culture building, but this work grows more manageable as foot-dragging becomes less comfortable and cooperation more appealing.

Moynihan's Two Truths

Mr. Baron's tale reflects a critical truth, one famously articulated by former US senator and Harvard professor Daniel Patrick Moynihan. Moynihan observed, "The central conservative truth is that it is culture, not politics, that determines the success of a society. The central liberal truth is that politics can change a culture and save it from itself."[22] When it comes to schooling, it is culture and professional performance that ultimately determine the success of a school or school system. But policy plays a critical role in making these things possible. (See "A Tale of Two Cages" for an illustration of Moynihan's dictum.)

A Tale of Two Cages

In his 2011 book *Class Warfare*, journalist Steven Brill reports on a twinned pair of New York City schools, offering a powerful glimpse of how cages can shape school culture and student learning.[23] Brill wrote of PS 149, which enrolled 433 students in K–8, and the adjoining lottery-filled Harlem Success charter school, with 631 students in grades K–5.

The schools share a building, including a gym and cafeteria; they're separated by only a fire door and some staircases. Yet the cultures were profoundly different. At PS 149, Brill found overwhelmed teachers and students wandering the halls; only one-third of students were proficient as measured by state reading and math assessments. At Harlem Success, teachers threw themselves into mentoring and collaborating, and about 90 percent of (the demographically similar) student body was proficient in reading and math.

When seeking "best practices," what the casual observer can miss is the degree to which those differences in culture and outcomes rest on profound differences in the cages inhabited by leaders of the two schools. At PS 149, the 167-page CBA tightly constrained what teachers would and would not do during their 6-hour-and-57.5-minute workday. It spelled out their 179-day work year. Educators at Harlem Success worked from about 7:45 a.m. until 4:30 or 5:00 p.m., tutored on Saturdays, taught several weeks more than teachers at PS 149, and were available by cell phone for parent consultations. PS 149 spent more per pupil than Harlem Success, but fringe benefits for teachers soaked up almost $4,000 more per pupil at PS 149 than at Harlem Success—erasing the advantage. PS 149 teachers received thirteen paid sick or personal days a year, with the average teacher missing eight days. At Harlem Success, the typical teacher missed 1.1 days. Because fewer dollars were tied up in benefits, substitute teachers, and the like, Harlem Success paid its teachers 5 to 10 percent more than similarly experienced teachers at PS 149 *even though it spent less per pupil*.

The principal of PS 149, Kayrol Burgess-Harper, told Brill that at least ten of her forty teachers were not effective, that "their attitude and lack of caring affects many others," and that she'd rated three unsatisfactory. As a result, her relationship with the union representative in her building was "really tense." Burgess-Harper was trying to help these weak teachers improve via observation and coaching, but felt she was making little headway. For one thing, Burgess-Harper told Brill, "If we went into a classroom every day, we'd be charged with harassment." On every count, life at Harlem Success was markedly different.

The cage is the web of rules, regulations, and routines that limit a school or system leader's ability to spend money wisely, use talent well, or create a culture where student learning comes first. Cage-busters work to create schools and systems where kids and teachers want to show up every day, dollars can be spent in ways that matter most, and staff are eager and able to focus on the work of teaching and learning. In that kind of environment, it's surprising how much easier it is to be an instructional leader.

Culture does not exist in a vacuum. *This* is what critics of teacher evaluation and the defenders of tenure miss when they insist that reform proposals are "attacks" on the profession. These changes are tools for creating a more responsible and professional culture. (Now, like any tool, they can be used well or poorly. And that's an issue we'll discuss a little later.) As University of Virginia turnaround impresario LeAnn Buntrock observes, "Culture is embodied in the policies and practices of a school or system; in what gets prioritized and enforced. You can't say you have a data-driven culture and then not ensure that teachers have time to hold data team meetings, or fail to hold teachers accountable for providing evidence of how they're using data to drive instruction."

Nina Gilbert is founder and executive director of the Ivy Preparatory Academy network, based in Gwinnett County, Georgia. The network's flagship, Ivy Prep, receives less per-pupil funding than any other school in the district. Yet, in 2010, 100 percent of Ivy Prep's predominantly low-income students met state proficiency standards. Ivy Prep offers a weekly four-hour Saturday academy. School starts at 7:30 a.m., dismisses at 4:00 p.m., and tutoring is available until 5:00 p.m. The average teacher salary is $43,000. When asked how she gets teachers to work long hours without extra pay, Gilbert says, "Teachers know the schedule when they come in. We built that into our mission; it's in our charter. So they come in knowing that's part of our day . . . They wouldn't teach here otherwise." That's cage-busting 101: build an environment where you change what's possible.

Cage-busters take care to craft routines that support the culture they're trying to create. As one Texas principal explains, "A little trick of the trade I've learned is that when you want to put a teacher on notice, you have to be strategic. It has to be clear that I'm not the only one who thinks the teacher's not up to snuff. The team has to have a laser-like focus and be consistent. If four different administrators observe a teacher for thirty to forty minutes, we're going to make sure that we're looking for the same things and that our write-ups are the same."

THE RED PILL YIELDS OPPORTUNITIES, NOT RECIPES

Taking the red pill can sound radical. After all, the cage-busting mind-set is not one that educational leaders have been trained or encouraged to embrace. On the other hand, it's really just about shaking off assumptions, asking hard questions, and finding smarter solutions. What's amazing is how rarely leaders in K–12 do these simple things.

Hospitals, football teams, newspapers, software firms, and universities specialize in order to use scarce talent smarter. Yet, if you suggest exploring such approaches to most school or system leaders, you'll hear that they have been proven "not to work" in K–12. You'll hear they visited a more conventional high-performing school where the results were great—so "let's focus on replicating those best practices." You'll hear that "any kind of specialization would undermine a professional school culture." You'll hear that "this is how we use dollars, time, and talent because . . . well, because that's the way we do things."

It's hard to know what to make of the claim that allowing people to spend more time on what they do well "doesn't work" in schooling or that, somehow, when it comes to schools, paying hardworking, talented employees more than their peers is a silly idea.

The aim of the cage-buster is not to "innovate" or "implement best practices." It's not to promote site-based governance or enhance school autonomy. It's not to be a "reformer" or "get students online." These things are all incidental. They may happen, but they are not the aim—and the labels can be a distraction. The cage-buster looks at every challenge by asking whether tools are being leveraged as fully as possible; whether time and talent are being used as thoughtfully as possible; and whether funds are being spent as effectively as possible.

Cage-busting doesn't tell leaders what they should do; it helps them see with fresh eyes and beginner's mind, and then empowers them to lead accordingly.

3

What's Your Problem?

"If people are informed they will do the right thing. It's when they are not informed that they become hostages to prejudice."

—Journalist Charlayne Hunter-Gault

"What's your problem, Kazanski?"

—Pete "Maverick" Mitchell, *Top Gun*

CAGE-BUSTING REQUIRES CLARITY. Ask yourself: What is *your* vision of a terrific school or system? Not just, How are kids faring when it comes to ELA and math? but, How many kids are mastering a second language? How advanced is the instruction? How engaged are the parents? How dynamic is the arts curriculum? How do kids behave in the hallways and cafeteria?

That's the school or system you want to lead. Take a moment to fix it in your mind's eye. Now, try to gauge the distance from here to there. That can help you resist the tendency to settle for "sucks less." It can swipe away the fog of platitudes. And it can backlight the bars that stand before you.

THE SMARTEST WAY FROM HERE TO THERE

A journey of a thousand miles starts with a single step. But taking that first step requires knowing where the heck you're trying to go. Until you're crystal clear on what you're trying to do, you risk getting stuck in the

"more, better" rut. Here's a simple exercise I often use when working with
school and system leaders:

> "You're in Washington, DC. You need to get to Los Angeles.
> *Question:* How fast can you drive there? Go."

Give or take, it's about twenty-five hundred miles. What inevitably happens is that folks turn to their iPhone to figure the distance and then calculate how long it will take to drive it, given the requisite rest stops, meals,
naps, and such. Most estimate three to four days. Then the MacGyvers go
to work. They start figuring out they can do it with friends, eat in the car,
and get there in forty-five or fifty hours.

Frequently, though, there'll be one or two people who have a different
answer. Instead of casually assuming that they should *drive* from DC to
LA just because I said so, they think about the *purpose* of the trip. Not seeing any reason they need to drive, they get unstuck and decide the point
is to *travel* from DC to LA. They hop online and find the quickest flight, a
nonstop that gets them there in five or six hours.

So, what's the best answer? For the cage-dweller, it's about forty-five
hours—since that's the fastest you can *drive* from DC to LA. But the cage-
buster is focused not on instructions but on solving the problem. The cage-
buster's best answer is "five or six hours." Why? Remember Pirsig's screw
from last chapter. Those who say five or six hours have set aside familiar
routines and gotten unstuck. They're focused on function, not form. This
requires blasting past routines, assumptions, and mental traps to focus on
what matters.

As superintendent in Arlington, Massachusetts, Nate Levenson en-
countered countless examples of assumptions that had hardened into "We
can't" or "We're not allowed." To combat this, he used the "Five Why" approach. He explains, "You ask the question 'why?' five times to understand
the root cause of a problem." He illustrates:

> *Question one:* Why do we have so many special education students be-
> ing educated out-of-district at the district's expense?
> *Answer:* We don't have programs to meet their needs in-district.
>
> *Question two:* Why don't we have programs to meet their needs in-district?

Answer: Their needs are so substantial it would be more expensive to have in-house programs.

Question three: How expensive would it be to have in-house programs?
Answer: We don't know.

Question four: Why don't we know?
Answer: We aren't sure what services we must provide or how much staff we need for each program.

Question five: Why don't we know what services to provide or how many staff to hire?
Answer: We don't have programs like these in-house, so we haven't seen them.[1]

Levenson recalls, "After some field research, we learned that we could run our own top-quality programs with identical staffing levels and services to the out-of-district schools for 40 percent less per student . . . Over the next few years, Arlington opened eight programs and saved more than five million dollars."[2]

OWN YOUR BELIEFS

Cage-busting requires clarity on what you're trying to do and what you think a great school or school system looks like. Saying "Raise test scores" or "Make AYP" are bad responses here. They're bad because they're secondhand goals, defined for you by policy makers and test developers. Now, don't get me wrong. Making AYP or raising scores are fine things, but they should be signposts along the way—not the destination. A good response identifies the destination and lights a path forward. A good response is that you want every eighth-grader to speak a second language, master algebra, or volunteer in her community. Knowing what you care about frees you to push back on the stuff that you don't think important.

For instance, Steve Dackin, superintendent in Reynoldsburg, Ohio, says, "My concern about the [highly qualified teacher] requirement is— I'm not. I'm less concerned about a credential than I am making sure the teacher is effective. My report card will speak for itself. We received an A on the last report card, and we hit twenty-six out of all twenty-six performance goals while reducing our expenditures."

Dave Wilson was asked to take over as principal at the high school with the worst graduation rate in Nevada. In addition to the usual problems, he also noted that, at a school where 55 percent of the students were Latinos in families pummeled by Las Vegas's collapsing economy, many absences were due to students working full-time to help support their siblings. He determined that perhaps more than half of the persistently absent students were actually mastering the content: "I decided that what matters is whether the students are learning the material, not whether they're necessarily sitting in classrooms."

Wilson says, "It turned out the principal has the authority to look at each case and determine whether to issue credit, despite the number of absences per semester. So I just said, 'If the student can pass the exams and demonstrate mastery, this is what matters.'" The result: a fifteen-point graduation boost in Wilson's first year. Is Wilson's strategy necessarily the right one? Nope. Might attendance be more important than Wilson allows? Sure. But Wilson owned his judgment and he led accordingly. How did the superintendent respond? Well, the superintendent was sitting at hand as Wilson told me this story. He said, "I just get out of Dave's way. I wish I had more like him."

PRECISION IS YOUR FRIEND

A cage-buster can't settle for ambiguity, banalities, or imprecision. These things provide dark corners where all manners of ineptitude and excuse making can hide.

Thus, cage-busters strive to see things clearly and discuss them precisely. Craig Pliskin, an assistant principal in Cypress-Fairbanks ISD outside of Houston, puts it beautifully: "There are four kinds of barriers. There's, 'We don't have to' or 'You can't make me,' which is culture. There's the legal, 'We're not allowed to,' response. There's, 'Why we can't do it,' which is about logistics. Finally, people will explain 'why we shouldn't do it.'"

These excuses thrive in ambiguity and shrink when subjected to scrutiny. "You can't make me" can be combated by making clear that they *do* have to, or by altering incentives so that they'll *want* to. "We're not allowed to" can be fought by finding specific policies or contract provisions that permit action or, more often, by showing that supposed prohibitions don't actually exist. "Why we can't" can be countered by scrutinizing resources to find a way forward. And that narrows objections to "why we shouldn't," a complaint that's surprisingly tractable in isolation. Specificity lights the way.

I recall meeting with a clutch of principals to discuss parental involvement and asking one principal from a high-performing school what percentage of her parents attended parent-teacher conferences. She said the figure was around 50 percent. I asked what she'd like it to be. She said 90 percent. Suddenly, instead of vague pledges to "boost parental engagement," we had an actual goal and a specific problem to solve.

Until that moment she'd been uninterestedly scrolling her iPhone. Now, she got interested—and unstuck. She said the school could have parents sign in on big nights to get hard numbers and track its gains. She could ask staff to visit habitually absent parents and perhaps drive them to school, if necessary. She could have teachers do more to ensure that notices made it home to parents or guardians in languages they understand. In hindsight, these ideas all struck her as obvious, leading her to good-naturedly grouse, "We should have started looking into these three years ago." Precise, identifiable problems lead to problem solving.

Cathy Mincberg, CEO of the Houston-based Center for Reform of School Systems, recalls:

> When I was on the Houston School Board, we constantly complained about the difficulty and cost of terminating administrators. When we asked why this was hard, the administration had many reasons. When I returned to the district as chief business officer years later, I asked the *lawyers* a different question: "How can we let an administrator go without having to go through a long-drawn-out process?" That simple question produced a solution. All we had to do was buy any administrator's term contract and renewal rights for reasonable consideration. All but a handful of current administrators took the option [which came with a one-time $5,000 to $15,000 bump in salary]. The district had to litigate one time. It won. After that, the provision was rarely exercised, but often used to negotiate a peaceful departure of someone who wasn't measuring up. This simple action had a huge impact on the quality of district administration.

Jeremy Hauser, academic manager in Clark County, Nevada, says, "What people tell you is not necessarily the whole truth, or the only truth. In our district, we wanted to use our ELL teachers differently, and began finding multiple states that have done so. After hearing those examples, you can't just tell me that it's impossible to do that because of federal mandates. You now have an example of someplace interpreting the law to let this happen. If some states are doing it, you can no longer tell me federal mandates prohibit it. When you get stuck is when you just accept the procedures of the district over your gut instincts about what's right."

Precision can surface solutions that are simpler than you might imagine. Years ago, I was researching reform in Buffalo and hearing about the system's failure to remove ineffective teachers before they got tenure. There was much talk about better recruiting and improved evaluation. Yet, it soon became clear that a key reason no one was denied tenure was that the system *had never bothered to generate the forms required to terminate a probationary teacher.* This little obstacle had gone overlooked and unaddressed for years. Imprecise critiques can lead us to miss obvious problems. (For more on how to make sure you're getting precise information, see "Get Your Information Straight from the Tap.")

Get Your Information Straight from the Tap

One big problem for school and system leaders is that information tends to be highly filtered by the time it gets to them. This is why it pays to take claims about what can or can't be done with a big grain of salt. President Franklin Roosevelt, a man who knew a little something about leadership, had a stratagem for dealing with this filtration problem. Historian Arthur Schlesinger explained that FDR believed a leader needed "to guarantee himself an effective flow of information and ideas . . . through a myriad of private, informal, and unorthodox channels and espionage networks. At times he seemed almost to pit his personal sources against his public sources."[3]

It's critical to verify the information you receive from staff because, as Warren Bennis, Daniel Goleman, and James O'Toole point out in *Transparency*, "When staff speak to their leader . . . the message is likely to be spun, softened, and colored in ways calculated to make it more accept-able." The result: a leader "who has a narrow view of proper channels for information often pays a high price for its orderly but insufficient flow." To avoid this trap, they advise finding ways "to get information raw."[4]

These cautions are doubly important for educational leaders, who find themselves in a world where consensus is celebrated, plain speak-ing can be perilous, and everyone is used to dealing in the lexicon of "must" or "can't."

How can raw information help? Consider the K–5 principal who says, "I'd really like to restore five days of music and art. We can swing it if we take another look at staffing in special education. We've got three FTEs working with nine students in a self-contained class. What if that third teacher spends some time supporting a couple classes with main-streamed kids and we use the savings to restore arts time?" The district official says, "Sorry, you can't do that." So the principal suggests, "How about if we bump up class size in phys ed, art, languages, and music?" Another district official says, "Sorry, you can't do that."

Well, why *can't* you? In this case, neither the special ed nor the elec-tive class size policies were as cut-and-dried as reported. It turned out the principal *could.* Saying "no" was just the default response of the special ed coordinator and associate superintendent for instruction. But the principal learned that only by getting her information straight from the tap—by talking to a friendly outsider, consulting a helpful attorney, and then using that information to talk precisely with district officials.

CALLING PROBLEMS BY THEIR GIVEN NAME

An ancient Chinese proverb advises, "The beginning of wisdom is to call things by their right names." Doing so helps focus the mind and pierce the fog of platitudes. It permits us to see problems and surface solutions.

There's great value in setting concrete, granular goals for students, teachers, schools, programs, offices, or the system. By *granular*, I mean specifically what you think a great school or school system looks like. What share of parents hear from their child's teacher in a given week? How fast do teachers get assessment results back? How many students are "advanced" in chemistry or biology?

Once you've set targets, gauge where you are. If you'd like to be at 50 percent of students mastering a second language, and you're currently at 40 percent, that's a *problem*. If you don't know how you're faring, because you don't track those data, that's a *big problem*. It's a problem even if your numbers are relatively good. Why? *Because you just said so.* When you identify objectives you deem important, and then determine that you're falling short (or don't even know how you're faring!), you've pinpointed problems.

And this is great! It generates clear, concrete goals. It flags precise opportunities to get better. And it enables you to identify and cast into sharp relief the obstacles in your way. If your teachers aren't reaching out to parents at the rate you think they need to be, is it due to lack of time? A dearth of contact information? Because the teachers don't know what to say? Because the teachers don't think it's important?

I recall teaching one principal who said it was hard to drive improvement because his school already fared well on California's accountability rubric and thus lacked clear, motivating challenges. A classmate asked if he had goals beyond California's reading and math metrics. The principal said, "In a perfect world, 100 percent of my students would be able to speak two languages." When asked what the number was currently, he said, "About 5 percent." I said, "So, you're failing there." He reflexively responded, "No, we're not." Then he paused, thought, and said, "Yeah, we are." He thought another moment, then said, "You know, saying it that way to our teachers and parents might help." He explained, "Not everyone is interested in our language offerings, which are mostly French and Spanish. I'd like to offer sign language. But I can't fund it. I want to bring in people that aren't credentialed to teach other languages, but we don't have any way to do that." Failing to focus on the concrete, the principal had been stuck.

Now, the principal quickly got unstuck. Could he get a waiver or memorandum of understanding (MOU) that would allow uncertified sign language instructors to come in and teach? (He didn't know.) Could he use Rosetta Stone or another computer-assisted provider to offer language instruction that he couldn't afford to staff? (He would ask.) Could he find a way to reconfigure his budget or staffing to fund language offerings? (He hadn't looked.) Identifying a problem unlocked a raft of potential new ways to tackle it.

Vikas Mittal, a professor of marketing at the Rice University School of Management, tells an instructive story about working with Houston principals who'd been losing students under the district's school choice plan. He says that many schools were busy "wasting funds on t-shirts and fancy brochures" without ever stopping to think what problem they needed to solve or what parents wanted. He recalls,

> One school was a mile and a half from the nearest bus stop. And the principal named all of the rules and reasons why the [public transit] bus wouldn't come directly to the school. But YES [Prep] and KIPP were using shuttles from the bus stop to the school. When I asked the principal, "What are you going to do?" the principal said, "I'll start an after-school drama and arts program." And I thought, "How is that supposed to help?" They were spending all that money on the drama program in the evening without rectifying the real problems.

Mittal says, "People mistakenly seem to think that marketing is about brochures, events, and gimmicks; good management instead focuses on the needs of students and families and how to meet them."

THE "CURLY RULE"

Now, you may well be asking, "Hold it. I can identify a dozen places I might do better. Fine. But what am I supposed to do with that? I can't tackle a dozen things at a time."

That's absolutely right. As we've said, that's part of the problem with the twenty-one-point plans of the ed leadership gurus.

The value of identifying all of these possibilities is *not* because you'll address them all right now. It's because it helps you get unstuck. It pierces the haze and lets you see where, why, and how you're falling short. Remember, while a lot of education thinkers tell you what your priorities are *supposed* to be, cage-busting doesn't. Cage-busting isn't about marching orders. It's about helping you figure out how to do better at those things *you* have flagged as important.

Put another way: you need to embrace the "Curly rule." What's that? Well, some readers may remember the 1991 Billy Crystal movie *City Slickers*.

Crystal plays Mitch, who, in the throes of a midlife crisis, heads out west. Along the way, Mitch finds himself alone with Jack Palance's grizzled trail boss Curly. Eventually, Curly warms to Mitch, telling him he's met any number of "city slickers" hoping to get their priorities straight.

Finally, as they're riding, Curly asks Mitch, "Do you know what the secret of life is?"

MITCH: No, what?

CURLY (*holding up index finger*): One thing. Just one thing. You stick to that and everything else don't mean sh*t.

MITCH: That's great, but what's the one thing?

CURLY (*smiling*): That's what you've gotta figure out.[5]

Vikas Mittal offers an observation that can help leaders apply the "Curly rule":

> The thing that boggles my mind is the district's belief that if we keep giving more and more information to parents, they'll see the light of day. With charter schools like YES and KIPP, it's not just about an information dump. Their parents have a much better sense of what it is that the school stands for . . . Businesses know [what they stand for] and everything is designed to accomplish that objective. KIPP and YES's positioning is designed around getting students to college—that means they don't do other things. They don't promise the best football team. The district schools try to be everything to everybody; in the process, they're nothing to anyone.

PROBLEM SOLVING, NOT "REFORM"

Precision, naming problems, and the "Curly rule" add up to the cage-buster's simple, clarifying mantra of: "What problem are you solving?" Cage-busters try to begin every conversation—with parents, board members, staff, and the pizza delivery guy—by talking about the problems they've identified and how they might solve them.

Is reading performance far below where it should be? Okay. Moral urgency is swell, but what are you going to do besides care more and work harder? You don't need "innovation" or "reform." You need to solve a problem. Why are you coming up short? Is it the curriculum? Amount of time on task? Caliber of instruction? Lack of student engagement? Lack of parental support? Some of these? All of these?

Define, as concretely as possible, the problem you're trying to solve. Remember, excuses love ambiguity. Once you focus on *this* problem, as it exists *here and now*, it's a lot easier to start identifying possible solutions.

Take professional learning communities. Nearly every school claims to be a professional learning community (PLC) or says that it wants to be one. Of course, being a PLC requires time for teams to meet and plan; timely data on student learning; and customized training and support. These are all good things that instructional leaders heartily endorse. The frustrating thing is that it's remarkably hard to make all this actually happen. Between contracts and master schedules, schools can't find the requisite planning time for teams. It takes days, or sometimes weeks, to get the results of formative assessments—and the data or the data analysis tools may not be granular enough to usefully inform instruction. Professional development is too often provided through drive-by workshops or in generic monthly staff meetings. A problem-solving approach can't birth a PLC, but it helps identify and deliver what is needed for PLCs to fulfill their promise.

Ultimately, a problem-solving focus helps you constantly circle back to the six questions that should guide every action you take:

Is X *important*?
If so, how well *should* we be doing when it comes to X?
How well *are* we doing with X?
If we're not doing as well as we should, how can we *improve* X?
What's *stopping* us from improving X?
And finally: How do we *remove, blast through, or tunnel under the bars* stopping us from improving X?

You can boil cage-busting down to those six questions. (For more help getting started, and examples of the kinds of questions worth asking, check out appendix B.) The rest of the book is basically an extended treatise on how to do this. It offers examples, flags opportunities, and highlights how some others have forged ahead. But let's keep it simple: leaders who wake up each day asking these six questions have a fighting chance to do something about the mountain. Leaders who don't, well—hello, Sisyphus . . .

TALENT, TOOLS, TIME, AND MONEY

Cage-busters focus not on "more, better" education but on finding ways to improve "teaching" and "schooling." And this is largely a question of finding smarter ways to employ *talent, tools, time,* and *money.*

Talent is all of the expertise, potential instruction, and mentoring that you might tap—whether that encompasses full-time classroom teachers, operational staff, local undergraduates, online instructors, part-time tutors, or volunteer professionals. *Tools* are all of the materials, resources, management techniques, training, and so forth that can help support talent, including the technology that allows us to better inspire minds, share expertise, track data, and deliver instruction. *Time* is all the student time and adult time you can use to promote learning. And *money* is, well, all the money at your disposal. We'll talk much more about all these in chapters 5 and 6.

The bottom line, though, is simple. Schools are in the people business, and the talent pool on which schooling draws has changed profoundly in recent decades. This means, like it or not, we need to rethink our assumptions about how schools ought to attract and use talent. Sixty years ago, more than half of all college-educated women became teachers; today, it's closer to 15 percent. Forty years ago, the average college grad expected to hold perhaps five jobs in the course of his career; today's grads expect to hold that many jobs by the age of thirty. Like it or not, schools no longer enjoy a monopoly on educated women and need to find new ways to recruit, use, and retain talented teachers.[6]

Today, even the most heralded charter and district schools tend to rely on "more, better" solutions: more school time, more talent, and staff working more evenings and weekends. The problem is that the supply of talent, energy, and passion is limited. That's why transformative improvement, in any sector, typically requires rethinking the way things are done. While educators sometimes balk at such talk, with some critics ominously warning (again) of "business" thinking, it's really just a question of making the best use of the talent, tools, time, and money at your disposal. In fact, such rethinking holds opportunities for educators to fill dynamic new roles, spend more time doing what they're best at and what they enjoy most, take on new responsibilities, earn more pay, and to do all of this without having to abandon teaching for administration. (For some additional guidance in how to use talent smarter and to create new opportunities for educators, see "Rethinking School Design to Create an 'Opportunity Culture.'")

Leaders need to ask whether they're squeezing all the juice they might out of the team they have. For instance, we know from time diaries that about 35 percent of the typical teacher's day is spent on tasks other than instruction—on assemblies, celebrations, attendance, paperwork, class disruptions, and the rest.[7] Can you reduce this by half? Doing so would boost each student's instructional time by more than one hundred hours a year.

IT'S NOT REFORM IF IT COSTS MORE

You may recall the 2011 movie *Moneyball*, starring Brad Pitt as visionary Oakland A's general manager Billy Beane. Based on Michael Lewis's terrific 2003 book of the same name, the movie tells the story of how a cash-strapped A's team learned to compete with richer ball clubs. Early in the film, Beane sits down with owner Stephen Schott to insist he needs more money. Beane starts by mumbling some encouraging words, then cuts to the chase:

BEANE: Um . . . we're not gonna do better next year.
SCHOTT: Why not?
BEANE: Well, you know, we're being gutted . . . We need more money Steve.
SCHOTT: Bill . . .
BEANE: I need more money!
SCHOTT (*quietly*): We don't have any more money.
BEANE (*pleading*): I gotta ask you, what are we doing here if it's not to win a championship? That's my bar. My bar is here. My bar is to take this team to the championship.

Rethinking School Design to Create an "Opportunity Culture"

North Carolina-based Public Impact has helped spell out some of the options for making fuller use of talented staff and new technologies. The goal is to forge an "opportunity culture" where opportunities reflect instructional excellence, leadership, and impact on students.[8]

Such schools create a number of new opportunities for educators to work with kids, take on new responsibilities, and cultivate new skills. A half-dozen roles Public Impact suggests include:

Blended-learning teacher: Extends reach by swapping enough teaching time with digital instruction to teach more students, in person or remotely.

Specialized teacher: Extends reach by teaching best subject(s) to more classes and students, in person or remotely. Other duties are reduced.

Teacher-leader: Extends reach by leading multiple classrooms (in a school or virtually) and a teaching team. Responsible for team and all students.

Professional tutor: Delivers assigned small-group and individual instruction; professional tutor is certified or experienced teacher now delivering this focused instruction.

Video-teacher: Records video units of instruction for repeated use by students learning digitally—in school, at home, or in community-based organizations.

Digital designer: Contributes to design of instructional software, using knowledge of subject matter content and student motivation.

Why bother with all of this? Well, for one thing, today's twenty-somethings think very differently about careers than did recent graduates thirty or forty years ago. Pollster Jean Johnson observes that, when talking to students at top colleges, one big concern about teaching is that "young people in their twenties have a hard time envisioning (and being excited about) doing the same job in the same way in the same place for several decades." That's one reason that barely half of young teachers say that they see teaching as a lifelong career. At the same time, there's much more interest in staying in education if there are opportunities for growth, new roles, and new challenges.[9] So, rethinking job descriptions is not just a chance to get more value from the talent we have, it's also a necessary adaptation in a labor market where old norms have changed.

SCHOTT: Bill, I'm asking you to be okay not spending money that I don't have. And I'm asking you to take a deep breath . . . and figure out how to find replacements for the guys we lost with the money that we do have.[10]

Moneyball is the story of how Beane learned to think differently, taught the A's to think differently, and, after sufficient ridicule, how the A's taught baseball to think differently. The lesson is explained by Peter Brand, the young baseball economist Beane hires to help him figure out how to do more with less:

BRAND: There is an epidemic failure within the game to understand what is really happening and this leads people who run major league baseball teams to misjudge their players and mismanage their teams.
BEANE (*intrigued*): Go on.
BRAND: Okay, people who run ball clubs, they think in terms of buying players. Your goal shouldn't be to buy players. Your goal should be to buy wins, and in order to buy wins, you need to buy your runs. You're trying to replace Johnny Damon. The Boston Red Sox see Johnny Damon and they see a star who's worth seven and a half million dollars a year. When I see Johnny Damon, what I see is . . . an imperfect understanding of where runs come from. The guy's got a great glove, he's a decent lead-off hitter, he can steal bases. But is he worth the seven and a half million dollars a year the Boston Red Sox are paying him? No! No! Baseball thinking is medieval. They are asking all the wrong questions, and if I say it to anybody . . . I'm ostracized. I'm a rebel . . . Mr. Beane, and if you want full disclosure, I think it's a good thing you got Damon off of your payroll. I think it opens up all kinds of interesting possibilities.[11]

It's always nice to have more money. But there's only so much money to go around. Taxpayers don't have limitless wealth, and policy makers are also concerned about funding health care, highways, public safety, higher education, and much else. Every dollar you need is a dollar that can't go to another school or another need. More to the point, depending on more makes us lazy and cautious. Necessity can help unlock our imagination. Everybody wants more; the real trick is to figure out how to get the job done with the money that is available. And that requires thinking like a moneyballer.

Cage-busters have a simple mantra: *It's not reform if it costs more. Reform* is finding ways to improve teaching, learning, and schooling with the resources you've got. Spending more money to get better is fine. But, if you spend more on anything, you'd better expect to improve. That's not reform, that's just a minimal test for not wasting money.

What do I mean? Adding all-day pre-K because you get millions in additional funding might be a swell idea, but it's not reform—it's just spending those dollars on one new service instead of another. Adding extra staff because you got grant funds? Not reform; just more money for more bodies. This is what we referred to in chapter 2 as "more, better" reform.

The only time cage-busters countenance "more, better" reform is when leaders use new dollars to vault themselves up the mountain. Using millions in new spending just to adopt "merit pay" at a few dozen schools? Not reform. But using funds to help convince the union to alter the CBA? Now, that's using new funds to make a lasting change. Example: Washington, DC was promised about $60 million by several major foundations if—and only if—teachers approved the performance-based contract negotiated by the Washington Teachers Union and Chancellor Michelle Rhee. In this way, the investment greased the transition from the old system to the new.

Now, let's be clear. I am *not* saying that schools have enough money. (I'm also unconvinced that they're underfunded.) I'm saying that cage-busters do the best they possibly can for their students with the talent, tools, and resources that they have. When you've wrung every last ounce out of what you've got, then, by all means, make the case for more.

In short, it's not that schools and systems have all they may need to meet our shared ambitions, but that they can and should do a lot better with what they've got.

LAZY MAN'S LOBSTER

Let me put this another way. Have you ever been to a restaurant and ordered "lazy man's lobster"? The dish is so-named for a reason. "Lazy man's lobster" is when the chef takes the lobster meat out of the shell for you so you don't have to get your hands dirty. It's convenient. And, if you've got a few bucks to spare, it's all good. But you don't always have those extra bucks.

"I need more money" is the lazy-man's-lobster approach to school improvement. Money is the lazy man's way to procure talent, tools, and time. You need more tutoring, more instruction, more guidance counseling? You can get it by altering rules, repurposing funds, or convincing parents or local professionals to pitch in. Money is just a convenient shortcut. You need more instructional time? Cool. What percentage of your teachers' time is currently spent trying to get unruly kids to behave? If you don't know, that's a problem. Find out. If it's 10 percent of their time, cutting that in half in a school with forty teachers is like adding two full-time positions—or about $140,000. That's right; improving student discipline is like getting an extra $140,000 a year.

Steve Dackin, superintendent in Reynoldsberg, Ohio, illustrates why money isn't the only way to solve a problem, just the easiest:

> Three years ago, to ensure that our graduates are career and college ready, we affectionately declared war on the senior year. We have entered into a variety of partnerships, so we now have, for example, a community college on one of our high school campuses. So now most seniors will not be taking traditional classes in our schools. They'll be out and about on college campuses, in internships, taking online courses or in a blended learning environment, taking dual enrollment college courses or attending our career and technical education centers.

To provide these services, Dackin has gotten creative:

> Keep in mind, I don't have any money. But I have premium space. We have all new or newly renovated buildings. So space has become a sort of currency for us. I invested $1.4 million in bond money to renovate for the college's needs. The benefit to us is a shared services partnership in which the college's professors deliver both high school and college credits to our students. We think this is going to be a new model in Ohio. It's not about adding funds; it's about taking dollars we have and spending them differently.

Rob Mancabelli, educational technology expert and author of *Personal Learning Networks*, observes, "The most common thing I hear when I bring up technology is, 'That's great, but we really don't have the money.' When I hear that, I ask the district to let me take a look at their budget. What I usually find is money being spent on nondigital things that would be completely eliminated by the new technology—calculators for the classroom, paper, ink, toner, postage, letterheads, and so on. All of these things that they're spending tens to hundreds of thousands of dollars on would be eliminated." When it comes down to it, Mancabelli says, "They usually have more than enough money, especially with how technology costs have fallen. It's a matter of shifting mind-sets about how to spend the money they have."

Dan Weisberg, executive vice president at TNTP, relates, on a similar note:

> [Houston superintendent] Terry Grier did something on professional development that I don't think any other district has done. He had a fairly typical central operation, with a bunch of people working on curriculum and presenting workshops, and no particular way to measure impact. He restructured that entire operation to create 130 new teacher development specialist positions. They're responsible for spending 100 percent of their time in the schools providing individualized support based on teacher needs identified in the new appraisal process. This had a marginal cost of zero. He just took the existing funding and repurposed it.

I've never yet seen a school or system that couldn't free up time or resources if leaders took a hard look at what they're doing. Start there.

THE "NEW STUPID"

It's hard to attend an education conference without being bombarded by talk of "data-based decision making" and "research-based practice." But unless we're careful, today's enthusiastic embrace of data can lead to a reflexive reliance on a few simple metrics and stand in for careful thought. Too often, the result can be something I've called the "new stupid."[12] The "new stupid" incorporates three key mistakes.

Using Data in Half-Baked Ways. I recall giving a presentation to a group of aspiring superintendents. They were passionate and eager to make data-driven decisions. But I got concerned as we discussed value-added assessment and teacher assignments. They'd recently read about the inequitable distribution of teachers within districts. The aspirants were fired up and ready to put this knowledge to use. To a roomful of nods, one declared,

"Day one, we're going to start identifying those high-value-added teachers and moving them to the schools that need them." I envisioned these well-meaning leaders shuffling teachers among schools, growing frustrated when results didn't translate across schools, puzzling over the departure of highly rated teachers, and wondering what had gone wrong. The key is not to retreat from data but to ask hard questions and contemplate unintended consequences.

Translating Research Simplistically. For decades, advocates of class-size reduction have referenced the findings from the Student Teacher Achievement Ratio (STAR) project, a class-size experiment conducted in Tennessee in the late 1980s. Researchers found significant achievement gains for students in small kindergarten classes and additional gains in first grade, especially for African American students. The results seemed to validate a crowd-pleasing reform and were famously embraced in California, where in 1996 legislators adopted a program to reduce class sizes that cost billions in its first decade. Yet, the dollars ultimately yielded disappointing results, with the only major evaluation finding no effect on student achievement.[13] What happened? Policymakers ignored context. STAR was a pilot program serving a limited population, which minimized the need for new teachers. California's statewide effort created a voracious appetite for new educators, diluting teacher quality and encouraging well-off districts to strip-mine teachers from less affluent communities. The moral: even policies or practices informed by rigorous research can prove ineffective if the translation is clumsy or context is ignored.

Giving Short Shrift to Management Data. Schools and systems have embraced student achievement data, but too many "data-driven" systems have given short shrift to the operations, hiring, and financial practices crucial to ensuring that talent, tools, time, and resources are used wisely and well. State tests offer little more than a snapshot of student and school performance, and few district data systems link student achievement metrics to operations, practices, or programs in a way that can help determine what is working. Successful public and private organizations monitor their operations extensively and intensively. FedEx and UPS know at any given time where millions of packages are across the United States and around the globe. Yet few districts know how long it takes to respond to a teaching applicant, how frequently teachers use formative assessments, or how rapidly school requests for supplies are processed and fulfilled.

USE DATA LIKE A PROBLEM SOLVER

Turning "data-driven decision making" into more than a platitude requires avoiding the "new stupid." How do you do that?

First, don't allow data or research to substitute for good judgment. (See "Getting Moneyball Right.") When presented with promising programs or reforms, ask the simple questions: What are the expected benefits? What are the costs? How confident should you be that promising results are replicable?

Second, cage-busters need to be sure they're collecting data with an eye toward solving problems. Student achievement data is terrific, but it doesn't tell you how effectively HR is recruiting or how well schools are communicating with parents. Such measures can help flag problems and suggest answers.

Third, data can be as important for illuminating challenges as for its ability to dictate solutions. After all, one popular justification for cage-dwelling inertia is, "There's no problem to solve." Without good data, it's hard to challenge such claims. The result, in the words of TNTP's Ariela Rozman, ĭs "dysfunction based around denial." For instance, in one large California district in 2008, the contract allowed forced placement of teachers into schools—even when principals didn't want them. Asked if this practice was a problem, HR officials told TNTP analysts, "Well, technically it's allowed, but it never happens. We pride ourselves on not doing that." However, the district had no data documenting what was happening one way or another. When TNTP gathered the data and surveyed principals, Rozman recalls, "Well north of half of the principals said forced placements happened regularly to them [and] some principals were saying it was a massive problem."

TNTP president Tim Daly notes, "When people don't want to look into a problem, they will sometimes *deny that the means to investigate it even*

Getting Moneyball Right

The movie *Moneyball*, drawing on Michael Lewis's 2003 book, explores how the Oakland A's used sophisticated statistical analysis to build winning teams. While it hasn't gotten much traction in traditional educational leadership, *Moneyball* has inspired many in school reform circles to think about how to use value-added metrics in the same way that A's general manager Billy Beane leveraged new econometric tools.

Here's the thing. Lewis made it abundantly clear in the book that the pre-Beane problem was not an absence of data. In fact, baseball has long been a geek haven *because* of all its statistics. The problem was that the stats—typically home runs, runs batted in, and batting average—were flawed measures of individual performance. They routinely understated (or overstated) a player's value by ignoring the stadium he played in, how often his teammates got on base, how well he fielded, and so on. The problem was less a lack of numbers and more a reliance on simplistic measures. Players who hit a lot of home runs were overpriced, while players who played on bad teams were often undervalued.

This is where value-added student achievement comes in. Value-added is potentially a very useful tool, but it's still in its relative infancy. Today's value-added metrics conflate the effect of support staff and teachers of record, capture a narrow slice of instruction, are exceedingly imprecise, and offer only an incomplete picture of the performance of perhaps 30 percent of teachers. Value-added can provide useful information, illuminate what might otherwise be overlooked, and help combat our tendency to misjudge certain teachers, schools, or programs, but it should not stand in for good judgment and common sense.

It's frustrating, but today's value-added measurements mean only that K–12 has finally caught up to baseball in its *pre*-moneyball era. We finally have simple, incomplete performance measures like home runs and batting average. These tell us something useful, but they'll lead us astray unless used carefully.

Paul DePodesta, the inspiration for Billy Beane's ubergeek right-hand statistician in the movie, cautions that the moneyball idea was never intended to replace human judgment. Rather, DePodesta has noted that baseball execs are "constantly trying to predict the future performance of human beings. We're trying to get our arms around that uncertainty. Scouts really help you deal with that uncertainty. On the other hand, we looked at it and said, 'How can we further decrease that uncertainty?' And being able to use data was one of the ways we could do that."[14]

exist." Working with one district to improve teacher evaluation, Daly says, "We asked [the HR director] for things like the GPA of people who applied to the district and their evaluations, and he told us flatly that none of this stuff existed because they had an antiquated data system that didn't store any of it. You could just tell that he had no idea whether it existed or not. My suspicion was that either he knew it existed, or he had no idea and didn't care. So we just went to the tech people, and asked, 'Do these data exist in the database?' And they said yes. Before the end of the business day, we had all of this information in hand."

Now, metrics need to measure what matters. A simple mantra is: *Always be sure that you're not working for your metrics and measurements, but that they're working for you.* Here are three more things to keep in mind when putting data to work.

Measure More Than Test Scores.   Be clear about the outcomes you'd like to see in a classroom, building, program, department, or district. Cage-busters don't just default to state achievement data. That data is valuable, but limited. It can't answer questions like: Are you using faculty time wisely? Is music and art instruction of high quality? Are high achievers mastering advanced science and language skills? Such questions flag opportunities for improvement and help fuel a problem-solving culture. While serving as chief of the Transformation Management Office for Washington, DC, public schools, Abigail Smith recalls that a big challenge was streamlining district operations. She says, "When you start measuring things like the number of days it takes to turn around a procurement, and you're literally sitting around with the leadership of a district and putting up names of the different procurement officers and what their turnaround rate is, it's brutal but it does move things. In terms of kick-starting that culture, that kind of accountability really helped."

Think in Terms of Root Cause.   Solutions that work in one place may not work somewhere else, if the challenges or conditions are different. It's easy to get this wrong, notes LeAnn Buntrock, executive director of the University of Virginia's program for training school turnaround leaders: "One thing I see often, and it just drives me nuts, is when you go into a school and the leader tells you they have a discipline problem. So, they say, since we have a discipline problem, we are going to institute a school uniform policy. And that's just fabulous if student dress is what's causing your discipline problems. But if you look at your data, you might notice, 'Well, actually, most of our discipline referrals take place when kids are getting off the buses. So we need to have more teachers there when kids are getting off the buses.' It comes down to figuring out the root cause of the problem."

Similarly, when serving as Delaware secretary of education, Maryland superintendent Lillian Lowery recalls,

> The state board was saying, "This is insane," because districts were writing new "data-based" corrective action plans every year and nothing was changing. So instead of taking data at face value, the delivery unit started using longitudinal data to check school and district plans. If a school came in and said, "We're going to work on fourth-grade math," we could look at their data and say, "You don't need to work on fourth grade, your fourth-graders have made three years' worth of growth. Your tenth-graders are the ones with the abysmal math scores." So we could focus them and say, "You need to do a root cause analysis." It was eye-opening for them.

Put the Action in Action Research. *Action research* is one of those awful ed-schoolisms, serving mostly to justify mediocre research. But in the hands of a cage-buster, it's a useful tool for identifying opportunities, illuminating barriers, and solving problems. Action research can help ensure that convenient metrics aren't narrowing your thinking. If you don't know what share of kids are fluent in a second language, that's a great action research project. If you don't know how often teachers are e-mailing, calling, or visiting parents, there's another. Action research is just another way of saying that you need to dig down to identify opportunities to do better.

THE POWER OF CREATIVE PROBLEM SOLVING

If you know your history, you know that the feds didn't get gangster Al Capone for the murders he committed, his bootlegging, or his larcenous

empire.[15] They got him for—yep—not paying his taxes! Creative thinking
has a remarkable power to help tackle stubborn challenges.

David Weiner, deputy chancellor at the New York City Department of
Education and the hero of our principal-moved-into-the-classroom story
from chapter 1, said he's been using the tax-evasion approach for years. He
says it can be tough to remove inept teachers for being "incompetent and
ineffective," but that it can be simpler to remove them for more mundane
transgressions:

> Getting a teacher out through the rating process is kind of like how the US
> government actually put Al Capone in jail for tax evasion. That's kind of
> what it's like as a principal. Given the rules and regulations, I would nev-
> er be able to prove this teacher was incompetent in terms of her teaching
> skills, because [the union would say] I don't know what I'm talking about, I
> never taught fifth grade—you know, a thousand different things. But I was
> always able to say, "You are not teaching social studies. I know because I sat
> in your classroom every day and for two straight weeks you did absolutely
> no social studies and I'm going to give you a U [unsatisfactory] rating for
> that." And the union never defended her. It's like putting Capone away for
> tax evasion; we write up the teacher and get rid of her not for being incom-
> petent but for not teaching social studies.

You don't have to solve every problem head-on. Doing so can be exhausting. That's the problem with so much well-intended ed leadership
advice. The emphasis on collegiality, stakeholder buy-in, and mentoring
means that many leaders run out of steam or get overwhelmed trying to
forge consensus and win everybody over—especially in schools and systems where turnover, attrition, new families, and local elections mean that
such efforts are never "done." Tackling what you can with shortcuts or
creative solutions can make it easier to isolate and solve real problems.

James "Torch" Lytle, veteran school and system leader and professor at
University of Pennsylvania, recalls that while he was a principal at University City High School in Philadelphia, he had one particular teacher
he thought was bad for the school. He says, "My sense was that he was
more concerned [with] his personal status and recognition than with his
students' success." He dealt with the situation in an unusual fashion: "One
of my early mentors taught me that as an administrator, and particularly

as a principal, you define yourself by the people you fire or offload . . . A trick I had learned as a central office administrator was to ask Human Resources for a W-2 (tax statement) run at the end of each tax year, with individuals rank-ordered by the total amount they had been paid for the year." When he did this, he "was stunned to find that [this teacher] had been paid $35,000 more than his base salary. I asked the district's controller to investigate, and learned that the teacher had listed himself on several different overtime payrolls—and on many occasions had submitted duplicate invoices. He had arranged to be paid from two or three different accounts for time worked on the same days . . . I initiated a formal evaluation process, which ended with his termination."[16]

There's nothing wrong with using ingenuity to make rules and policies work for you. This is what union locals, recalcitrant vendors, and pushy special interests do—they take the letter of the law and stretch it to their ends. Cage-busters employ that same savvy in the service of great teaching and learning.

Lock onto that mental picture of what you think schooling should look like, and make that your North Star. What are ways to accomplish that vision smarter and better? And what rules, boundaries, and bars stand in your way? Once you're thinking that way, you're ready to bust that cage. Now, it's time to explore all the ways to proceed, and that's easier if we understand the bars that may stand in your way.

4

Seeing Through
the Shadows

"The real world is beyond the mind's ken; we see it through
the net of our desires . . . To see the universe as it is, you must
step beyond the net. It is not hard to do so, for the net is full of
holes. Look at the net and its many contradictions."

—Sri Nisargadatta Maharaj

"Behold human beings living in an underground den, which
has a mouth open towards the light and reaching all along
the den; here they have been from their childhood, and have
their legs and necks chained so that they cannot move, and
can only see before them . . . Above and behind them a fire is
blazing at a distance, and between the fire and the prisoners
there is a raised way; and you will see, if you look, a low wall
built along the way, like the screen which marionette players
put in front of them, over which they show the puppets."

"I see."

"And do you see," I said, "men passing along the wall
carrying all sorts of vessels, and statues and figures of animals
made of wood and stone and various materials, which appear
over the wall? Some of them are talking, others silent."

"You have shown me a strange thing, and they are strange
prisoners."

> "Like ourselves," I replied; "and they see only their own
> shadows, or the shadows of one another."
>
> —Plato, *The Republic*

A "WHAT PROBLEM ARE YOU SOLVING?" approach can help a cage-buster find a way through the bars of the cage. The problem: the bars of the cage are swathed in shadow. The cage-buster must first find the bars if she is to cut, smash, or slip through them. This requires piercing the darkness.

In practice, cage-busting actually makes doing so easier. Why? By seeking out the specific, cage-busters illuminate the possible and backlight real impediments. If you merely say, "I want to give a raise to teachers working in hard-to-staff schools, but I can't," you're stuck. After all, it's not clear why you "can't." Is it due to contract? State law? District policy? In truth, most leaders just know that they've heard or been told that they can't. When you start asking and acting, things get clearer.

IS THAT BAR REALLY THERE?

Cage-busters actively assess the bars in their way. Some bars are thick, anchored in concrete, and hard to budge. Others may prove to be little more than shadows. It's useful to think of these bars as arrayed along a *cage-bar continuum*.

There are certainly plenty of *solid bars* out there. States like West Virginia and Pennsylvania mandate seniority as the sole determinant when making layoffs, leaving districts with no wiggle room.[1] Six states require charter schools to operate in accord with all the provisions in the local district's CBA.[2] In Virginia, several superintendents sought to change state policy so that students could have multiple chances to demonstrate mastery on the state's Standards of Learning assessments. As Fairfax County superintendent Jack Dale puts it, "The state board said 'No.' Not only that, but 'Hell, no.'" That's a solid bar.

Other bars are *illusory and self-imposed*. In New York City, the district was having a hard time getting principals to honestly assess and write up their low-performing teachers, since each negative piece of feedback was subject to a three-step grievance and arbitration process. Dan Weisberg, who served as the district's chief executive of labor policy and implementation, explains, "The final two steps were a big deal, because [principals] had to leave their building and go downtown, which could take hours. Principals complained about it and used it as an excuse [for] why they couldn't document poor performance when they saw it." So, according to Weisberg, "[Our team asked the principals], 'Why couldn't you attend these hearings by phone?' And the answer we first got was 'No, we can't do it. We've never done it that way.' And we said 'Where is that in the contract? Where is that in some policy?' And the answer is, nowhere. So we just did it. It was a small thing, but it showed principals that we cared, that we understood this was very burdensome and we were trying to make their lives easier . . . It had a concrete impact in encouraging principals to take action to document poor performance."

Distinguishing the things you can do from those you can't also makes it easier to tell allies and supporters where you need their help. In the words of education attorney Melissa Junge, "The beauty is, once you've gone through a process of looking at your own practices and searching for additional flexibility and you've found some hard stops, then you really have something useful with which to approach [state or federal officials] . . . If you haven't done that sort of self-inventory, it's hard to see what's a hard stop legally."

In practice, cage-busters frequently navigate what Newark superintendent Cami Anderson terms the *messy middle*. Obstacles in the messy middle are more than illusory, but can frequently be managed with know-how, political maneuvering, or elbow grease. For instance, key CBA provisions can be maddeningly ambiguous. There's a provision in the Little Rock, Arkansas, contract that stipulates, "An individual teacher's lesson plan book shall be subject to the review of the principal at any time," before also stipulating that "Teachers shall not be required to make their lesson plan books available on a scheduled basis."[3] There's a *lot* of gray there.

In Montana, state rules on class size dictate that the maximum class size be no more than twenty students in kindergarten and grades 1 and 2; and no more than twenty-eight students in grades 3 and 4. The law then takes pains to specify, "An overload of five students per classroom is considered excessive."⁴ This would suggest the actual class size limits are four students higher than at first appearance. Such language casts plenty of shadows, and a cage-buster learns to distinguish shadow from substance.

MAKING SENSE OF POLICY

I work in a DC think tank and regularly teach education policy. So it's no surprise that I spend more time thinking about public policy than educators who are busy, you know, teaching kids or leading schools. Even so, I'm surprised by the distaste for policy I so often encounter among school and system leaders. The consensus seems to be that policy is something idiotic state and federal officials do to amuse themselves and annoy practitioners.

I'll be blunt: ed leaders need to get over it. Public schools spend public dollars and hire public employees to serve the public's children. For better or worse, they're going to be governed by public policies. Whether made by legislators or bureaucrats, and in Washington or locally, those policies sketch what educators can and can't do, how money is to be spent, how performance will be judged, who can be hired, and much else. We'll talk in the chapters to come about how to use and influence policy; for now, my aim is to make sure we're clear on what policy is, what it does and doesn't do, and how that can help a cage-buster distinguish solid bars from shadows.

Policy Deals with the Floor, Not the Ceiling

First, understand that policy makers are not seeking to make your life difficult. Trust me on this. They're responsible for spending billions in public funds and for the public's kids. They know that if someone somewhere misspends funds or harms a kid, they'll hear about it—and may get blamed for it. This means that they don't gear policies to the needs or strengths of all-stars; rather, they work with an eye to what bad actors might do wrong.

Think of a teacher adopting classroom rules like "Keep your hands to yourself" or "Phones off." These rules generally aren't targeted at eager or well-behaved students, but at the disruptive. Except in the rarest of cases, policy is not a tool for promoting excellence.

Second, policy must be uniformly applied. Going back to the Enlight-enment, the whole logic of democratic law making was to stop laws from being applied selectively so that kings couldn't create different rules for you and for me. Because rules are being applied across the board—to good actors and bad actors alike—they can't be based on trust or good inten-tions. (So, for instance, legislators can write turnaround policies for all schools that objectively perform below a certain level, but they can't treat those schools differently based on whether or not they trust the princi-pal or the faculty.) Meanwhile, since policy makers aren't worried about people who want to do the right thing, these universal statutes and rules are inevitably written with an eye to those they don't trust.

Policy Can Make You Do Things, but It Can't Make You Do Them Well

Here's a simple rule of thumb: policy makers can make people do things, but they can't make them do them well. Policy is a blunt tool. School and system leaders will frequently tell legislators about their model program and then later wonder, in frustration, "Why don't they just have people do X? It works." The problem is that policy makers don't really have the levers to make schools or systems do X. They can require schools or systems to com-ply with punch lists—hire a parent liaison or set aside forty minutes a day for literacy instruction—but they can't require them to do any of this *well*.

The trouble is that most of what we care about when it comes to teach-ing and learning is about *how* you do these things, rather than *whether* you do them.

Take school turnarounds. I recall talking to a New Jersey reporter about a local turnaround effort. Despite an emphasis on engaging families, a man-datory planning meeting called to get parental input had drawn just a single parent. The reporter found it troubling that the school had done little more than send notes home in student backpacks to announce the meeting. If you think parent engagement matters, you need to get those parents there by hook or by crook. However, policy can't make anyone "do whatever it takes." All it can do is require that you have the meeting and send a note home with every kid. It can't make you live, breathe, and own the effort.

In fact, for all the enthusiasm around school turnarounds, there's a real question about whether many school leaders are taking advantage of the opportunities that these policies can provide. In a 2012 analysis, University of Washington researchers reported that, with a few exceptions, schools and systems in Washington State were approaching turnarounds in ways only marginally different from past improvement efforts. Not surprisingly, despite the hard work of administrators, principals, and teachers, the majority of schools showed little evidence of the bold changes that federal School Improvement Grants were supposed to produce. Policy can push districts to launch turnarounds, but it can't make school or district leaders carry them out aggressively or effectively.[5]

The Policy Maker's Limited Toolbox

In the end, policy makers really only have three crude tools at their disposal. They can *give away money* for particular purposes, tell you *what you must do*, and tell you *what you can't do*. That's about it. Yet, with just these three blunt instruments, they are under immense pressure to make the world a better place.

When they do give money away, policy makers are expected to make sure it is spent responsibly. The thing is, they really only have two ways to police how money is spent. They can regulate *inputs* by writing rules about how you can spend it (how many students per class, how many days school has to meet, and so on). This is the dreaded red tape. The hitch is that all the input rules written to combat malfeasance, stupidity, and missteps apply to everyone. Every time someone does something stupid or wrong, public officials feel compelled to respond with another rule or regulation. Rules written to make sure a bottom 20 percenter doesn't misuse IDEA funds apply to everyone, creating paperwork and restrictions for even the most trustworthy leaders. Given that this goes on month after month, year after year, it's easy to understand how the red tape accumulates—and can eventually thicken into bars.

The other option is to regulate *outcomes* by insisting on certain results. This requires leaning on tests or other performance metrics (and implies that something has to be done if a school or system doesn't deliver the expected results). This is a nice alternative to red tape, if people agree the outcome metrics are fair, accurate, and complete. Of course, when it comes to K–12, that tends to be a sticking point.

One final strategy is to trust people to do the right thing—except that policy makers get lots of grief if it turns out money was spent in ineffectual or problematic ways. You want to know why policy is so frustrating for you? It's because it's equally frustrating for those making policy. Yet, cage-busters must appreciate the design of the cage if they hope to escape it.

Big P Versus *Little p* Policy

It's useful to be clear on the distinction between what I call *big P* and *little p* policies. *Big P* policies are formal statutes and contractual provisions that present stubborn and hard-to-change barriers. These include things like teacher tenure laws, curricular mandates, and seat time requirements.

Little p policies, on the other hand, are local policies, accepted practices, or district conventions that can be more readily altered. They include school staffing, class schedules, dress codes, disciplinary norms, teacher evalua-tion, hiring practices, and much else. Much of what teacher leaders, prin-cipals, and district officials say they "can't" do anything about is of this ilk.

Big P policies are often statutes, which means they've been passed by the US Congress or your state legislature. Other times, they've been hand-ed down by federal or state courts. *Little p* policies are more likely to have been enacted by your school board or merely adopted by the system. Oc-cupying that messy middle are regulations that federal and state officials issue to implement statutes or court decisions.

Determining whether a given concern is a *little p* policy is often the key to determining whether quiet politicking, a memorandum of understand-ing, or creative thinking can solve the problem, or whether much more is necessary.

Federal Policy

Federal law is the source of many real and rumored obstacles, with poli-cies adopted as far back as the 1960s having congealed into regulations that can feel unmovable. As Federal Education Group attorneys Melissa

Junge and Sheara Krvaric have noted, "It is hard to overemphasize the number of federal compliance requirements that apply to states and districts. The Office of the Inspector General once estimated that Title I alone contained 588 discrete compliance requirements, and even this number does not provide a full picture."[6] One common result, violating every precept of cage-busting, is *defensive spending*—with districts more intent on keeping their books clean than ensuring they're spending dollars as effectively as they can.

Yet defensive spending makes sense if we consider what gets states and school districts into trouble. All recipients that spend more than $500,000 per year of federal funds must conduct an annual organization-wide audit of their federal program administration, including a review of internal systems such as procurement, payroll, inventory, and financial management.[7] Mostly, explain Krvaric and Junge, people get into trouble when they fail to "meet technical compliance requirements." Thus, they end up spending a lot of time and energy complying. The most common sources of noncompliance are requirements governing *time and effort* and *supplement not supplant*.

Federal law requires personnel paid with federal funds to keep "time-and-effort" records that track the time they spend on federal programs. The idea that staff paid with federal funds should be doing what they're supposed to makes obvious sense, but the practical result tends to erect bars and make it tougher to spend dollars wisely. The problem? Staff supported by multiple funding sources—such as those in a comprehensive early literacy program or school improvement efforts—become a bookkeeping nightmare. So districts tend to run programs in silos, just to be safe. This means that smart efforts to weave together extra formative assessment, reading instruction, after-school coaching, ELL instruction, and the like are frequently not pursued, just because allocating and documenting the costs and personnel can seem so intimidating.

Rules governing *supplement not supplant* apply to the largest federal K–12 programs, including Title I and IDEA. They require that states, districts, and schools use federal funds to provide eligible students with extra services, staff, programs, or materials they would not normally receive.

Like *time and effort, supplement not supplant* is sensible in theory. The problem is that districts and schools have to prove that each expenditure is an "extra" they would not have paid for, absent federal funds. The result: auditors tell districts they can't use Title I funds for things like an additional section of ninth-grade English to boost literacy skills or attendance incentive programs at schools with high absenteeism. Why? Because it's not clear that these things are extras. It's easier to spend federal funds on clear extras—like field trips—than on educational programs. This then shapes the use of state and local funds because, as Krvaric and Junge explain, "The easiest way to show that something is 'extra' is to build a budget in layers; in other words, to first budget costs supported by state and local funds, and then budget federal costs."[8]

Complying with the federal rules is a big deal. Violations bring headaches and can hurt a career. In 2010, for instance, the US Department of Education's inspector general questioned $107 million in salary charges in just one district, due to problems with the district's time-and-effort recordkeeping.[9] Krvaric and Junge note, "Even if [the Department of Education] ultimately does not require funds to be repaid, the threat of repayment, along with newspaper stories about funds being questioned, and the increased scrutiny that a state or district face" can leave leaders nervous about breaking with routine.[10] They note the irony that rules "designed to protect federal funds and better serve students can actually curtail *effective* spending and stifle innovation" due to fears they "could trigger additional scrutiny and raise audit risks."[11]

The complexities of implementing federal law in fourteen thousand districts and one hundred thousand schools have yielded a vast web of rules. As these rules are explained by federal officials to state program coordinators and then to local officials, the requirements and restrictions can make the messy middle look like an impenetrable wall. This is especially true given that state and local Title I and IDEA coordinators are in positions funded with federal dollars, receive their training at federally sponsored seminars, and generally view their job as ensuring compliance with federal law.

How can a cage-buster hope to steer clear of these obstacles? For starters, keep in mind that, as Council of the Great City Schools executive director

Michael Casserly notes, when it comes to federal law, "Unless something is otherwise prohibited by some provision in the statute or under the General Education Provisions Act, it's actually allowed." For district and state leaders, this means that silence is a license to lead. Unfortunately, says Casserly, many district and state leaders seem to think they are allowed to do only what federal law specifically permits. He says, "In [one southern district], the staff was under the impression that because Title I didn't specifically indicate that you could set additional goals beyond NCLB targets for SIG schools, it was forbidden. But after we helped straighten the superintendent out, he went ahead and set the additional stretch goals that he otherwise had been told by his staff he wasn't allowed to do."

State Policy

Since 90 percent of school spending in the United States is supported by state and local funds, most policy is made at the state and local level. State policy is generally the result of a three-part process. First, the legislature typically enacts broad policies, governing things like accountability, teacher evaluation, and the school calendar. Second, the finer details of such policies are generally determined by the state board of education. Third, the state education agency (SEA) then crafts the rules and regulations required to put those policies into effect. Most major federal education programs are also "state-administered," meaning the SEA ensures that districts comply with federal requirements. In doing so, SEAs can layer on additional requirements—sometimes creating confusion about what's permissible.

Each SEA is led by a chief, usually called the superintendent, secretary, director, or commissioner of education. Ironically, SEA activities are largely funded by federal dollars.[12] Those funds are exclusively tied to specific programs and employees, and—like local superintendents—state chiefs often feel they have limited control over how they are allocated. Federally paid employees are often physically separated from state employees and regarded as privileged, with their own networks, federal ties, and training.

SEAs face serious challenges. The Center on Education Policy has noted their difficulty attracting and retaining qualified staff, with state officials blaming uncompetitive and inflexible pay scales and balky hiring process-es.[13] States generally can't compete with the pay offered to senior adminis-trators in school districts. In Colorado, assistant commissioners are paid $125,000 to $150,000. Nebraska's top pay grade maxes out at just under $110,000; Indiana's at $135,000.[14] Meanwhile, superintendents in districts with forty thousand students routinely make more than $200,000 a year, and their top deputies frequently earn $150,000 or more. State officials are blunt about the challenge. "The minute we get [data specialists] trained, somebody out in the private world offers them $30,000 more, and they're gone," says one.[15] Another state official explained, "People who are really savvy with technology . . . you can't afford them on government salary schedules."[16] That's a problem.

There are frequently challenges with civil service rules and SEA cul-ture. Elizabeth Shaw, formerly an executive director at the Louisiana De-partment of Education, relates how an SEA division director attempted to rate an ineffective staff member as a 2 on a five-point scale during a performance evaluation. She recalls that the manager produced "an entire binder of documentation citing the employee's performance problems af-ter which every employee who reported to [the manager] was interviewed en masse (without him present) and encouraged to air all of their concerns with his management style. At the end of the process, the civil service di-vision overturned his rating. The underperforming employee was given a higher performance rating and retained."

In the end, she says, the manager was "cut off at the knees" by "the public nature of the civil service investigation and subsequent reversal of his rating."[17] (For some thoughts on how to tackle some of the challenges in SEAs, see "Cage-Busting in the SEA.")

District Policy

Local policy is in the hands of the school board in each of the nation's fourteen thousand–odd districts. Boards are much maligned for failing to provide strong leadership, being heavily influenced by the demands of employee groups, wading into micromanagement, and being prone to pet-ty bickering. In a few districts, mostly located in urban areas, boards are

Cage-Busting in the SEA

SEAs are as desperate for cage-busting leadership, and as ripe for it as any district, operational unit, or school. In fact, a new generation of cage-busting state chiefs—many of them quoted in this book—have forged ahead in states across the land.

When Clark County, Nevada, superintendent Dwight Jones was state chief in Colorado, he partnered with a local foundation to work at bringing more talent to the agency. He recalls, "I attracted some private financial support. As a result, some of my top staff were on loan from the private foundation. A public-private partnership like that matters a lot. For staff on loan, we developed a [memorandum of understanding] that said the staff answers to me but salaries would be paid by the private foundation." This provided crucial flexibility. Jones says, "If I had to work within the confines of the rules and regulations of the state department of education, I don't think we could have achieved half of what we did."

Susan Zelman, president of Zelman Education Consulting Group and former Ohio superintendent, sought outside help to tackle the disarray that greeted her when she took the helm of Ohio's SEA. She says, "There were no standards, although they claimed to have standards. They had assessments, but nobody knew what the heck was on the assessments. There was no vision, no mission about the agency." Zelman enlisted the local business community to, in her words, "put Humpty Dumpty back together again." She says, "I got executives on loan to come in and work with me. I had a human resource person from Procter & Gamble and a technology person from Worthington Industries. And the first thing I needed to do was fire the HR person—who was a transportation guy—and really create a whole HR system for the agency."

Lisa Graham Keegan, CEO of the Education Breakthrough Network and former state superintendent of Arizona, recalls, "When I went into office, there were only twelve out of over three hundred people in the SEA that were in discretionary positions [positions not covered by state civil service rules]. Arizona is a right-to-work state, but . . . everyone in the office had come through the school system and it was unionized and that's how the department was." Over her tenure, Keegan boosted the number of discretionary positions to a third of the department. She says, "Every time we had an open position we tried to uncover it. And if somebody was in a position and wanted to move up to a higher po-sition, they had to agree to uncover the position and opt out of the civil service protection." Keegan notes that many regulations are "my-thology, not fact." She explains, "You can do a lot of things. You can also excuse yourself from doing them by believing a bunch of people's shticks about what you can't do. I was told you couldn't uncover these positions. That's not true; it's just that nobody did it."

appointed by mayors. These boards are less subject to the failings noted above, but mayor-appointed boards have raised their own concerns, most notably a lack of transparency. A particular challenge for elected boards is the difficulty they have sticking to one course or agenda. An even bigger challenge may be that board members, whether elected or appointed, have little appetite for conflict or negative publicity, and thus typically boast a feeble track record when it comes to negotiating firmly, pushing back on the federal government, or standing up to aggrieved employees or com-munity members.

All the laws, rules, and regulations made by federal officials, the SEA, and the school board trickle down in complex and uncertain ways. The press to comply with federal, state, and district policies overwhelms most superin-tendents and leads them to organize their district as a series of silos. Mean-while, crucial district functions like human resources, information tech-nology, and finance are charged with merely keeping the trains running.

As a result, the mission of key units gets defined as keeping the machin-ery humming and the district out of trouble, rather than focusing on the problems that need solving. Superintendents defer to the presumed exper-tise of special ed or Title I coordinators, who flatly announce what is or is not permissible with a focus less on solving problems than on what federal and SEA officials have historically deemed unobjectionable. In frustra-tion, one district leader says, "I see Title I as a means to an end, where Title I staff see it as the end."

Melissa Junge and Sheara Krvaric recall working with an SEA that wanted districts to use federal funding to implement "expansive reforms focused on the issues contributing to poor school performance . . . like low attendance, behavioral problems, or low literacy rates." The SEA encouraged districts "to think in new ways about how to use federal Title I dollars to implement school interventions outside of just traditional reading and math interventions." To the SEA's surprise, no districts took advantage of the opportunity. The reason turned out to be the state's online application for Title I funds, which "contained a drop-down menu where districts could select the costs they wanted to charge to the grant . . . but the menu was limited to items like 'reading intervention,' 'math intervention,' or 'Title I teacher.'" These traditional, narrow options discouraged unconventional approaches, despite the SEA's intent.

Former Delaware secretary of education and current Maryland state superintendent Lillian Lowery says sometimes local interpretation of a state regulation can be unduly restrictive. When Delaware districts sought to use Teach For America corps members, she recalls, "There was some really hard pushback at the local level among some of the boards of education that said TFA teachers did not have the criteria to be highly qualified. They could not get their heads around the fact that [TFA corps members] were being certified as they were teaching. It took our policy and legal folks and my actually going to board meetings to present to them our policy and regulations to convince them it was OK."

MAKING SENSE OF COLLECTIVE BARGAINING

The biggest frustration that most school and district leaders wrestle with is the teachers' contract. Because of what's in it, what they think is in it, and what might be in it, would-be cage-busters routinely find themselves rolling the boulder when it comes to problems involving teacher assignment, compensation, hiring, professional development, instructional time, and much else. Contracts, like statute, include solid bars, illusory bars, and a whole lot of messy middle. Unfortunately, most advice on educational leadership manages to skip past such niceties, or how to lead in light of them.

For instance, one can read the entirety of books penned by the most commonly assigned authors in educational leadership courses without coming across one mention of "union contract" or "collective bargaining." The list of such books is vast, including such familiar titles as *What's Worth Fighting for in the Principalship, Change Leader, Leaders of Learning, School Leadership that Works, What Great Principals Do Differently, Rethinking Leadership, Strengthening the Heartbeat, Shaping School Culture, Leading with Soul,* and *Reframing the Path to School Leadership.*[18]

Real or imagined limitations on one's ability to rethink pay, hiring, evaluation, teacher assignment, professional development, or the school year and school day can prompt leaders to ignore these issues in order to focus wholeheartedly on culture and coaching. But, whatever its surface appeal, this is the path of Sisyphus. The sheer scope of teacher collective bargaining agreements ensures that some provision will almost assuredly touch upon virtually any serious effort to solve problems, much less rethink teaching or learning.[19]

MAPPING THE CBA LANDSCAPE

Where to start? First, cage-busters need to understand what they're obliged and *not* obliged to bargain. Public-sector collective bargaining is illegal in Georgia, North Carolina, South Carolina, Texas, and Virginia.[20] So, if you're in one of those five states and you see problematic provisions in district rules or policies, the district leadership (and maybe that's you) has got some explaining to do.

In states with collective bargaining, state laws typically spell out three categories of bargaining subjects: mandatory, permissible, and prohibited. That is, there are things you must bargain over, things you may bargain over, and things that you're not allowed to bargain over. As the National Council on Teacher Quality's (NCTQ) report *Invisible Ink in Collective Bargaining* makes clear, a mandatory subject of bargaining in one state may be a prohibited subject in another.[21] Legislatures can also change the rules if and when they desire, making it critical to check on the current rules of the road in your state.

The chart in figure 4.1, constructed from data available in the NCTQ's contract and policy database as of September 2012, provides a general

FIGURE 4.1   State law provisions for bargaining as of September 2012

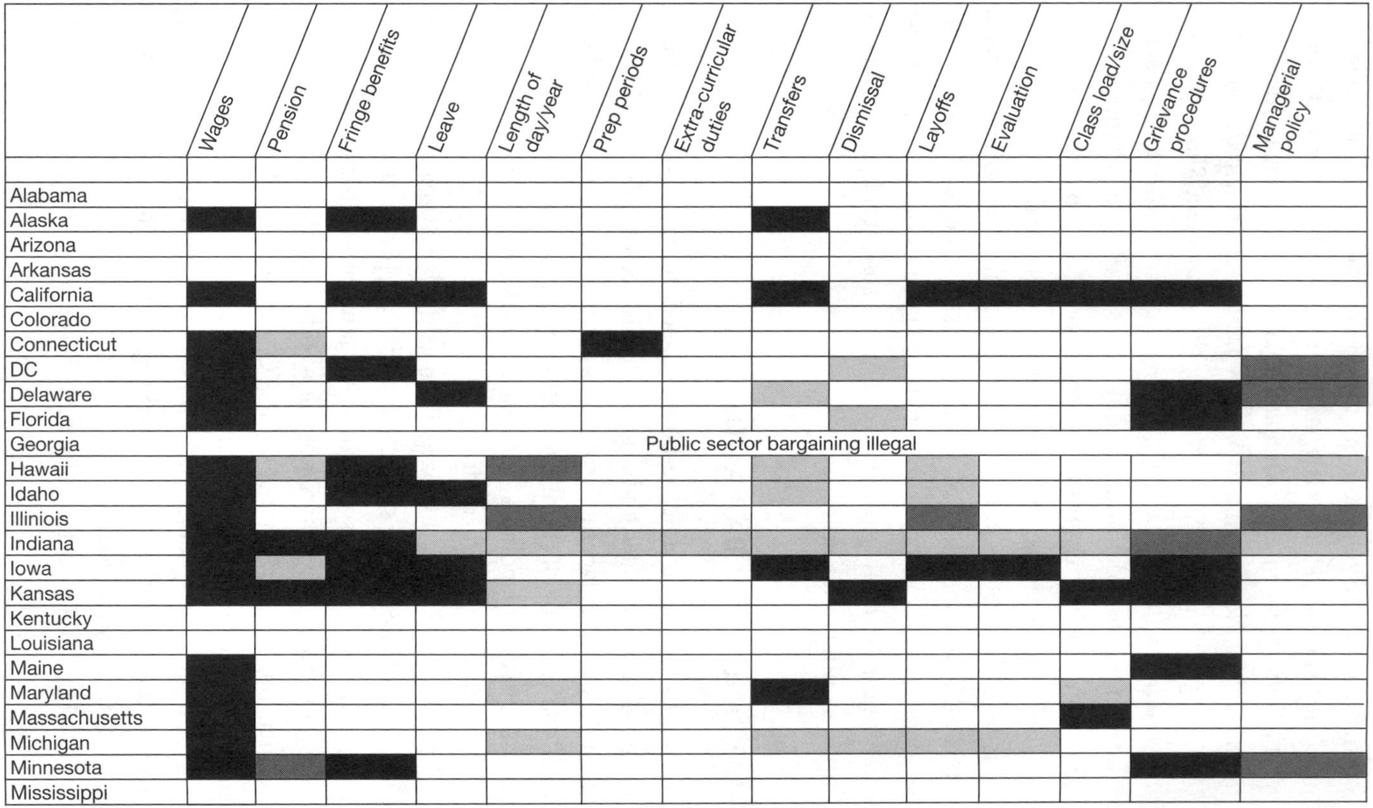

State law provision on whether leaders have to bargain over . . .

Missouri	
Montana	
Nebraska	
Nevada	
New Hampshire	
New Jersey	
New Mexico	
New York	
North Carolina	Public sector bargaining illegal
North Dakota	
Ohio	
Oklahoma	
Oregon	
Pennsylvania	
Rhode Island	
South Carolina	Public sector bargaining illegal
South Dakota	
Tennessee	
Texas	Public sector bargaining illegal
Utah	
Vermont	
Virginia	Public sector bargaining illegal
Washington	
West Virginia	
Wisconsin	
Wyoming	

Legend:
- ■ mandatory subject of bargaining
- ▨ permissive subject of bargaining
- ▨ prohibited subject of bargaining
- ☐ issue not addressed in state statute or no state statute regarding public sector bargaining

Source: National Council on Teacher Quality

overview of the national collective bargaining picture. It highlights whether fourteen issues—wages, pension, fringe benefits, leave, length of the school day and year, prep periods, extracurricular duties, transfers, dismissal, layoffs, evaluation, class size/load, grievance procedures, managerial policy—are mandatory, permissible, or prohibited subjects of bargaining for each state and for Washington, DC. As of September 2012, the four states with the largest number of mandatory subjects of bargaining were Nevada (9); California (8); Kansas (7); and Iowa (7).

Generally speaking, wages are the most common mandatory subject. Thirty-three states require leaders to bargain over wages.[22] In other states, the rules vary. In Wisconsin, for instance, wages are a permissible subject under state statute—districts can choose whether to bargain over salaries. In North Dakota, wages are not addressed in state law.

In nearly every state with public-sector collective bargaining, policy makers have also prohibited districts from negotiating over certain subjects. In 2011, Idaho and Indiana passed laws that prohibit systems from negotiating over transfer procedures. Wisconsin's controversial 2011 collective bargaining law restricts public-sector CBAs to wages and wage-related benefits. Statutes in Kansas, Indiana, Maryland, Michigan, and Wisconsin prohibit districts from bargaining over the school calendar.[23] Tennessee, Wisconsin, Michigan, and Indiana restrict bargaining over teacher evaluations.[24]

How do you use the chart in figure 4.1? The simplest way is to find your state and identify prohibited subjects of bargaining. If you've got problematic contract provisions in one of those areas, you've spotted a bar that's pretty easy to address. After all, the current restriction in the CBA is illegal.

In Alabama, Arizona, Arkansas, Colorado, Kentucky, Louisiana, Mississippi, Utah, West Virginia, or Wyoming, there are no state statutes regarding public-sector bargaining. In those states, your obligations may be found in the thicket of case law, composed of judicial opinions, state labor relations board decisions, and state attorney general opinions. Given these complexities, it's no wonder leaders are often unclear about what they're able to do.

Crucially, keep in mind that the chart in figure 4.1 is a starting place—it's an illustration of where matters stood in 2012. As NCTQ notes, the data is limited to state statutes and does not incorporate language that can be found in case law, arbitration decisions, or attorney general opinions. This chart is not intended to be definitive or the final word. Rather, it's a guide, a tool that you can take in hand when you sit down with an attorney and use to flag some of the things you should be sure to ask her about (much more on all this in chapter 5).

Monuments to Cage-Dwelling Leadership

Former Milwaukee superintendent Howard Fuller, who had previously served as secretary of the Wisconsin Department of Employee Relations, noted many years ago that the Milwaukee Public Schools contract grew from a slender eighteen pages in 1964 into a "sometimes impenetrable document" of ten times that length. He observed that there's also "a 'contract behind the contract' [which] includes the 1,700 [memoranda of understanding], nearly 300 grievance-arbitration rulings, and various state declaratory rulings. Together, they comprise more than 2,000 documents. No more than a handful of largely anonymous management and union staff understand them."[25] The haziness of all this is the killer.

Contracts can include any number of ridiculously minute provisions. The topics addressed in CBAs extend far beyond bread-and-butter questions of salary and benefits. In Oklahoma City, the contract has a section entitled "bulletin boards," which dictates that "The Board shall make available for exclusive use of the Union at least one (1) bulletin board, a minimum of eight (8) square feet located in each faculty lounge at each school for the posting of official Union material properly identified as such."[26]

In Eau Claire, Wisconsin, the contract sets out a "standard day" for K–5 teachers in painstaking detail:

> A standard day shall be defined as 435 minutes, excluding lunch but including a morning homeroom period of 7–15 minutes, e.g., where teachers will supervise students entering the building, take roll, take lunch count, make announcements, etc. The teaching day shall not exceed 349 minutes of classroom teaching, thirty (30) minutes for lunch and thirty (30) minutes of recess. Outside of the forty-five (45) minutes guaranteed prep time and a thirty (30) continuous minute block for lunch daily, up to eighteen (18) hours per year of the standard work day (an average of six (6) minutes each day—thirty (30) minutes per week) may be assigned each teacher for supervisory duties.[27]

Contracts routinely spell out procedures for evaluating teachers, allowances for preparation time, regulations on the use of substitute teachers, stipends for overseeing extracurricular activities, protocol for disciplining students, the extent and nature of professional development, and much else. CBAs are also cluttered with more idiosyncratic provisions. In Chicago, the contract specifies, "In all schools where an intercom is used, an oral signal shall be given to indicate the intercom is beginning to be put into operation, or a light shall be installed on each outlet to indicate when the intercom is in operation."[28] The Orange County, Florida, contract promises, "Each school shall provide . . . head lice shampoo when not provided by Workers Compensation."[29]

It's easy to blast teachers unions for problematic CBAs. But it's vital to remember that every one of those provisions in every single agreement *has been bargained and agreed to by district officials.* As analyst Mitch Price reminds us, "[CBAs] are signed by two parties—both the teachers union and the school district negotiated and ultimately agreed on the provisions in the contract."[30] District leaders share the blame for dumb or destructive provisions. Indeed, those provisions are monuments to cage-dwelling leadership.

The Price of Timidity: Ambiguity and Past Practice

In studying CBAs, Price has reported that most contain "ambiguous" provisions that "were not clearly restrictive, but neither did they explicitly authorize school-level autonomy or flexibility." In other words, there was less of the highly restrictive stuff mentioned above than you might expect. Price observes, "Ambiguity can be good for aggressive principals looking for greater flexibility and willing to push the envelope, but bad for cautious or timid principals looking to the CBA for guidance, permission, or authority before acting."[31] Contracts routinely contain flexibility that administrators don't know about or choose to ignore.

Indeed, policy analyst Coby Loup and I reported in 2008, CBAs in K–12 have often been used to excuse "inert, inflexible, or lethargic management. While hardly any labor agreements are truly conducive to effective leadership, [in the nation's fifty largest districts] only nine of the fifty labor agreements examined are egregiously restrictive . . . Most districts operate under labor agreements that are notably vague on just what management can or cannot do when it comes to compensation, personnel, and work rules."[32]

Ambiguous contract language permits competing interpretations of what a leader can do. In practice, unions often welcome ambiguity because they're confident that principals, superintendents, and school boards won't take advantage or will fold when it comes to crunch time. Stephen DeVita, general counsel for the school district of Loudoun County, Virginia, explains how thoroughly management had ceded its role to the union when he became chief legal counsel in Cleveland, Ohio: "When the new administration and I came to Cleveland in February of 2007 . . . the place was in shambles, and the union was calling the shots on everything. Principals were calling the union to find out how to interpret particular clauses in the contract."

There is another way. Adrian Manuel, principal of Kingston High School in Kingston, New York, thought his students needed more one-on-one time with teachers. He recalls, "I wanted to create an advisory period. Well, my school's union rep said, 'How can you add on this new contact period?' Once I heard her say 'contact period,' I knew she was thinking about the contract. I said, 'This isn't a new contact period. You already have language about homerooms. I'm just extending that from five minutes to fifteen. It's like homeroom but just more structured.' In the end, she said, 'I don't see why you can't do this.' It stemmed out of me looking at the contract."

When it comes to exploiting ambiguity, concerns about past practice are one oft-cited obstacle. (And it can be; see "The Evergreen Problem" for a particularly insidious variation on this.) *Past practice* is the importance accorded to established practice when determining whether there are informal but established routines that a district can't change except with a union okay. In truth, says education and labor attorney Harry Pringle, "There is probably no more misused term in labor relations." Brockton, Massachusetts, superintendent Matt Malone says, "There's this concept of past practice, where we use past practice like a law; it's a bunch of crap. When changing a past practice, simply write the union a letter telling them what you are going to do and then do it." For instance, Malone changed the district's past practice in regards to snow days. "On days that we had a delayed start,

The Evergreen Problem

District leaders often agree to certain provisions in the spirit of cooperation or with specific understandings about practice. If things change,
they figure they'll just remove the provision later. Or so the logic goes.
Unfortunately, as Mitch Price notes, it's never that easy: "Since subsequent contract negotiations typically begin with the current CBA as
a starting point, once a provision is in the contract, it is often hard to
remove it."[33] And for those district leaders operating under a contract or
state statute that contains an *evergreen clause*, things are even trickier.

Evergreen provisions stipulate that contract terms remain in force until
a new contract is put in place, making it nearly impossible to get something out of a CBA if the union wants to keep it. Evergreen applies to
many public-sector agreements. The rationale is that, since public employees are limited in their right to strike, these provisions help level the
playing field. For instance, the contract in Clark County, Nevada, stipulates that it "shall continue from year to year . . . unless either of the parties shall give written notice to the other . . . of a desire to change, amend,
or modify the Agreement and until a successor agreement is reached."[34]
In practice, evergreen clauses give very little incentive for unions to agree
to new contract terms, especially in times of fiscal distress.

The upshot for leaders is that evergreen clauses can make it immensely hard to get a clean slate once language has been ceded.

Of the eighty "contract-type" union agreements in the National Council on Teacher Quality (NCTQ) database, more than one-third (twenty-
seven) have evergreen provisions.[35] Additionally, some states, including
Missouri, Nebraska, Washington, and New York, have evergreen laws in
their statutes governing labor relations.[36]

In January 2012, *The Atlantic* reported that, due to a little-known
rider in the teachers' contract, Buffalo, New York's school system was
paying for teachers' plastic surgery at a price tag of $5.2 million an-
nually.[37] The rider, added to the contract in the 1970s, was originally
intended to cover "serious reconstructive surgery." However, as minor
plastic surgery procedures became more common, the use (and cost)
of the provision skyrocketed.

Despite public outcry, district leaders have been unable to eliminate
the provision. The stumbling block is New York's Triborough Amendment, which is a state evergreen clause. Though the Buffalo teachers'

contract expired in 2004, this amendment has allowed the old provisions to roll over from year to year—meaning that union members kept annual step-and-lane hikes and the free plastic surgery through tough economic times. In the words of Amber Dixon, interim superintendent of the Buffalo School District, "The urgency of negotiating a new contract isn't really there. You get to keep your benefits. You get to keep your cosmetic rider. You get to keep your 2.5 percent step increase. It makes getting back to the table difficult."[38]

Idaho state superintendent Tom Luna says evergreen provisions can completely change the dynamics of labor-management negotiations. "When I was elected to the local school board in the mid-1990s, I was surprised how many things there were in the master agreement that included an evergreen clause," Luna recalls. "I had no ability to change or influence them because they were evergreened. My hands were tied. When you have an evergreen clause, then one side never has the ability to remove things from the contract . . . As the school board, we couldn't even set the calendar. Then the voters want to hold the school board accountable, even though their hands were tied ten or twenty years ago when these things were negotiated away." When he became state chief in Idaho, Luna helped pass legislation that forbids contracts from containing evergreen provisions and that limits the length of CBAs to one year.

teachers were coming in one hour late with the kids rather than coming in at the regular start time or as close as possible to the regular start time given safety conditions," says Malone. "And, to be fair, they claimed past practice. But I could not find anything to substantiate this so I wrote them a letter that told them what I was requiring, asked them to comment, considered their suggestions, then finalized the new expectations."

As Malone suggests, past practice is often more malleable than many leaders imagine. Leo Casey, executive director of the American Federation of Teachers' Albert Shanker Institute, says of past practice, "It's a way to keep the district from unilaterally changing contracts and for unions to make sure that the district [pays] attention to its own written regulations in areas like class size. It doesn't privilege informal practices . . . maybe if it's something chiseled into state practice, but it would have to be a pretty high burden of proof. I've never seen a union local or a district just say in a grievance or anywhere that it was established practice to do something and get away with it."[39]

BE CAREFUL OF WHAT GETS INTO THE CBA

Even though state laws restrict what districts can negotiate away, you'll find districts across the United States that have agreed to CBA provisions on subjects that the legislature has made it illegal to bargain over.

Many times I've chatted with superintendents or board members who complain vociferously about provision X, only for it to become clear that the giveaway was entirely voluntary—*because, at some point, the district bargained over something it didn't have to.* When asked about this, they're surprised to hear it was optional or else they're fatalistic, explaining, "We've always done it that way."

For example, while would-be reformers urge states to do away with seniority-based layoffs, many districts are already free to do so. Indeed, the bulk of large districts using seniority-driven layoffs do so of their own volition. Seventy of the ninety big district contracts and board policies in the NCTQ database declared seniority to be the sole determinant when making layoff decisions. Of these seventy districts, two-thirds were in states that do not mandate the use of seniority.[40] District leaders, with no mandate or pressure, chose to negotiate deals that prevented them from protecting effective teachers.

In Massachusetts, for instance, local districts were long free to establish layoff procedures.[41] However, nearly 7 percent of districts negotiated CBAs that make seniority the primary factor in layoffs.[42] Low-income districts are much more likely than others to ignore performance and rely on seniority alone. The unions deserve responsibility in this; equally culpable, however, are the superintendents and school committees who bargained these agreements.

Consider the case of Kent Intermediate School District in Michigan. In 1994, the Michigan Legislature passed the Public Employment Relations

Act, which, among other things, made the "contracting out" of services a prohibited subject of bargaining.[43] However, in March 2010, Kent and nine other school districts in Kent County signed a CBA that included the provision: "All districts agree not to privatize any KCEA/MEA unionized services for the life of this agreement."[44]

Sued for a "blatant violation" of state law, Kent and the union representatives admitted that the provision was unenforceable. Kent's legal counsel said, "We can put that provision in there, but it is not enforceable. The districts knew it was unenforceable. The [Michigan Education Association] knew it was unenforceable . . . [It was added] in the spirit of collaboration."[45]

While district leaders may think illegal giveaways are easy, costless ways to score points with teachers and improve relations with the union, such maneuvers can go awry. For one thing, my experience is that district leaders hardly ever get the credit or goodwill they think they will. In this case, more significantly, Michigan's Mackinac Policy Center noted, "While [the Kent situation] was supposed to be a limited, one-year agreement, there will be strong economic and political pressure to include this in later contracts. Absent a public or legal challenge, this temporary agreement will likely become permanent, hamstringing future boards."[46]

Kent's situation was hardly unique. Michigan statute reads, "Collective bargaining between a public school employer and a bargaining representative of its employees shall not include . . . establishment of the starting day for the school year."[47] Yet the Detroit CBA includes a schedule that specifies a day "schools open for teachers and students."[48] Kansas law prohibits districts from bargaining over the school year, stating, "Matters which relate to the duration of the school term . . . are not subject to professional negotiation."[49] However, the Wichita CBA stipulates, "The Superintendent and the UTW President will review all requests submitted to extend the school year prior to April 1 of each year"; that "their joint recommendation shall be subject to Board approval"; and that "staff members who do not support the extended year concept shall have the right to transfer."[50]

In Maryland, the school calendar is a prohibited subject of bargaining. Yet, Anne Arundel County, for example, operates under a CBA that reads, "TAAAC [the Teachers Association of Anne Arundel County] shall name two (2) members to the Board of Education annual calendar committee from its Unit I membership. The representatives shall participate in the deliberations of the committee, present the position of TAAAC on calendar items, and assist in drafting the proposed calendar to be presented to the Board."[51] Similarly, in Prince George's County, the CBA requires the district to prepare a calendar in accord with stipulated guidelines and with heavy involvement of union representatives.[52] Such provisions, of dubious legality, limit the district's ability to craft a school year based on student needs.

This kind of weak-kneed "collaboration" is destructive on three counts. First, while the provision may be unenforceable, such decorative touches can become codified or harden into conventional wisdom. Second, it sets a precedent for districts voluntarily tying their own hands. Third, such concessions don't strengthen collaboration so much as make management look weak and easily bullied. Properly understood, state prohibitions are a gift to leaders wishing to avoid unnecessary fights. If the law says you can't give the language away, then you don't need to spend time or energy making the case—you should just shrug and say, "Sorry, my hands are tied."

Meanwhile, scour your existing agreements, with an attorney and copies of the relevant state laws, to see whether you've got language that violates statute. If so, it's an opportunity to dismantle some bars. Indeed, most contracts have what's known as a "severability" or "savings" clause; this allows a provision to be struck or renegotiated if it's found to violate state law.[53] In such cases, it may suffice to inform the union that the district can no longer honor the provision, and then ask the appropriate state authorities to make clear that the district will be in jeopardy if it abides by the language. Even if that's not feasible, you'll have identified clearly problematic provisions that can be rectified when it's time to renegotiate.

Today, cage-dwelling is so pervasive that district leaders have proven only too willing to give away their newfound autonomy even when states change statutes to recapture management prerogatives. One glaring example involves the Milwaukee Public Schools. In anticipation of Wisconsin's 2011 Act 10, which restricted the scope of bargaining and required teachers to contribute to the cost of their health care and pensions, MPS in 2010 renegotiated its CBA with the Milwaukee Teachers' Education

Association. The district committed to paying the full cost of teachers' health and retirement benefits—a total of $184 million in 2010–11 alone. This meant MPS would be unable to redirect tens of millions of dollars from benefits into classrooms. Cullen Werwie, spokesman for Wisconsin governor Scott Walker, notes that Milwaukee was one of many districts that failed to take advantage of the changes to state law. Werwie recalls, "About two-thirds of the districts either re-upped their contracts once Act 10 was announced but before it took effect or signed an agreement prior to Act 10 being announced but after Governor Walker was elected. A lot of it is political," he muses, with district leaders and school boards intent on placating employee unions, even if that means fewer dollars for programs and instruction.

In Indiana, the legislature also moved in 2011 to limit the scope of collective bargaining. Yet, dozens of districts went ahead and left restrictive language intact, even though it now violated state law. Indiana state chief Tony Bennett says, "There were systems that went on with business as usual, just leaving the silly stuff in the contract. I think many of those see this as the path of least resistance. They don't want to create an uncomfortable life for themselves in the communities in which they live. You had NEA Uniserv leaders urging superintendents to leave the language in. They were saying, 'Come on, just leave it in. What's the harm? What difference will it make? Nobody will ever find out.'"

Bennett explains that some superintendents took full advantage of the law. What they did, he said, was "sit down with general counsel and to take everything out of current contract that doesn't comply with the new statute. Then they can walk into negotiating session and say, 'This is what we're negotiating on.' That method has tended to be very effective at eliminating noncompliant language. The districts that have really taken advantage of this, they see huge differences."

SEEING STOP SIGNS AT EVERY PASS

The cage is real. There are real bars and frustrating restrictions. But cage-dwelling leaders have supersized these by being too cautious when it comes to compliance and too cavalier when negotiating contracts. School and system leaders too often regard even ambiguous laws, contract provisions, and policies as stop signs—and attorneys, Title I directors, and policy makers as traffic cops. Leaders warily eye statutes, regulations, policies, and contracts as something to fear and rarely see the law as a tool they can wield to tackle problems or bust the cage. Meanwhile, the American Association of School Administrators reports that superintendents are generally uninterested in these legal questions.[54]

Understanding the construction of the cage is essential if you're to escape it. Next time a state or district official tells you that you can't organize special ed this way, staff schools that way, or structure a program like so, ask, "Why not?" Ask her to point out precisely where the prohibition lies. Where is it written down? If it's not written down, what's the basis for the prohibition? If it is, how hard (or easy) would it be to change it? When you start to ask these questions, you'll be surprised how readily the "culture of can't" starts to melt away.

Serious leaders have an *obligation* to start removing the obstacles in their way. We'll explore much more about how to do this in the next few chapters. But, let's be sure to keep the purpose in mind. It's not to catalog dumb rules, pick fights, or (God forbid) glorify lawyers. Rather, it's to stop rolling the boulder so that we can focus more intently on promoting great teaching, learning, and schooling.

5

Swinging That Louisville Slugger

"I'll tell you, Hugh," the Boss said. "You sat in your law office
fifteen years and watched the sons-of-bitches warm chairs
in this state and not do a thing . . . Then I came along and
slipped a Louisville Slugger in your hand and whispered low,
'You want to step in there and lay round you a little?' And
you did. You had a wonderful time. You made the fur fly . . .
You want to keep your Harvard hands clean, but way down in
your heart you know I'm telling the truth."

—ROBERT PENN WARREN, *All the King's Men*[1]

WE ASK LEADERS to deliver transformative change, but don't give them
the tools. Hell, they're told to keep everything tidy and their hands clean.
That's a recipe for ineffectual chair warming. Fortunately, you don't have
to take that Louisville Slugger to every law or contract provision—just the
ones that are in your way right now. And you don't have to do it alone.

This chapter covers two distinct (but profoundly linked) topics—both
intended to ensure that you're not trying to do this by yourself. The first
discusses how educational leaders can turn lawyers and the law into agents
of school improvement. The second is how to attract, cultivate, and manage talent, a task made immensely easier by aggressive, smart lawyering.

Chris Barbic, founder of the Houston-based YES Prep Public Schools,
led YES when it was named the best place to work in Houston, the only time

a school or school system has been so honored. Yet, when this culture-first leader took the helm of Tennessee's new Achievement School District in 2011, he concluded that anyone's first move in that role ought to be: "Get a great lawyer, understand the legislation, and understand what you can and cannot do right out of the gate." Barbic learned this the hard way:

> I didn't find out until three weeks after I was here that we couldn't hire anybody at the school level. The way the legislation was written, we can fire whoever we want if we take over a school, but we have no hiring authority. So, I'm sitting in this meeting and say we need to start thinking about what teachers and principals we want in place and everyone said, "What do you mean?" I said, "Well, we're going to be hiring people" and they were, like, "You know that you can't hire anybody, right?" I went through the roof. I asked, "How are we going to turn a school around if we can't hire anybody?"

AMBIGUITY DOESN'T MEAN YOU CAN'T

If there's one lesson to take from chapter 4, it's that uncertainty shouldn't prompt paralysis. Cage-dwellers are forever explaining what they can't do, what they wish they could do, and what they're not permitted to do. Much of the time, they're wrong.

When we take the cage-bar continuum described in chapter 4, we can readily identify five kinds of situations leaders face. There are those things:
You can already do
You might be able to do
You can do if you're a little creative
You can do if you alter little p *policies*
You can do only if you change big P *policies*

You Can Do It, You Just Don't Know It

The lowest-hanging fruit is the stuff that leaders are already allowed to do and just don't know about, or think about. David Weiner moving his desk into that teacher's classroom back in chapter 1? Clark County's Dave Wilson revamping the rules regarding student absences and course completion (chapter 3)? Scott Mendelsberg figuring out how to get bilingual students college credit (chapter 1)? All classic examples.

When Michelle Rhee became chancellor in Washington, DC, everyone "knew" that layoffs required losing the most junior teachers, regardless of need or performance. But Rhee's team looked at the municipal regulations governing "reductions in force" (RIF), which said that city agencies had to take four things into account: professional credentials, agency needs, unique skills, and seniority. "Everybody had assumed you had to weigh those four things equally," recalls current DC Public Schools chancellor Kaya Henderson, then Rhee's deputy. "But we asked, 'What if we wanted to make evaluation count for 75 percent and seniority 5 percent?' And we learned that citywide regulations and the district personnel manual lay out how you do a RIF, but that agencies have the right to determine some things, including how the four components are weighted." So the district went ahead and weighted school needs at 75 percent, unique skills at 10 percent, professional credentials at 10 percent, and seniority at 5 percent. Though the move has been challenged multiple times by the Washington Teachers Union, the district has prevailed on each challenge. "For a lot of the stuff we did, it was really about asking the question, reading carefully, and then maximizing the opportunity," Henderson notes.

Nobody Yet Knows What You Can, or Can't, Do

Leaders face endless questions about how to apply new laws and regulations, how to interpret broad language, or what new officials will support. Put plainly: nobody knows exactly what a new law, rule, regulation, or contract provision means until the pushing and prodding sorts it out.

Massachusetts commissioner of education Mitchell Chester recalls that the law authorizing the state to take control of the Lawrence school system was vague. Yet he was disinclined to go back to the legislature for clarification, given the muscle it took to pass the law in the first place. So, instead, he remembers, "We moved forward with the assumption that we've got the maximum authority you can infer from the language of the statute. It doesn't seem far-fetched to assume that the legislature wanted to provide the tools necessary to pursue substantial reform." That said, Chester was aware of the risks: "It could very well get challenged in court. In addition, you can anticipate that my authorizers, including the state board and governor, are likely to be lobbied by adults in the system who are losing power and control and who would advocate incrementalism rather than substantial reform. So you need to weigh the pluses and minuses of how to proceed—and your attorneys should be your partners every step of the way."

Things That Are Doable but Require Some Creativity

Then there are those things that you can do with a chisel, quick thinking, or a bit of elbow grease—things that you've heard you can't do but that, when you dig a little, turn out to be manageable. School leaders encounter versions of these all the time when it comes to staffing or budgeting.

In Sacramento, many turnaround schools were staffed with bright young teachers, says Heather Zavadsky, author of *School Turnarounds: The Essential Role of Districts*. But the state's seniority laws meant many of these teachers would be the first to go during layoffs. So the district engineered a workaround: "The superintendent fought hard with the union, and he negotiated that if a teacher had been specifically selected for a turnaround school, and the district could document that the training was different and specific, then the teachers would not be subjected to seniority-based layoffs. The district was smart about it. They literally scheduled the training at a different time of the year and carefully documented how the training was different." As a result, "Sacramento was able to preserve their young, talented teachers. That made a big difference in maintaining the core."

Things That Require "Little p" Changes

There are times when no waiver, sidestep, or workaround is possible, and you need to change the policy in question. While annoying, this can be readily managed when dealing with those *little p* policies discussed in chapter 4. Such policies can often be modified by the school board or the superintendent.

In Louisiana's East Baton Rouge Parish (EBRP), for instance, the district tweaked its declaration of intent process to give principals more time to plan for vacancies. "One of the things that districts really struggle with is that teachers don't announce that they're retiring or leaving the district until summer," says TNTP's Ariela Rozman. "Teachers fear there might be personal repercussions if a principal knows of an upcoming departure, so the district is left playing guessing games as to how many vacancies they will have come fall. Then you're stuck with all these vacancies at the last minute and you're desperate to fill them." EBRP accelerated the formal declaration of intent by a month and established informal one-on-one conversations between principals and teachers. Rozman says, "One of the things that our people came up with that I thought was really clever was surveying teachers. We don't even need to know who you are; just tell us what subject you're in and whether you're planning to leave and then we can plan accordingly. That way, you don't have to make it an awkward thing with your principal where they are angry that you're not staying. That type of thing is new and different for a lot of districts, but it's a pretty simple solution to a common challenge."

Things That Require "Big P" Changes

Finally, there are the hard stops. This is when you run into bars erected by a *big P* policy—these are the cold, steel bars of the cage. Remember, these are policies that have been adopted by legislatures, passed by referenda, or written into state constitutions and where the wiggle room has been wrung out. *Big P* barriers include things like statewide class size mandates or laws that prohibit starting school before a certain date. Truth is, it's hard to do much about *big P* bars. That said, marking them is crucial because it makes it possible to tell friends, allies, and would-be reformers what policy changes you need them to pursue.

Kim Wooden, chief student services officer in Clark County, Nevada, precisely identified a once-murky hard stop, making it possible to address. She recalls,

> We were trying to expand the community-based instruction opportunities for kids with disabilities. The way we've understood the law, students have to be in the "immediate vicinity" of an instructor while participating in community-based activities. That makes these activities really expensive and difficult. I said, "What does this really mean? Can we do anything to get around that rule?" So, my special education executive director came back and showed me what was published in one of the district manuals. And though it cited state law, it was someone's interpretation of what the statute said rather than the text of the law. It included things that aren't in

the law. The statute does, in the end, say students need to have "immediate supervision." But now we know just what we're dealing with and can seek a more helpful interpretation, come up with solutions, and research how other states and districts deal with this issue.

Only when they had clarity on where the problem was could Wooden and her team begin tackling the *big P* barrier.

GETTING THE LAW ON YOUR SIDE

Just about every K–12 policy, process, rule, regulation, contract provision, and question you can think of has a legal dimension. School start times? Check. Transportation and safety? Check. Mandatory class sizes? Yep. Salaries and benefits? Yep. Work rules and professional development? You bet. Requirements for spending Title I, special education, or Title II dollars? Of course.

All this means that cage-busters need to make the law a tool of reform—to make ambiguity and uncertainty work for them. This requires smart, creative, tough-minded legal assistance. Francisco Negrón, general counsel at the National School Boards Association, notes, "A good general counsel . . . will tell you how to achieve what you want and how to do it within the law."[2] Whether this help is funded by the district, provided by donors, or offered pro bono by local firms is immaterial.

There are some leaders who manage to do this without help. Adrian Manuel could provide a clinic on this score. Upon becoming principal at Kingston High School in Kingston, New York, Manuel says, "The very first thing I did was have the secretary make photocopies of every contract— teacher, support staff, clerical—for all the administrators. We have four assistant principals and one vice principal. At the first couple of meetings I gave them copies and said, 'How many of you have read through these things?' Some people have been there for nine or ten years and hadn't read through it. I said, 'You all have two weeks to read these. I want you to write any questions you have, identify where you have leverage points, and earmark pages where you're confused. We're going to spend the next couple of months talking about those things.'"

Most leaders aren't Adrian Manuel, and that's fine. But they just need to recognize that, and to call in the necessary support. What happens when you don't call in support? Education attorney Sheara Krvaric says, "We see two things in this field. You have one group that says, 'I know what's right, so I don't care what the law says. I'm just going to go forward recklessly.' That's silly. Somebody is going to call you out, and a good initiative is going to crumble because you have a scandal. But then you have the other camp which says, 'I don't care what the right thing to do is, the law says I have to do it this way.'" Both approaches are losers.

Unfortunately, the whole subject of the law and how to make it work for you has been largely ignored when it comes to educational leadership. A look at the relevant professional publications for the period from January 2009 to September 2012 illustrates the point. Over that span, *Educational Administration Quarterly* featured just one mention of *general counsel* or *legal counsel*, and just four mentions of the word *attorney*—and none of those involved using attorneys to address legal questions. *Educational Management Administration & Leadership*, in total, included just one mention of the terms *attorney, general counsel*, or *legal counsel*. Meanwhile, *Improving Schools, Management in Education*, and the *Journal of Research on Leadership Education* made no mention of any of those terms.[3]

Stop Getting Bullied

In a sector that prizes consensus and rewards longevity, it's easy for leaders to get intimidated when unions push or teachers and parents "lawyer up." Ronald Valenti, former superintendent of New York's Blind Brook School District, says, "In this business, superintendents should all be more conservative than not . . . because mistakes can come back to bite you. I don't know of any superintendent terminated because he or she introduced the wrong reading curriculum. I know of several superintendents who have lost their job because of financial mismanagement or legal misjudgments."[4] The problem is that it's like appeasing a schoolyard bully. A failure to push back means you wind up getting pushed around. Indiana state superintendent Tony Bennett says, "I always tell people, 'When they want to play a game of chicken and you don't blink, next time you win.' The next time, they'll believe."

Meanwhile, lawyers who work for districts tend to play defense. There's a professional inclination for lawyers to focus on avoiding unpleasantness—*unless you tell them otherwise.* If you want them to help you solve problems, you need to say so. TNTP's Dan Weisberg says, "When I first got into education, I was amazed how rarely I heard, 'We're doing this because this is the right policy for kids,' and how often I heard, 'We have to.'" He recalls that, when he started out as chief of labor strategy for the New York City Department of Education, he constantly heard that there had to be five negative letters in a probationary teacher's personnel file before the district could "discontinue" the teacher. Yet, when he looked more closely, it turned out that one letter could suffice if the principal had a legitimate performance concern. Funny thing: even after extensive training of principals and their managers, Weisberg continued to hear the five-letter myth. Where was it coming from? "It turns out that in many cases it was coming from our own district lawyers in the field," he says.

One system administrator muses that district counsel "fixating on compliance aren't doing it for fear of their own job. Instead, I see them trying to protect the image of the school system. With any potential conflict, it's all about, 'Make it go away.'" One veteran education attorney says, "I think it's a cultural mind-set, [a] fear that you will give the wrong answer and someone will get questioned . . . When people feel under the gun, the incentive for the inside counsel is to be as within-the-lines as possible." This mind-set is crystal clear in the National School Board Association's Council of School Attorneys' mission statement, which stipulates that the group's primary purpose is to "improve the practice of school law *and prevent lawsuits against public schools*" (emphasis added).[5] There's nothing wrong with this, per se; but it doesn't say anything about assisting their clients to provide great teaching and learning, and it sure does seem to encourage a defensive posture.

When it comes to school law, union grievances, and the threat of lawsuits, it's not clear that the ingrained skittishness of school and system leaders is entirely justified. For instance, education law scholar Perry Zirkel has found that school systems fare much better in court than the prevailing wisdom seems to suggest. When it comes to terminating tenured teachers, for example, he notes, "The prevailing belief is that the outcome of litigation is usually in favor of the plaintiff-teacher, not the defendant-district. Quite the contrary. School districts consistently win the vast majority of the court decisions concerning the involuntary cessation of a teacher's employment based on incompetency. In a comprehensive canvassing of court decisions . . . I found that the defendant-districts prevailed with more than a 3-to-1 ratio."[6]

Other analyses of district-union clashes turn up similar findings. A breakdown of state board decisions compiled by the Maryland Negotiation Service between 1969 and 2010 found that the state board sided with district management twenty-eight out of thirty-six times in disputes regarding the scope of collective bargaining.[7] An analysis of the Minnesota Bureau of Mediation Services database of representation decisions found that the district prevailed over the union's grievance or interpretation in seventeen of the twenty-one cases since 2001.[8] The Iowa Public Employment Relations Board database of K–12 professional grievances shows that districts prevailed in twenty of the thirty-seven available decisions since 2000.[9] In Washington State, the Public Employment Relations Commission has compiled a database of decisions, including unfair labor practice complaints. Of the forty decisions recorded between 2010 and early 2012, districts prevailed in thirty-three.[10]

While district leaders are leery of conflict, it seems they fare better than they might expect when they stand up to union complaints. Now, it's important not to make too much of these findings. We know districts tend to proceed very cautiously and selectively, which helps to explain their hefty winning percentage. But these results do imply that many districts could push a lot harder than they do and still expect to have a reasonable chance of prevailing.

Given these possibilities, why don't leaders press? Well, for one thing, cage-busters can encounter intimidating threats of legal action—especially in special education. Ann Bonitatibus, associate superintendent in Frederick, Maryland, says, "Deaf parents of a child who was hard of hearing demanded interpreter services. They anticipated a future need, but it wasn't our responsibility to pay now for something not needed in the present. They were insisting, saying the [Individualized Education Program] mandated it. But that wasn't in the IEP. Their child was highly successful wearing hearing aids and didn't need an interpreter." What happened next may not surprise veteran principals, though Bonitatibus's response is less typical. She recalls, "In the middle of a meeting, the parents literally ripped the hearing aids out of their child's ears. They said, 'We are not going to put the hearing aids back, so now you must provide an interpreter.' And my response was, 'No. And I may have to consider reporting neglect to child protective services if you choose not to provide the hearing aids.' The parents filed a suit and it went to the state board; the school system prevailed."

Nobody likes it when you push back, but sometimes that's what it takes. While charter schools are supposed to enjoy enhanced autonomy, they can be bullied just like districts or district schools. Donald Hense, chairman of the Friendship Public Charter School in Washington, DC, notes that his school was being bombarded with demands by the Office of the State Superintendent of Education (OSSE). He says:

> It's hard to manage the voluminous requests made by OSSE and still have time to run a school . . . OSSE has fifty, sixty, maybe seventy people sending e-mails. We had to hire a general counsel specializing in special education just to be able to respond and force OSSE to [back off] or change policies when necessary. They may not like being challenged, but it's been necessary to maintain Friendship's independence.

Realizing the promised autonomy of chartering, says Hense, has required an attorney willing and able to keep bureaucrats at bay.

Standing firm is tough. So leaders often conclude it's not worth the time, energy, political capital, or hassle. The problem: letting them bully you ensures you'll be stuck in that cage. A better course is to go and get someone who'll swing that Louisville Slugger for you.

You Need a Consigliere

You may recall Francis Ford Coppola's classic 1972 movie, *The Godfather*. In it, young Michael, played by Al Pacino, takes the reins of the family business from his father, Don Corleone. At one key point, Michael explains that his brother, Tom Hagen, is no longer going to be his personal adviser. He says, Tom "is no longer consigliere. He's going to be our law-yer in Vegas. That's no reflection on Tom, but that's the way I want it." Surprised, Tom asks, "Why am I out?" Michael responds, "You're not a wartime consigliere, Tom. Things may get rough."

What you're looking for is counsel that can assist you when things get rough. You need someone aggressive, wily, and intrepid, who can help fig-ure out what's possible and what's not. You need a lawyer. They need not work for the district. They can work for a local law firm, happen to have a child at your school, or even agree to lend a hand from afar. How do you know when you've found the right lawyer? Robert Sommers, veteran superintendent and former education adviser to the governor of Ohio, re-calls he knew he had the right lawyers when they would say, "Where do you want to get? We'll find a way to get you there." (See "What Lawyers See When Scrutinizing a Contract" to get an idea of what they can tell you.)

Once you find your consigliere, how do you use her? What do you ask her? There are four key rules to guide you:

Always Start with "What Problem Are You Solving?" The goal is to help you solve problems. It all starts with you being clear about what you're trying to do and what problem you're trying to solve. You're setting the course; your consigliere's job is to help get you there. As attorney Sheara Krvaric explains, "The most successful clients that we work with have a goal in mind, they know what they want the outcome to be, and they're firm on the outcome, but then they [search out ideas] about what might be the best path to get there. The problem is that people think a lawyer's job is to tell you what to do. That's not our job. Our job is to tell you risks. Our job is to say, 'Option A has this risk, option B has this risk, and there's option C that you never thought about.' The effective leaders are the ones that know what they want to do, want to hear different approaches for how to do it, and then are willing to make a decision."

Find a Consigliere Aligned to Your Values and Priorities. If you want lawyers to act more like cage-busters than padlocks, you need to make that clear. You need to find someone who's committed to your aims and

What Lawyers See When Scrutinizing a Contract

I've noticed that when district officials see top-shelf education attorneys in action, they grasp the possibilities pretty quickly. But when discussing contracts or regulations in broad strokes, the opportunities may not be as obvious. So, for illustration's sake, let's take a look at a couple points from a memo that one top-shelf litigator crafted to help a district make sense of its collective bargaining agreement.

Legal Issue: Evergreen Status

The memo noted, "The District's CBA contains an unenviable 'Term of Agreement' provision which provides that the contract 'shall continue from year to year thereafter unless either of the parties give written notice . . . [of] a desire to change, amend, or modify the Agreement and until a [new] agreement is reached.'"

Counsel recommended, "Set an aggressive negotiating schedule to achieve a new agreement prior to expiration. Consider establishing 'grounds rules' for the negotiations (the [state statute] alludes to this) which include a mutual commitment to have a new agreement in place prior to expiration. This way, the District can continuously cite . . . that provision when negotiations are slowed or become bogged down, and announce intentions to file a breach of contract lawsuit or unfair labor practice charge if the union drags its feet in meeting that deadline."

Counsel also suggested, "The 'evergreen clause' refers to a party's written notice of intent to 'change, amend, or modify' the contract, but not to 'terminate' it. An aggressive strategy to consider is for the District to send a notice of contract termination (as of the expiration date of the contract), and, if no successor agreement is reached by contract expiration, argue that the evergreen clause is inoperable due to the termination notice. There exists federal NLRB precedent which distinguishes the amendment/modification of a contract from termination of it, and it is this precedent on which the District would rely."

Legal Issue: Extra Pay for [Extracurricular] Duty Schedule

Counsel recommended, "Consider negotiating definitive amounts for these extra duty positions (as opposed to payments that are calculated as a percentage of the teacher's ordinary pay). This way, the amounts do not increase automatically with each wage increase. Also, a union is less likely to want to extend collective bargaining negotiations simply to make advancements in this area, if they are otherwise satisfied with the negotiated deal."

Legal Issue: Sick Leave

Counsel recommended, "Redefine the phrase 'immediate family' to exclude siblings, in-laws, and others living in the employee's household. This will comport with the Family and Medical Leave Act, and thus is easily defensible at the bargaining table. Conform this definition with immediate family for bereavement leave."

Legal Issue: Disciplinary Procedures

Counsel recommended, "My reading of [the provision] confirms that the District may insist upon a union representative appearing within the 'reasonable notice' period and, if the representative does not appear, require the employee to choose whether to proceed without the representative or decline to participate. I recommend applying this provision strictly as written, and also strengthening it by adding the following final sentence: 'If the employee chooses not to be interviewed, the District shall proceed on the information available to it, and any statement by the employee thereafter (including at arbitration) shall not be considered in determining whether reasonable causes for discipline existed at the time of the District's decision.'"

This stuff can be a little dense, I know. But it's worth a careful read. If you start to look at contracts this way, it shows the cracks, suggests targets of opportunity, and can help build leverage for the next negotiation.

is comfortable embracing your values and priorities. Newscorp vice president Peter Gorman recalls that, while serving as superintendent of Charlotte-Mecklenburg Public Schools, "We specifically interviewed law firms to look for someone who truly believed that what we were doing and thought what we were talking about was fair, legal, and consistent." TNTP's Dan Weisberg explains, "Converting the mission of the legal team is vital. In a school district, you're in a compliance culture . . . where people are very nervous about making any decisions without getting approval from a lawyer. But while many district lawyers see their job as being about risk avoidance, good lawyers are skilled at finding creative ways to help their clients reach their goals. All it takes is a difference in viewpoint. The goal is not to make sure there is no legal risk, which is impossible in a district undertaking serious reform. The goal is to increase student achievement. If you change the mission of the general counsel's office [that way] . . . then you've got a sea change."

Work Closely with Your Legal Team. Treat your consigliere as a partner and an ally. Don't expect her to know exactly what you need. Make yourself clear and stay involved. Push. Ask questions. Gain enough familiarity so that you understand the challenges and opportunities. I know you didn't get into schooling so you could act like an attorney. And you don't need to. But remember "beginner's mind." Just as a school or system leader should know enough about budgeting or technology that they know what questions to ask, the same is true here. Alan Bersin, former superintendent of San Diego and secretary of education for California, after working for decades as a successful attorney, says, "District leaders don't need law school, but they do need to get smarter about the law and legal process. The law is not a black box . . . It's a matter of judgment. Lawyers must be asked for risk assessments, not for decisions masked in the form of advice. A good lawyer would never just say that you can't do something, and a competent CEO would never take just that as a final answer."

Prepare for Some Tough Choices. Pushing means you'll be in for some turbulence—no matter how measured your efforts. You'll need a consigliere who has your back when it counts. Stephen DeVita, general counsel for Loudon County, Virginia, notes that this mind-set doesn't come naturally to those in K–12: "There are too many leaders who come out of the teaching profession, and they have this desire to be loved. That makes it difficult for them to make tough choices and reach out and ask, 'Show me another way. If going down road A is not legal, is there another way to get to point B?' Oftentimes, the answer is, 'Yes, there is, but you're going to have to go to the legislature, lobby the mayor, or stand up to the union president.' And a lot of times these leaders don't want to hear that because it has the potential for a certain amount of conflict."

It's not enough to find your consigliere; you need to allow him to get a grip on that Louisville Slugger. Melissa Junge says, "K–12 leaders are so compliance focused that . . . questions are framed as black or white, never gray. Lawyers aren't viewed as people who can help find areas of flexibility or identify paths to accomplish goals." If you treat your attorney as a gate-keeper, he'll wind up functioning as one.

How to Find Your Consigliere

It's tough to find a consigliere. As system leader, you've really got three options. If your district has a general counsel (GC), start there. The problem is that GCs aren't necessarily equipped or inclined to play this role. You may find they've got latent skills, if you offer them direction and encouragement. If not, you'll need to replace them—or look elsewhere. A second tack is to use *outside counsel* (lawyers retained by the district). A third approach is to draw on local law firms or attorneys to provide pro bono support.

School leaders have more limited options. A lucky few might be able to turn to the district's staff (though that's feasible only in larger districts and if the superintendent's got staff attorneys convinced that they're supposed to help you solve problems and not just keep the peace). Occasionally, a school leader can turn to the district's outside counsel. But a school leader's best option may be connecting with local attorneys who are excited to help promote school improvement and who regularly provide pro bono support to worthy causes or clients.

Professionals want to make a difference. Yet, when attorneys reach out to schools or districts, they're often asked to do little more than serve as reading buddies for second-graders. Better plan: put their expertise to work, especially if you can find folks specializing in employment, regulatory, administrative, or contract law. Go out and find these individuals, if necessary. Talk to local lawyers and law firms. Reach out to Education Pioneers, a nonprofit that each summer places hundreds of law school, business school, and graduate school students in school systems, SEAs, and other educational enterprises.

The American Bar Association reports that nearly three-quarters of attorneys provide an average of forty-one hours of free legal counsel each year.[11] This means that in Michigan, where there are over thirty-two thousand active lawyers, it's a safe bet there are over 1 million pro bono hours performed every year; in New York, the figure is 5 million. Given that many law firms expect attorneys to devote some time to pro bono causes, you might just be surprised that even a small firm may offer up dozens of hours of free counsel.

When districts are hiring attorneys, a promising source of talent may be new law school graduates, particularly the hundreds who've previously taught via Teach For America or participated in Education Pioneers. Recent grads will be inexperienced and untested, but they'll also be free of the defensive mind-set and frequently willing to work long hours cheap. Now, it's hard for districts to compete with the salaries being offered by private sector firms. But each year, over 10 percent of graduates from the top twenty law schools (or more than seven hundred new lawyers) take jobs in the public sector that offer a median salary of $52,000.[12] They go to work in district attorneys' offices and at nonprofits because they're eager to gain hands-on experience and do important, socially meaningful work. Every survey of this population tells us that many of these people are passionate about schooling.[13] States and systems should pursue these folks, with their energy and fresh eyes.

Seeking out grads from top schools is by no means all that states and districts should be doing. For one thing, systems don't need Ivy Leaguers— they just need smart, enthusiastic grads eager to work hard. "This work doesn't take attorneys from the top law schools," says Dan Weisberg. "You might even do better with the people coming out of the eighty-fifth ranked law school. You just need people with smarts, commitment, and guts."

You Found Your Consigliere . . . What Now?

Leaders are sometimes uncertain what kinds of questions to ask a consigliere, or what might be possible. So, let's flag a few examples of the kinds of things that an A-list consigliere might suggest. (See "Five Places in Your CBA to Look for Leeway" for a few more.)

Five Places in Your CBA to Look for Leeway

The University of Washington's Mitch Price is one of the nation's leading authorities on CBAs in schooling. He has documented how districts and charters voluntarily tie their hands and fail to take advantage of existing freedoms. Fortunately, in "Teacher Union Contracts and High School Reform," he has also flagged easy opportunities to do much better. Price suggests five places where every district and school leader should look to see if there's room to run.[14] These are provisions that leaders often don't take full advantage of, and that they sometimes don't even know about.

"Best Interest of the District" Exceptions

Many CBAs contain clauses that "allow the 'best interest' of the district and/or students to trump other factors, considerations, and/or contract provisions, such as seniority." Price provides an example from the Columbus, Ohio, contract: "Correct and proper operation of the school district will necessarily require that involuntary transfers be made. In making involuntary transfers, the wishes of the individual teachers will be honored to the extent that these considerations do not conflict with *the instructional requirements and best interests of the school district and the pupils*."

Special Sections That Grant Reform-Related Opportunities

Many contracts contain special provisions that touch on issues such as "small learning communities, site-based management, new schools, restructuring, and closing the achievement gap." In Seattle, the CBA grants specific autonomies to schools participating in the "partnership for closing the achievement gap." These include flexibility permitting "staff in designated schools [to] be eligible for incentive pay" and "hiring incentives to attract qualified candidates for hard-to-fill positions."

Exceptions for Special Instructional Skills or Qualifications

Price writes, "A number of CBA provisions allow for exceptions to a seniority-based hiring or transfer system in special instances where a less-senior candidate possesses special instructional skills or qualifications." In Los Angeles, for example, the contract states, "When there is an over-teachered condition, the teacher with the least District seniority

(continued)

. . . will be displaced unless it is reasonably determined at the discretion of the immediate administrator that such teacher *possesses special instructional skills or qualifications* needed by the pupils and the educational program at the school and not possessed by another teacher available to fill the need."

Provisions Allowing Consideration of External Job Candidates

Contracts sometimes allow external, out-of-district candidates to be considered alongside internal candidates for transfers and vacancies. Price writes, "In Oakland . . . the contract states that as part of the transfer process the principal requests from the district human resources office 'a list of eligible candidates who have submitted timely transfer requests, *as well as any qualified applicants recruited by the Employer.*'"

Allowances for Different Daily Schedules

Many contracts contain language allowing for alternate schedules. In Tacoma, Washington, the contract states: "Employees at a school site may voluntarily work an alternate schedule . . . in response to program needs and services." Employees at a school can implement an alternate schedule by gaining district approval and approval from 75 percent of the school's teachers.

Does your contract include language like this? If so, are you taking full advantage? Might you be able to use it in new, smarter ways? If these provisions aren't in your contract, they belong on your wish list for your next negotiation.

Take the familiar step-and-lane teacher pay scale. Plenty of superintendents grumble that paying strictly for years of service is a not-great way to pay teachers but say there's not much they can do about it. Even worse, their GC may suggest that evergreen provisions leave them without recourse, even when the contract expires. Attorney Lyle Zuckerman, who does a lot of education law from his perch at the New York firm Vedder Price, notes that it's not quite so cut-and-dried. He explains that some contracts define steps in terms of years of service. If so, districts have to keep paying accordingly when the contract is evergreened. But there are other contracts that don't specify what constitutes a step. In those cases, there are options. One might declare that granting steps for years of service has been a convention rather than an obligation, and that no steps will be granted until a new deal is signed. Doing so can create bargaining leverage and give teachers cause to lean on the union to work with you to get the deal done. Of course, the union will push back, so—as we'll see in chapter 7—it's crucial to be prepared.

In a similar vein, states like Arkansas, Illinois, and Maine permit districts to extend the probationary status for teachers by an additional year. The Arkansas code reads, "'Probationary teacher' means a teacher who has not completed three (3) successive years of employment in the school district in which the teacher is currently employed. A teacher employed in a school district in this state for three (3) years shall be deemed to have completed the probationary period; however, an employing school district may, by a majority vote of its directors, provide for one (1) additional year of probationary status."[15] Smart school and system leaders can use that extra time to evaluate new hires, weed out weak teachers, and rigorously police quality. (See "Beating Tenure to the Punch.") But district leaders have to ask for that time—and remarkably few even know they can.

A hard look at staffing rules can turn up intriguing flexibility. Missouri has firm caps on the number of students per teacher.[16] The regulations also stipulate, however, that class size "may increase by as many as ten (10) students for any period that a teacher assistant assists the classroom teacher full time." A teacher assistant needs only "sixty (60) semester hours of college credit" and "a general understanding of the objectives of public education."[17] This is an invitation to rethink class size by, for instance, using work-study or internships to tap into local college students interested in community service or preparing to become teachers.

Many state legislatures have given cash-strapped school districts flexibility that can provide powerful negotiating leverage. In New Mexico, the statute governing collective bargaining has an emergency provision that allows public employers to "take actions as may be necessary to carry out the mission of the public employer in emergencies."[18] This provides leeway to push cuts or policy changes that might be nonstarters in flush times. Ohio statute allows municipalities, counties, and townships to declare

Beating Tenure to the Punch

Tenure makes releasing your low performers more difficult. But cage-busters never mistake difficult for impossible. More immediately, tenure heightens the import of being smart about policing quality *before* teachers get tenure.

"In our district, teachers have three one-year contracts at the beginning of their career," says one Ohio superintendent. "There is no law that makes you rubber-stamp people once they reach a certain number of years. So we have raised the bar on tenure. The principal has to advocate for that teacher, they have to come with evidence about that teacher's performance, and they need to understand that we are making—from tenure through the end of that person's career—about a $1 million investment. Is that teacher really worth $1 million? And we have turned people down for tenure; it was not pleasant. Last year, four people that were up for tenure did not get it, because they were not the quality that we were willing to hitch our horse to their carriage for the rest of their career."

In fact, twelve states give district leaders an avenue for extending the probationary time for tenure decisions.[19] In Maine, the provisional time before a teacher is granted tenure is two years. But state statute also allows the commissioner to grant an additional extension of up to two years based on, "(1) The recommendation of the superintendent; (2) The recommendation of the support system that includes" a Teacher Action Plan, specific steps to achieve the plan's goals, and criteria for measuring progress.[20]

A similar law is on the books in Nebraska: "Probationary certificated employee means a teacher or administrator who has served under a contract with the school district for less than three successive school years in any school district, unless extended one or two years by a majority vote of the board in a Class IV or V school district."[21]

Yet, remarkably few districts take advantage of these provisions or are even aware of them. A representative from Little Rock couldn't remember when the district had last requested additional time. The district doesn't keep any data on this, nor does the Arkansas Department of Education. In fact, it proved impossible to find a state that claims to track this information. A representative from Portland, Maine, said that, despite Maine's law, the district's HR department wouldn't extend the probationary period. In Omaha, Nebraska, an HR representative said the district never extends the probationary period.

themselves in a state of "fiscal emergency." If a court or arbitrator OKs the declaration, entities are free to submit a "detailed financial plan" with actions that promise to help "avoid any fiscal emergency condition in the future."[22] California Public Law Group attorneys Jonathan Holtzman, K. Scott Dickey, and Steve Cikes explain, "A declaration of fiscal emergency may prove to be a critical tool in maintaining public service levels, limiting or eliminating the need for layoffs, and avoiding municipal insolvency through bankruptcy." Of course, they also advise steering clear of fiscal crisis by negotiating far-sighted CBAs "that preclude increases in salaries where the funds have not been certified as available in the budget or by supplemental appropriation."[23]

An aggressive legal posture can save big bucks. Buffalo, New York, benefited from a March 2011 decision by the New York Court of Appeals, which held that school district employees were not entitled to annual salary step increases during the city's thirty-eight-month wage freeze. The ruling saved the school district $148 million over the next three years. Superintendent James Williams said the ruling supplied "leverage to have a serious conversation about improving the quality of education."[24]

GET THE RIGHT PEOPLE IN PLACE

In chapter 1, I told the story of visiting the Fairfax County turnaround school where the principal treated turning over more than half her staff as an afterthought.

Fairfax County superintendent Jack Dale later noted how remarkable it was that the principal and her team had glossed over this critical piece, saying, "It was fascinating that she forgot to mention that. Because when we're talking to principals turning schools around, we talk a lot about the need to change people. I was kind of taken aback that she didn't even mention it." To my mind, the principal's omission wasn't all that unusual. She did what ed leadership authorities recommend, which is to focus on the uplifting, team-building stuff and not on that unpleasant mountain.

But trying to transform organizations through culture alone is a classic recipe for rolling the boulder. In his seminal management book *Good to Great*, Jim Collins observed a commonality among the successful companies he studied: "We expected that good-to-great leaders would begin by setting a new vision and strategy. We found instead that they *first* got the right people on the bus, the wrong people off the bus, and the right people in the right seats—and *then* they figured out where to drive it. The old adage 'People are your most important asset' turns out to be wrong. People are *not* your most important asset. The *right* people are."[25]

One veteran HR executive who has worked with school districts says, "Leaders need to be unapologetic about addressing mediocrity. Until you're ready to do that, you're not serious about improvement." He recalls working with one highly regarded district where, "The HR director was lamenting the pain of having to lay people off based on performance. He said, 'Oh my God, I hope I don't have to go through that again.' He was acting as if it was some huge burden that he had to go through. So I put my arm around him and said, 'Do it because you believe in it. Those teachers that you kept are going to perform great for you. It's a long-term journey.'"

Of course, culture is essential. The mistake is imagining that culture is some kind of ephemeral thing that can spring forth anywhere, anytime, solely through good intentions. Cage-busters find ways to build teams that will promote a culture of great teaching and learning. Abigail Smith, former chief of the Transformation Management Office at DC Public Schools, says of her work in Washington, DC, "The investment we made in recruiting talent is a huge part of getting around incompetency and bureaucracy. That's because you have people coming in who say, 'I'm going to figure out a way around this dumb obstacle,' and then do it."

As a superintendent implementing performance-based evaluation in Charlotte-Mecklenburg, Peter Gorman says, "We found that we had to change our HR chief because we had one who always said, 'Oh no, you can't do that. We can't get rid of that.' And eventually we had to say 'enough is enough' and put our foot down. We burned through at least three HR chiefs in the five years I was there, and that was because those people just accepted that poor performance was OK."

High-performing schools and systems are uncompromising when it comes to seeking talent. At YES Prep, Chris Barbic's team was maniacal about hiring. "We spent a ton of time up front on our selection process," he says. "There's an art and a science to recruiting and selection, and a lot of charter management organizations are good at the art. But we also got very good at the science. We did a personality profile of every single high-performing teacher that we had. We did the same personality profiles on teachers in the bottom 10 percent. Our high performers shared traits that our low performers didn't. We were super picky about who we hired. And if that meant we left a position open, we would rather not fill it than stick a warm body in there."

Nina Gilbert, executive director of the Ivy Prep Academy network of charter schools, says, "I can figure out if someone is right for the team, because I'll say, 'Look we don't have air [conditioning]. Some days there is no toner in the copier. Some days you may read in the press that our school is closing because of low funding or a denied charter petition. I need to know that you can teach through that.' Listening to their answers lets me know if they're the right people."

Leaders often complain about the types of teachers they're seeing from local colleges of education, as if they're powerless to change things. When Terry Grier was superintendent in Akron, Ohio, he and his staff were concerned that the teachers they were hiring "did not possess the skills necessary to be successful in a rapidly changing urban setting." Grier held a meeting with leaders of the local colleges of education to tell them things had to change or he'd stop accepting their student teachers or hiring their graduates. "After I spoke, you would have thought someone sucked the air out of the room," says Grier. "A representative from Kent State said, 'Terry, let me get this straight. You want us to change how we are preparing teachers to teach, even though we have one of the best training programs in the country?' I responded, 'Yes. Allow me to use a crude analogy to make our point. You sell cars, we're your largest client, and we want you to make some modifications to the engines of the cars we purchase.' Finally, Bill Muse, president of the University of Akron said, 'You're absolutely right. You're our largest customer, and if you want a different engine, we'll work with you to design that new engine.'"

Rewarding Your Stars

Schools and school systems generally operate today on the implicit assumption that most teachers will be similarly adept at everything. This may have made sense fifty years ago, when we had a deep talent pool of willing teachers and few tools for customizing teacher roles or gauging performance, but today it is a costly legacy. A fourth-grade teacher who is a terrific English language arts (ELA) instructor might teach reading for just ninety minutes a day. This is an extravagant waste of talent, when one can stroll down the hallway and see a less skilled colleague offering ninety minutes of pedestrian reading instruction. One move to consider is rethinking schedules and student assignment so that the exceptional ELA instructor can teach reading to many more kids, and then reshaping responsibilities, recognition, and compensation accordingly. Job descriptions and salary ought not be inviolate; they should be tools for finding smarter ways to attract, nurture, and use talent.

Any would-be cage-buster can list his or her *stars*: people whose motivation, skill, effort, and performance are unquestioned. What can you do to attract more of those folks, to get the most value out of the ones you have, and to increase the odds that both old stars and new ones will stick around? Here are a few tips that can help:

Make Sure You're Systematically Doing the Easy Stuff. TNTP's Dan Weisberg notes that high-performing and low-performing teachers leave the profession at about the same rate. Today, just 37 percent of high-performing teachers (as measured by growth on student assessments) report that their principals encourage them to stay at their school the following year.[26] Weisberg says, "District leaders and principals need to be identifying their best performers and attempting to get them to stay by whatever means necessary. It starts with doing no-cost things like saying to them, 'I think you're a great teacher, and I want you to stay' or, 'Do you really want to teach AP chemistry next year in addition to your ninth-grade algebra class? Because if that's interesting to you, I'll make that happen.' Good principals are doing that every day, but there's no systemic effort. And there's no obstacle to that."

Get Creative About Rewarding and Acknowledging Talent. When Michele Evans was superintendent of Canton City, Ohio, she allowed star performers to step into new roles. She recalls, "My director of K–12, who was doing a great job supervising buildings, told me he was really interested in HR. And I said, 'Okay, you got it. So now he has buildings that he supervises but he's also in charge of the HR function, which I think is smart because I've seen so many people in HR get isolated from the organizational issues that HR often causes. So he's out in the buildings, he can see the effects of the decisions that we make, and I think it makes him stronger in both areas.'"

Get More Value Out of Stars, and Reward and Inspire Them Along the Way. What I'm talking about is that dreaded word *productivity*. While it's gotten a bad rap in K–12, it refers to nothing more than how much good a given employee can do. If one teacher is regarded by colleagues as a far better mentor than another, or if one reading instructor helps students master skills more rapidly than another, that teacher is doing more good than others—*at least in that particular area*. Rewarding prized mentors who choose to work with more colleagues or boosting pay for terrific classroom teachers who choose to take on larger student loads (and then holding them accountable for results) allows you to make fuller use of the talent you have even as you recognize and reward excellence—always, of course, assuming these opportunities are *offered* to your stars and *not* just one more thing on their plate.

It's Not Okay to Be Bad at Your Job

For reasons that are never quite clear, folks in K–12 sometimes have trouble saying, "It's not okay to be bad at your job." It seems an obvious point. Yet, my national study of ed leadership preparation in 2007 found that just 3 percent of instruction on personnel management related to teacher dismissal. At twenty of thirty-one programs studied, not a single week of instruction even mentioned teacher termination.[27]

When ed leadership icons Andy Hargreaves and Michael Fullan advise, "The worst thing to do is to write off apparently poor or mediocre teachers as dead wood . . . try doing the hard thing, the right thing, the ethical thing, and explore ways of bringing these teachers back," they are condemning leaders to spend a lot of time and emotional energy trying to take the worst performers and raise them to mediocrity.[28]

KIPP Academies cofounder Mike Feinberg approaches the issue somewhat differently. He says, "Picture Eduardo Espinoza, who's sitting front and center in that classroom but isn't learning. I tell KIPP school leaders, 'Two years ago you sat at the kitchen table with Eduardo's mom telling her you would do whatever it would take to get him to and through college. So, are you going to keep your word?'" He says, "If teachers are not good and kids are not learning . . . the bottom line is the teacher needs to go." When all is said and done, there's no excuse for being bad at one's job. That said, it's ludicrous and self-defeating to suggest that firing lousy employees is some kind of improvement strategy by itself. Feinberg notes, "You can walk around with a bloody hatchet saying, 'This is great, I fixed my school,' but if you've got high turnover, it's a lose-lose. Why are you losing all your people? If they say, 'No, I'm getting rid of bad hires,' then it's a question of why you're hiring bad teachers in the first place."

Newark superintendent Cami Anderson offers a terrific illustration of how to tackle the "culture of can't" and get serious about job performance, from her time as area superintendent for New York City's alternative schools and programs. She recalls that the district had two "conventional wisdoms" when it came to evaluating guidance counselors and social workers: "The first was you'd be violating student confidentiality if you observed guidance counselors or social workers interacting with kids one-on-one, and the second was, if you weren't licensed as a clinical supervisor, you didn't have the authority to evaluate or document performance for these people." Anderson says she had to "debunk these urban myths" before addressing staff performance. "I finally pulled the contract, asked our labor lawyers to take a look, and found out that the contract is relatively silent on how guidance counselors and social workers are evaluated. We had more latitude, not less, when it came to these individuals." Anderson instituted a performance-based evaluation system for these staff, and says, "This piece was key when you're working with kids in jail and kids who've dropped out. Outcomes like attendance and retention started going up."

Policing Personnel Makes Culture-Building Easier

The New Teacher Project reported in 2009 that 81 percent of administrators and 57 percent of teachers said there is at least one tenured teacher in their school who is performing poorly. Yet half of the districts studied did not dismiss a single tenured teacher for poor performance during the years in question.[29] School leaders have habitually given weak teachers a pass, with the tacit approval of risk-adverse district leadership. "I think in many cases there is a disconnect between what people in the principal's office believe will be rewarded and what a [cage-busting] superintendent actually wants," explains TNTP president Tim Daly. "If they document poor performance and initiate a dismissal, these principals don't believe they will be supported in a difficult decision or that they will be seen as doing the right thing." Instead, he says, they fear they'll be hung out to dry.

Changing that is a matter of culture. But changing culture requires changing routines and expectations. The Teacher Performance Unit in New York City was launched to ensure that lawyers were supporting school leaders and not hassling them about paperwork. David Weiner, now deputy chancellor in New York but then a principal in the system, says, "[The TPU] was hugely beneficial to principals, because, before that point, principals were always nervous about writing people up and what the [union] is going to think and the threats they would make. The TPU shifted the mind-set to say, 'Oh, you're writing these people up? Great, let's get someone there to help you and to make sure that you're doing everything correct so you don't get hung up on some sort of ridiculous procedural hiccup.'"

Culture, coaching, and inspiration are terrific things. But when staff don't share a common vision, it's tough to build a coherent culture. Jay Steele, associate superintendent of high schools in Nashville, recalls that when he came to the district, he "had to . . . remove some people to get this vision moving forward. It's about holding the schools accountable and removing barriers, and a lot of those barriers were people. Out of eight schools, four were implementing the [program effectively] . . . The other four were not . . . So we had to hold them accountable. Those four principals are gone—I removed them right away. That made everybody fall in line."[30]

Setting a tone early can help encourage low performers to leave of their own accord, says Walter Jackson, principal of Alief Taylor High School in Houston. "I came to a campus in great distress. We had to change the culture. Our [new] culture was, 'There are no excuses—these are poor kids from single-parent or no-parent households. It is what it is.' Saying that made a lot of faculty uncomfortable. Those are the ones who jumped out when they got the chance. They didn't want to work under those demands." Maryland state superintendent Lillian Lowery recalls that, when she was Delaware secretary of education, one turnaround school "decided to have critical conversations with every teacher about the aggressive nature of the partnership zone. The administration would say, 'Do you think you can do this work or not? If you don't, let us help you find another placement somewhere else.' About one-third of the teachers left just based on those conversations." When staff want to be in a school or system, it's a whole lot easier to forge a coherent culture.

As state chief in Colorado, Dwight Jones took over a troubled state agency that required a lot of changes. But he avoided firing a lot of employees by creating an environment where the wrong people would choose to get off the bus:

> For instance, one senior staff member came to work at 9 or 10 and would leave by 2 or 3. I realized that if I expect every employee to work hard, it has to start at the top. That begins with me. To change the culture, I have to model what hard work looks like. So I put this employee on a schedule. I required [her] to notify me before leaving work each day. The individual chose to retire very shortly after I arrived. While a lot of other personnel changes followed, most folks left on their own. As a result, I was only forced to move five people. Once I built the new system, the rest of the employees saw that accountability and culture had changed, and they left on their own.

Be Measured—and Fair

It's an easy mistake for leaders to pursue a more performance-focused culture in a manner that can feel like an assault on the teachers. States and districts across the country have adopted teacher evaluation systems while doing too little to ensure that principals are effective evaluators and before adopting similar expectations for system or school leaders. Peter Gorman, vice president of Newscorp's education division and former Charlotte-Mecklenburg superintendent, sketches a smarter path. He says, "In Charlotte, we faced the same challenges everyone does where people say you cannot remove low-performing employees. When we'd go to release low performers, we'd find that they had years of outstanding evaluations. This is going to sound simplistic, but I told our team the first thing is we had to start by telling the truth to people about performance. I started with the direct reports to me. We were on a four-point scale and we had very senior folks—assistant superintendents, area superintendents—for the first time getting, like, a 2.8 or a 2.5 on their evaluation. They nearly had a heart attack. They said, 'Oh my God, am I going to be fired?' And I said, 'No, it's being transparent about your performance, helping you get better.' . . . I've learned that, when you go to change the evaluation process, it's a process that takes stages. So it was me and the executive staff one year. The next year we got it right for principals. The year after, assistant principals. Only then did we start with teachers."

Sometimes, would-be cage-busters can fall into a trap where they give the impression that they think firing people is the way to improve schooling, or that improving teaching and learning is mostly a question of evaluation and pay. First, it's crucial to keep explaining that the whole point of busting the cage is to create the conditions where instructional leadership will stick and where powerful cultures can more easily take root. Second, keep in mind that a lot of teachers don't like working down the hall from laggards. These teachers agree it's important to do a better job of moving out lousy practitioners. FDR Group and Education Sector have reported that 55 percent of teachers say that, in their own district, "the process for removing teachers who are clearly ineffective and shouldn't be in the classroom—but who are past the probationary period—is very difficult and time-consuming." Forty-six percent of teachers say that they personally know a teacher who is "clearly ineffective and shouldn't be in a classroom," and 49 percent say that the union "sometimes fights to protect teachers who really should be out of the classroom."[31] If leaders present their case calmly and fairly while acknowledging and addressing legitimate concerns, they may find more support than they'd expect.

SEEING THE LAW AS IT IS

I started this chapter with some thoughts from Willie Stark, the legendary Boss in Robert Penn Warren's *All the King's Men*. It's worth sharing a bit more of Willie's wisdom as we close:

"Hugh," the Boss said, and grinned, "The trouble with you is you are a law-yer. You are a damned fine lawyer."

"You're a lawyer," Hugh Miller said.

"No," the Boss corrected, "I'm not a lawyer. I know some law. In fact, I know a lot of law. And I made me some money out of law. But I'm not a lawyer. That's why I can see what the law is like. It's like a single-bed blanket on a double bed and three folks in the bed and a cold night. There ain't never enough blanket to cover the case, no matter how much pulling and hauling."[32]

Cage-dwellers have come to see laws, rules, regulations, and contracts as immutable, inviolate things. That's why you'll so often hear, "We're not allowed to do this" or "We're required to do that." That's how we've built the "culture of can't." Willie Stark knew better. And cage-busters do too. The law's meaning is always contested. If you're not yanking back on that blanket, it just means that the union lawyer or federal grants official is going to wind up snug and comfortable. And you'll have no one to blame but yourself.

The law is a tool. Lawyers are allies who can wield it. Now, keep in mind: cage-busters don't need to be legal experts; they just need to know enough law so they can use it to ask the right questions. Understanding the bars of the cage can help you see which are stout, which are frail, and which are illusory. Finding your consigliere and giving her that Louisville Slugger can help you start to crash through bars that once looked impenetrable.

In the end, though, any leader's ability to serve kids is a question of making smart use of talent, tools, time, and money. Of these, the most critical is talent. Thus, it's no surprise that so much cage-busting is about finding ways to be smarter about recruiting, using, and retaining talent—and addressing ineptitude. These aren't alternatives to building cultures and improving practice, they're tools for doing so more intently and effectively. I'll say it again: you don't engage in cage-busting *instead* of focusing on talent and culture, you do it precisely so that you can focus more effectively *on* talent and culture.

In chapter 6, we turn to other key tools in the cage-buster's toolbox. We'll focus on opportunities to spend resources smarter and to take full advantage of technology and talent.

6

Everyone Knows
Where the Booze Is

IN A PIVOTAL SCENE in the movie *The Untouchables*, Sean Connery's veteran cop Jim Malone, Kevin Costner's Elliot Ness, and their little squad stride out of the police station and into the streets of Chicago. They're finally going after gangster Al Capone's illegal booze. They've barely crossed the street when Malone stops short, in front of the post office.

MALONE: Well, here we are.

NESS (*puzzled*): What are we doing here?

MALONE: Liquor raid.

NESS (*bewildered, eying the police station just behind them*): Here?

MALONE (*dryly, and very patiently*): Mr. Ness, everybody knows where the booze is. The problem isn't finding it, the problem is, who wants to cross Capone?

School and system leaders have a wealth of opportunities to use limited talent, tools, time, and money to promote great teaching and learning—if they look for them and have the will to act on them.

For starters, educators have accepted routines and procurement rules that inflate costs and leave them gasping for the dollars to fuel improvement. David Hardy, CEO of the charter school Boys' Latin of Philadelphia, says, "At my last charter school, I got a $55,000 grant. We planned to hire a reading teacher and set up a computer lab. But one of the grant rules was that you had to hire at the district's pay scale. We could have hired a reading teacher for $40,000, but the district's reading teacher scale was $80,000. That put an end to that. When it came to the computers, we had to buy them off the district contract. So we ended up getting nine computers for $55,000. By the time the district got them installed, they were obsolete. So I got someone to give us $25,000. With that, we got fifteen terminals, a server, and printers; and we got all for less than $25,000. That's what anyone with good sense would do."

OfficeMax routinely identifies 15 to 25 percent cost savings when asked by districts to scrutinize spending on office products, print and document services, furniture, technology, janitorial supplies, and the like. "Most districts don't have a clue what the total cost of ownership of these things actually is," says Andrew Kniberg, manager of OfficeMax's education division. Eliminating a central warehouse and moving to an on-demand model for supplies and print services can, for instance, yield big savings. Kniberg says that OfficeMax often receives a warm reception from CFOs. The catch: many districts don't act to realize these savings, because boards and other district leaders are reluctant to trim jobs or upset longstanding relations with vendors. A few years ago, OfficeMax partnered with one of the nation's largest districts, identifying $7 million in potential purchasing and materials savings. Yet, even in the midst of a shortfall measuring in the hundreds of millions, the district failed to act on any of the recommendations. One observer explained, "There's always another excuse, another sign-off to get, and another cabinet discussion about potential impact on support staff morale. This was a hundred teaching positions we could've saved. You'd think that would get people moving. You'd be wrong."

Districts routinely leave low-hanging savings unrealized. Several years ago, New Orleans feared it had long-departed employees on the payroll. To verify which employees actually were in the system, all employees were required to physically pick up a particular paycheck. Hundreds of checks went uncollected. Consultants estimated that the district probably had well over a hundred dead employees on payroll, and many others illicitly collecting pay. (Funny postscript: the exercise was foiled when payroll staff decided they ought to mail out all the uncollected checks.) While it may seem crazy, Cami Anderson says this type of thing happened all the time in New York City: "In District 79, we found that payroll was still paying people who had moved to Florida, passed away, or transferred." I asked one seasoned education consultant about this phenomenon, saying it seemed astonishing that major school systems were paying dead people, *in the twenty-first century!* In response, she patted my hand, saying, "Oh, you dear thing. *All* the districts we work with are paying dead people."

Washington, DC, chancellor Kaya Henderson found $10 million to launch a competitive "Proving What's Possible Fund" that supports school-level problem solving around time, talent, and technology. All of the funds were repurposed from existing sources. She explains, "We were funding things centrally, nonprofits or interventions, for ten schools here or fifteen schools there. But when you looked at the results, they were uneven at best." What types of savings did she identify? "One outfit was getting $1.9 million to be in ten schools. Now, everybody said, 'I want them.' Of course, everyone would like ten extra bodies for free. But when you looked at the results, in some schools scores went up, in others they went down. They were supposed to be doing literacy interventions, which wasn't their expertise. I asked, given that trained professionals have uneven success, why they thought people trained over a couple of weeks were going to be able to solve problems for struggling readers?" Henderson zeroed out the initiative and put the savings into the fund. She and her staff also leveraged existing School Improvement Grant (SIG) dollars. "Previously, we would just give the whole lot of [SIG] cash to schools. We reserved half of the school SIG money for the fund. Now, schools have to explain what they're going to do with $400,000; they can't just replace the librarian who got cut last year or replace everything that never worked before."

Everyone knows where the booze is: the question is who is ready to do something about it. One problem is a K–12 culture where the words *productivity* and *efficiency* are often regarded as heresy. Nate Levenson, formerly superintendent in Arlington, Massachusetts, and now managing director at the District Management Council, says, "The idea of measuring return on investment can be uncomfortable. When I was superintendent, I was asked to approve a $150,000 purchase of new materials for our elementary writing program. Before answering, I asked how many students would be using the new materials and what gains we might expect in writing ability. The angry response surprised me . . . [The reply was] 'The question is offensive. If only one student benefits, then that should be enough.'"[1]

Readers will note that most cost-saving options entail finding ways to get more value out of current staff or make do with fewer staff. Skeptics will ask, *Why would cage-busters pick on their employees?* The answer was provided more than half a century ago by infamous criminal John Dillinger. Asked why he robbed banks, Dillinger memorably responded, "Because that's where the money is." In the typical school district, around 80 percent of spending is devoted to salaries and benefits; meanwhile, 90 percent of instructional expenditures go toward salaries and benefits for instructional personnel.[2] That's where the money is. If schools are to do much better with the dollars they have, it requires rethinking how those dollars are spent. And that means changing what employees do, how they're used, and how they're paid.

I don't know how many dollars per pupil it takes to run a great school. But I do know that every school and every system I've seen can do much better with the resources it already has. (See "Four Common Mistakes When Facing Tough Times . . . and a Wiser Course.")

THINK *BANG FOR THE BUCK*

Educators make a well-meaning mistake when they focus on academic outcomes without also focusing on cost-effectiveness of programs and personnel. In fact, what usually results is a well-intentioned variant of the "new stupid." Well-run organizations worry—*of course*—about performance, but *also* the cost of the time, talent, and tools that produce those outcomes. The relationship of results to costs is sometimes referred to as *return on investment,* but it's fine to just think of it as the bang you're getting for each buck you spend.

Today, it's easy to find out how well a school or system is faring in terms of academic outcomes, but it's harder to gauge bang for the buck. Performance outcomes are generally discussed without much regard for

Four Common Mistakes When Facing
Tough Times . . . and a Wiser Course

There are four bad habits that school and system leaders fall into when it comes to thinking about spending and school improvement. Each was brilliantly illuminated in a 2011 *Phi Delta Kappan* article by scholars Rick Ginsberg and Karen Multon.[3] It's worth quickly touching on each, because the responses that leaders shared offer classic examples of where the "culture of can't" kicks in:

Excuse-mongering: One superintendent opined, "I feel as though I am at a point where I have to say that it is OK for some kids to fail because we cannot provide the extra help they need." Hold up, there. When police budgets are cut, we'd be ticked if the police said, "Hey, we can't keep you safe. Deal with it." It's not okay to use tight budget cuts as an excuse to accept mediocrity. Every leader, public or private, has good budget years and bad ones. Cage-busters do the very best they can with the resources they have.

Imagining that progress only comes with new dollars: One superintendent lamented, "You can't push forward with new innovations without the funding to see them through." That's silly. The most innovative organizations in the world are cash-poor start-ups that have to find smarter solutions. In education, though, *innovation* has typically meant "more, better" reform. Districts didn't rethink staffing or school libraries when they got computers or Internet connectivity, they just laid these alongside what was in place. This is why education is perhaps the only sector where the introduction of the personal computer has yielded a *decline* in measured productivity.

Seeing every budget cut as debilitating: One principal said, "It is impossible to make cuts in a district and not have it impact teachers and students. We cut a secretary and many tasks are now falling to teachers. This takes up their precious time to prepare for students . . . We cut a mail delivery person, and now secretaries and paras are having to do curbside pickup and drop-off of mail so the mail can travel on buses." By this logic, no organization—not the US military, US Postal Service, or General Motors—can ever trim spending or personnel without compromising quality. Impending cuts offer a chance to ask how time is being used, how roles are defined, and

(continued)

what tasks are unnecessary or can be rethought. In reality, public and private organizations routinely make cuts that boost productivity and strengthen their culture. The challenge is to prune wisely so as to emerge leaner and healthier.

Countenancing rather than condemning unacceptable employee responses: One principal said, "I was and continue to be surprised at how some people react. I had typically reasonable people telling me that they weren't going to do their job . . . We have taken a huge step backwards in our communication, trust, and cooperation." Surprised? When "reasonable people" announce their intention to shortchange kids, a cage-buster's first instinct is not to worry about communication but to insist that adults behave responsibly.

Chicago mayor and former White House chief of staff Rahm Emanuel has sketched a far wiser response to tough times, namely: "You never want a serious crisis to go to waste."[4] For more than a half century, until 2009, K–12 schooling spent more dollars per pupil each year than the year before. The problem with this is that no one makes tough choices in flush times. It doesn't matter if you're a hardhearted for-profit CEO or a cuddly koala of a nonprofit executive; nobody is eager to squeeze costs, shut down inefficient programs, or trim employees. A leader who tries to do this when times are good just seems mean. But tight times allow cage-busters to tackle problems that otherwise get swept under the rug, reexamine old priorities, and pursue overdue cuts.

whether they're achieved while spending 20 percent more or 20 percent less. Consequently, school and system leaders focus on boosting achievement but pay far less attention to cost-effectiveness. And, since trimming staff or squeezing expenditures are sure to complicate a leader's life, it's no surprise that superintendents and principals—even those recognized as head-knocking reformers—only pursue efficiencies in spending and staff intermittently and reluctantly. Yet, getting the same achievement results for 10 percent less means a district is freeing up millions to add services or invest in programs, staff, and practices that can drive improvement. Here's a simple rule of thumb: if school A is posting results that are 50 percent better than school B's (with similar students), but is spending 50 percent more, we ought to hesitate to suggest that it's a better school—much less some kind of model. If you're serving similar students in similar circumstances and spend 50 percent more, you need to be 50 percent better *just to tread water.*

The fact is, some schools and systems get far more bang for their buck than do others. In 2011, the left-leaning Center for American Progress (CAP) studied district spending and performance, taking into account the students served. Other things being equal, districts with below-average productivity spent $950 more per student than above-average districts to produce the same academic outcomes. The authors observed, "If school systems spent their dollars more productively, many would see large gains in student achievement."[5] In California, all else being equal, low-productivity systems could boost achievement by 25 percent if they spent dollars more efficiently. In Arizona, the figure was more than 36 percent. In Wisconsin, CAP compared the districts of Oshkosh and Eau Claire, noting the two are similarly sized and have similar demographics. Yet, in 2008, Oshkosh spent about $300 per student less to produce similar student outcomes.[6]

STRETCHING THE SCHOOL DOLLAR

There are many ways to think about how to use resources smarter. A good place to start is just by measuring costs more accurately. A powerful but underused tool in education is the concept of *unit cost.* The University of Washington's Marguerite Roza, perhaps the leading authority on this topic, explains that breaking down costs to per school or per pupil terms can help make sense of spending. Otherwise, it can be hard to know what it means that a new program will cost $3 million a year or that a new data system will cost $20 million.[7]

Breaking out unit costs can make clear that a "cheap" program has an exorbitant per-pupil cost, or that an "expensive" data system will actually cost $10 per student per year over its lifespan. For example, I recall working with one district that broke out the amount it spent on substitute teaching each year and realized its per-teacher cost ranged from $300 at one school to as much as $2,000 a year at another. As Michele Evans, former superintendent of Canton City, Ohio, schools explains, "When you look at exorbitant costs per participant it changes the conversation. People have to understand that they are making a choice to pay for this and is that how you really want to spend your money? . . . At one point in time I thought, 'Oh, this is just an academic exercise, it's really kind of tedious.' But it really did [force] conversations about where we're really willing to put our money."

For instance, technology and program investments are often discussed with a tone of "gee whiz" enthusiasm. But they should be scrutinized in terms of *opportunity cost*—in other words, What could we do with those same dollars if we spent them otherwise? Are we spending half a million dollars on iPads for a middle school so that kids will use them to do Web research and take the occasional quiz—while faculty continue to teach, use time, and assess as they always have? If so, it's a big outlay for little obvious benefit. How big a bang are we really seeing for each dollar spent?

When it comes to stretching the school dollar, there are two broad strategies: *optimizing* and *rethinking*. Optimizing is about doing familiar things better, while rethinking is about devising better, cheaper, smarter, faster ways to use talent, tools, and resources.

Optimizing the Familiar Things

One way to get more bang for the buck is to improve the operational efficiency of today's schools and systems. This includes straightforward steps like using buses more efficiently or constructing class schedules in more cost-effective ways.

In Clark County, Nevada, with more than 350 schools, bus drivers were starting and ending every day by walking into an office to punch their time card. This meant a driver's shift would start a few minutes before and end a few minutes after she started driving, costing the district about five minutes per driver per day. This added up to thousands of hours a year. The district installed a device that would clock drivers in when they started the bus. It cost a couple hundred thousand dollars to install these devices in the entire fleet, but the savings paid for the installation in fewer than two years—and then started to save the district hundreds of thousands annually.

Vince Bertram, CEO of Project Lead the Way, recalls that during his tenure as superintendent in Evansville, Indiana,

> We rethought our facilities. One example: we closed our central office. We had a warehouse full of supplies and, over a few months, we went to just-in-time delivery for everything. We went to suppliers and said, "If we're going to do business with you, you're going to deliver directly to our schools. We're not going to warehouse anything." That warehouse today is the central office. We stopped warehousing, closed the central office, closed three other buildings that housed central office staff, and then renovated the warehouse and moved everyone into it. That saved us over $1 million.

Automation and streamlining can eliminate waste. Lynn Bragga, budget director at Richmond Public Schools in Virginia, says the district used to spend $52 million a year for supplies. Half of those purchases were documented only by paper receipts. An audit found some schools paying $1 a box for paper clips that cost less than thirty cents a box under a centralized contract.[8] In Chicago, where the system had too many managers, duplicative functions, and haphazard job titles and salaries, restructuring the central office helped the district save $25 million a year.[9] One veteran business manager recalls, "We found that supplies sat on our warehouse shelves for years, when the industry standard for 'turn rates'—the number of times an item is replaced—is closer to six to twelve times a year." She says part of the problem is the lack of importance district leaders accord to operations: "Leaders who want to be cage-busters need to stop using the non-education side of the house as a place to dump nonproductive school administrators."

Michael Casserly, executive director of the Council of the Great City Schools, has observed that the median district uses 87 percent of its bus fleet on a given day, while low performers use just 69 percent. In a district with one hundred buses, moving from the bottom to the middle in bus utilization would allow a district to sell sixteen vehicles. At the expected rate of depreciation, that would yield savings of about $320,000 a year.[10] With regard to custodial services, a district with 10 million square feet of buildings and a below-average assigned custodial workload of 14,792 square feet per custodian could save $5 million annually by increasing the workload to the median of 25,536 square feet. Given that a district with about fifty schools serving thirty-six thousand students could easily have

5.5 million square feet of floor space, such districts could be eyeballing savings of nearly $3 million a year.[11] Once you start seeking such savings, you'll be surprised how many possibilities suggest themselves.

Rethinking Schooling

Cage-busters work hard to optimize schools and systems. But they're not content merely doing the same things better. They also seek smarter ways to use teams, data, and technology to deliver teaching and learning in better, cheaper, and faster ways.

Steven Wilson, founder of Ascend Learning charter schools, notes that at SABIS International Charter School in Springfield, Massachusetts, students are placed in grades by skill level, not age, allowing teachers to succeed with classes of thirty or more students. SABIS founder Ralph Bistany says, "We need to define the word 'class.' Every course has a prerequisite—concepts that the course is going to use but not explain. That list of concepts determines who belongs in the class and who doesn't." SABIS dramatically outperforms the local district, even though its class sizes are eight students larger and it spends nearly $1,000 less per pupil. Indeed, at SABIS, low-income and African American tenth-graders outperform the average student statewide on the state assessment.[12]

John Chubb, CEO of Education Sector, has written about the potential savings of redesigning schools to take advantage of new instructional technology. "Consider a conservative model of what is now possible," Chubb writes:

> Elementary students might work online one hour per day, middle school students two hours per day, and high school students three hours per day . . . If online instruction is supervised in double-sized student groups in grades K–8 and triple-sized groups in high school, the teacher savings are, for elementary schools, 7 percent fewer teachers; for middle schools, 14 percent fewer teachers; and for high schools, 29 percent fewer teachers . . . The teacher savings from online courses could average nearly 8 percent annually—or $800 per student in a $10,000 per-year per-student school budget.[13]

California-based Innosight Institute, under the leadership of Michael Horn, has played a valuable role in helping school and system leaders rethink school design using technology. Along with his colleague Heather Staker, Horn has sketched tech-infused models that offer ways to stretch dollars and talent while providing chances to customize instruction and boost instructional time.[14] Each model offers the chance to rethink the shape of teaching and schooling in order to dramatically boost learning and generate new efficiencies. A few options include:

Rotation: Within a given course or subject, students rotate between learning "modalities" (like small-group instruction, whole-group instruction, online learning, and so on). For instance, the KIPP Los Angeles Empower Academy equips each kindergarten classroom with fifteen computers. During the day, the teacher rotates students through online learning, small-group instruction, and individual assignments. Unlike conventional efforts to wedge computers into classrooms, the presumption is that a rotating set of students should be engaged in computer-assisted instruction throughout the entire day. Rocketship Education students rotate out of their classrooms to a learning lab for two hours each day to receive extra math and reading instruction via online learning. (See "A Look at Rocketship's Hybrid Model.")

"Flipped" classroom: Students have more opportunity for face-to-face teacher-guided practice in class because they use online instruction to learn course content at home or off-campus after the school day. The most famous example of the flipped classroom may be the Khan Academy, which offers thousands of instructional units in math and science and is partnering with a number of schools and systems to flip STEM instruction. Another example is the Stillwater Area Public Schools in Minnesota, where students in math classes in grades 4 through 6 watch ten- to fifteen-minute online videos after school hours and follow those up with comprehensive online assessments. At school, they then work with their teacher on applying and practicing what they've learned.

Flex model: Instruction is delivered primarily online, and students move on a customized, fluid schedule at school that takes advantage of various instructional modalities. Teachers provide face-to-face support through activities such as small-group instruction, group projects, and individual tutoring. At San Francisco Flex Academy, online-learning provider K12 Inc. delivers the curriculum and instruction while classroom teachers offer targeted interventions and supplemental support.

Self-blend: Students choose to take one or more courses entirely online to supplement their traditional instruction. Students may take online courses either at school or off-site. Quakertown Community School District in Pennsylvania, for instance, offers students in grades 6 through 12 the option of taking one or more online courses after they've completed a cyber orientation course. Students can work on these courses any time during the day, including at in-school "cyber lounges."

One illustration of how these models might work can be glimpsed at the School of One, a New York City program for teaching math in grades 6 through 8. Rather than employ a conventional curricular scope and sequence for an entire class, the School of One unpacks each grade level's math objectives into its component parts. Think of an iPod rather than an old LP record. Where a record used to require that the listener play it from beginning to end, MP3 technology makes it possible to customize the sequence as the listener prefers. The School of One organizes instruction

A Look at Rocketship's Hybrid Model

In his 2012 article, "Learning Labs 101," journalist John Fensterwald has provided a terrific account of how Rocketship Education uses technology and a redesigned school day to increase instructional time, get more value from staff, and stretch the school dollar.[15] As he describes it,

> The Learning Lab at Los Sueños Academy, in downtown San Jose, is not unlike the computer labs you'd find at many elementary schools—it's just much bigger. Tightly packed computer cubicles, one hundred in all, form long rows along the 2,000-square-foot open-plan room. The size of the lab reflects the outsize ambitions of Rocketship Education, the Palo Alto–based nonprofit organization that runs Los Sueños and four other charter schools in San Jose. In fact, the lab is the financial and academic

key to Rocketship's ambitious mission. Cofounder John Danner aims to expand rapidly by using fewer teachers and paying them better—all while transforming how they teach.

Fensterwald explains,

> The 100 minutes a day that Los Sueños students spend in the Learning Lab supplement the five hours of classroom instruction required by California law. But the time spent in the Learning Lab also replaces one out of four teachers per grade in every Rocketship school. That adds up to about five fewer teachers per school, at an average savings of $100,000 per teacher (including the cost of benefits), or $500,000. Rocketship uses that money to pay for the aides in the Learning Lab, two additional administrators at each school—and 20 percent higher pay for teachers.

He continues,

> At any time of the school day, the Learning Lab at Los Sueños is at least three-quarters full . . . After shaking hands with a learning specialist as they enter the room, the young "Rocketeers" go straight to their stations and log on. Except for some antsy kindergartners and first-graders, students stay more or less focused on their monitors. The few who dawdle or pester a neighbor get a reminder—or if they persist, a red written warning. There are purple slips, too, for exhibiting Rocketship core values: persistence, responsibility, empathy, and respect. The lab is overseen by five aides.

Fensterwald further observes,

> In an area carved out in the center of the room, classroom aide Katya Silva tutors five fourth-graders who were identified as below basic in reading. Today, they are reading "Mrs. Hen's Plan," a two-page story about a hen's efforts to hide her egg from a farmer. The day's goal is to focus on words related to cause and effect. After students take turns reading aloud, some haltingly, they underline clue words—as, so, because—that can help them decipher meaning. A mother of two children at Los Sueños, Silva was an active volunteer before she was hired as a Learning Lab specialist at about thirteen dollars per hour. Some of the specialists are new college grads exploring teaching as a career.

A cage-buster doesn't regard the Rocketship model as a miracle cure. Rather, she asks: What problems can the Rocketship model help you solve? And How can you make these tools and strategies work for your students?

using the iPod intuition. It uses pre-tests; brief, near-daily unit assessments; a slew of instructional modalities (large group, small group, online tutoring, computer-assisted, and so on); and an organizing algorithm to customize scope and sequence to each student's individual learning needs. Students skip over objectives they've already mastered and learn different objectives using the instructional approaches deemed most appropriate for them. They spend more on certain learning objectives when they need to and race ahead when they are able. In many ways, the School of One is simply using technology to facilitate and make practical an amped-up version of the student-centered instruction that Ted Sizer and Deborah Meier were touting more than twenty years ago.[16] By combining all the math courses at the school into a common, flexible enterprise, it becomes possible for teachers to differentiate instruction, share instructional responsibilities, and collaborate in ways that are usually impractical.

The School of One model suggests a number of new efficiencies and opportunities. Just for starters, teachers are typically absent seven or eight days a year. In most schools, learning pretty much stops during those days. The School of One design means an absent teacher no longer interrupts learning. This change, all by itself, effectively adds about seven or eight days of free instructional time per year. Now, let's be clear: the point is not that School of One is the "model," but that there are powerful opportunities to think smarter about organizing and supporting teaching and learning.

For those who think this all sounds too radical, consider what American Federation of Teachers founder Albert Shanker had to say on the subject a quarter century ago:

> What we need to do in schools is go through a process of rethinking like the one the Japanese [auto industry] went through . . . We have to give teachers an opportunity to work individually with students—coaching them in writing, expression, persuasion and critical thinking . . . We have to use the new technology which we now have instead of the obsolete factory batch processing system which is failing . . . Schools need no longer assume that the only way to learn is through lecture and blackboard. Students can learn through a videotape, audiotape, computer, an older student or a community volunteer.[17]

YOU CAN *CREATE* RESOURCES

It's easy to *say*, "Everyone knows where the booze is." But the real trick is that getting smart about using talent, tools, time, and money allows you to create new resources. Done right, it can be possible to operate as if you've managed to bump your budget by 10 or 20 percent, or more. Remember the lesson of lazy man's lobster: money may make things easier, but anyone who has changed his car's oil or cut his own hair knows there are lots of ways to get things done, even when dollars are scarce. You'd be surprised where you can find hidden resources; even a restrictive union contract may offer hidden nuggets. (See "Turning a Contractual Burden into a Benefit.")

Turning a Contractual Burden into a Benefit

One inspired district found a way to turn a burdensome CBA provision into an asset, leveraging its class size clause to strategically assign kids and reward effective teachers. Typically, provisions requiring districts to pay a penalty for exceeding contractual class sizes are nothing but a headache for district leaders. Meanwhile, teachers grumble about the extra students—even with the extra dollars.

In this district, however, the leadership worked with outside friends to craft a better solution. They decided to start offering terrific teachers the chance to teach more students and to reward those teachers if they *chose* to shoulder a slightly heavier load. As part of this move, the district boosted the oversized class bonus from $1,000 to $2,000 per student, a figure that still saved the district money while making the opportunity more appealing to teachers.

The district had principals give their most effective teachers the first crack at taking additional students. When they realized that taking five kids would amount to a $10,000 bonus, many strong teachers were eager to take more kids. This meant that more students were winding up in classrooms with the most effective instructors. (To deal with parents who might not want their child in a larger class, the district offers them the chance to opt out, saying, "If you'd like, we can move your child out of this class into one of the smaller classes." Perhaps because the

(continued)

teachers with the extra students tend to be the teachers parents are clamoring for, just about all parents pass on the offer.)

This move has yielded a cultural shift. Teaching a larger class is now regarded as a badge of honor. Parents can live with larger classes, if that's what it takes to get their kid into a class with the most desired teachers. In short, creative application of existing CBA provisions changed incentives in a way that's shifted the culture even as it's helped to reduce costs, reward excellence, get more kids in classrooms with great teachers, and avoid giving oversized classes to less accomplished or unwilling teachers.

Now, you'll sometimes hear that teachers don't want more students, even if they're paid more. Not so fast. Center for Reinventing Public Education researchers Dan Goldhaber, Michael DeArmond, and Scott DeBurgomaster observe that this is true if teachers are just asked about teaching more kids for more money in the abstract. However, when teachers are asked whether they'd want two fewer students in each of their classes or a salary increase of $5,000 (a rate that would be a financial wash in most districts), they report that more than 80 percent of teachers prefer the raise.[18]

Use Time Wisely

As we've noted, most school spending is devoted to compensating staff. You're paying these folks for their time. Cage-busters make smart use of the time they've bought. This is the key to some of the approaches popularized by Doug Lemov in his influential book *Teach Like a Champion*. Lemov notes that tightening up something as simple as how a teacher passes out paper can yield big time savings in classrooms where a teacher is passing out a dozen things a day:

Assume that the average class of students passes out or back papers and materials twenty times a day and that it takes a typical class a minute and twenty seconds to do this. If . . . students can accomplish this task in just twenty seconds, they will save twenty minutes a day (one minute each time) . . . Now multiply that twenty minutes per day by 190 school days, and you find that [the time saved is] thirty-eight hundred minutes of additional instruction over the course of a school year. That's more than sixty-three hours or almost eight additional days of instruction.[19]

Time teachers spend passing out paper is instructional time stolen from students. And the dollars that fund that time are wasted. If you're seeking funds for a longer school year or school day, first make sure that you're making full use of the time you've already got. Stop wasting time on unproductive tasks. Administrators and teachers once had to spend a lot of time filling out forms by hand and mimeographing materials; today, computers, printers, and data systems can speed things up considerably. The trick is making that happen. Newark superintendent Cami Anderson says eliminating time-consuming tasks can help principals focus on what matters. When she started in Newark, she recalls, "I 'unmandated' three-fourths of the training we were providing. I made anyone who wants to send an e-mail to principals go through one point person so that principals get one bulletin a week rather than dozens of e-mails. We reduced the number of things they were required to report to the district over the year to four pieces of paper from four binders."

Get More Time . . . for Free

How do you get more time? Recall Nina Gilbert's discussion of Ivy Prep back in chapter 3. The rules, regulations, and policies that restrict time are permeable. Just look at charter or district schools that have extended the school day and year. The key is not only to get the extra time, but to get it at a good price. That's tough, but it's doable. One option is creating schools or programs where staff opt in, allowing expectations to be established up front. This won't be easy, but many districts have the ability to waive policies or CBA provisions for "innovative programs" or turnaround schools. In St. Paul, Minnesota, for instance, the CBA reads, "The contract may be amended to allow unique and innovative programs . . . When it is determined that an exception to the terms of the labor agreement is warranted, the District and union *will grant waivers as necessary* [emphasis added]."[20]

Such language is more common than you might think. Of the sixty-three CBAs from districts in states that require collective bargaining in the National Council on Teacher Quality database, 57 percent contain provisions that explicitly allow for waiving the contract language.[21] Thirty-three CBAs contain a general waiver process by which any school site can request a waiver from the agreement, while four limit the waiver process to a particular subset of schools (such as elementary schools or innovation schools). The most common process for requesting a waiver, present in fourteen CBAs, involves securing the support of two-thirds or more of the school staff for the request and approval by a committee of union and district representatives. Such a requirement would often make for an exhausting slog behind the boulder, but the climb can be made much easier if leaders have planned ahead and found ways to constitute communities of the willing.

Leverage Community Resources

You want to extend learning time? Offer more mentoring? Provide tutoring? The assumption is that these are often prohibitive because of the added cost for teachers and staff. Yet, communities throughout America boast adult populations with remarkable stores of talent, expertise, and energy. The Woodrow Wilson National Fellowship Foundation has reported that more than 40 percent of adults with college degrees are interested in teaching.[22] Notice they haven't said they want to be *teachers*—just that they're interested in teaching. Those millions of educated adults are one hell of a potential asset. Much of what teachers do requires specialized skills. But there is a lot that teachers do—supervising study hall, tutoring, coaching debate teams, counseling alienated teens, to name a few—that others may be able to help with, and even do as well as the pros. The challenge is to identify problems and then tap those people in a way that creates a torrent of talent, not just the occasional homeroom volunteer or reading buddy. How do you alter statute or contract so that security-cleared community members are able to more fully pitch in during the school day? The Rocketship Academies use volunteers to supervise and support students in tandem with full-time instructors and computer-assisted tutoring, making it possible to shrink class sizes and add instructional time. Boston-based Citizen Schools, now operating in more than a dozen districts, helps recruit and train local professionals to teach engaging, weekly after-school seminars, for free.

Use People Smarter

If you walk into an elementary school and ask the principal to show you his best and his worst fourth-grade reading teachers, he'll have little trouble doing so. Yet, dollars to doughnuts, you'll see each teacher teaching reading to the same number of students for the same ninety minutes. They'll each then also teach art for thirty minutes, police the cafeteria for twenty-five, do their turn at bus duty, and all the rest. More times than not, those principals will also tell you that reading is the most important thing their school teaches—that, if kids are reading proficiently, everything else is possible. Yet those same principals won't see anything peculiar about how schools are staffed until you ask them what they'd think of a hospital that asked its cardiovascular surgeons to do cardiovascular surgery just ninety minutes a day, and to spend the rest of the day doing patient intake, delivering food to patients, and organizing medical supplies. If you've got employees with scarce skills, it's ludicrous not to do your best to take the fullest possible advantage of their talent. In fact, with enough creativity, you could conceivably get thirty-five hours a week of great reading instruction from that one terrific reading teacher—that's *seven times* as much instruction as she's providing today.

Tap Your Team's Skills

When schools or districts want to do something new, the impulse is to pay someone new to do it. That's a classic lazy-man's-lobster approach. A better option is to surface and take advantage of the talents of those you already employ. In *Working for Kids*, veteran principal and University of Pennsylvania professor "Torch" Lytle explains how he unearthed new resources by tapping faculty talents:

> There were two ways we built human capital at University City High School. One was learning about the underutilized or overlooked talents of people on our staff, and then building around them . . . Two of our security officers who were also outstanding professional musicians volunteered to work with our music teacher in developing a jazz band. Our school psychologist had a Web design business; we built a high-end computer lab, he began teaching Web design courses, and soon we had a student-operated small business of our own. A computer teacher started a Cisco-certified computer network training program and a computer-building and -repair shop; her students operated the business and were paid as hourly employees . . . Learning about these hidden talents and then encouraging faculty and staff to use [them] for the benefit of our students was a quick and powerful way to build our capacity.[23]

In a particularly entrepreneurial twist, Lytle recalls, "The teacher who did our school scheduling was extraordinarily skilled and key in . . . designing and putting in place our small learning community organization. Recognizing his talents, I suggested to the school district central office that, for a fee, our leadership team would be willing to provide technical assistance to other high schools as they undertook similar reorganizations. Within a year we were earning $250,000, paid by charge-backs from other schools and added to our school's budget."[24]

Tom Payzant, Harvard professor and former superintendent, observes it's crucial to have the talent you need, but, "I did not go into any of my superintendencies bringing a whole crew with me. I've found in every place I've been that there are always people in the organization that may be hunkered down somewhere and now have had the opportunity to lead. You can find some real talent there."

IT'S NOT JUST ABOUT THE MONEY

K–12's leadership experts have historically pooh-poohed talk of efficiency because they deem such crude concerns as undignified or a distraction from what really matters. Cage-busters regard such sentiments as flat wrong. Thinking about bang for the buck brings healthy discipline. It helps ensure that resources and personnel are being used to serve kids best. It discourages the temptation to cling to ineffective programs and practices. Going after the booze doesn't just better position schools and systems to be academically successful; it helps forge stronger, performance-oriented cultures. There are a couple of tips worth keeping in mind when it comes to the culture-building side of all this.

The Truth Shall Set You Free. Because public schools spend public funds in the public eye, it can be tempting to massage the numbers in order to avoid negative publicity or having to make unpopular decisions. Erie, Pennsylvania, superintendent Jay Badams notes just how deep the reluctance to share bad news can be. He recalls, "We had an audit report that was hilarious. I had just taken over our first board meeting, and we had our auditors there. They're looking at me sideways, like they're afraid they're going to get whacked by a rolled-up newspaper if they tell the truth, but they wanted to tell the truth. I was, like, 'Well, say it.' So the auditor said, 'We've spent about six to eight million dollars more than we took in.' Sure, it's bad news. But such truth-telling makes it possible to get serious about pinpointing challenges, chasing away excuses, and solving problems. Absent honesty, it's hard to earn credibility as a disciplined leader or to educate the public on what needs to change.

Sometimes Programs and Positions Should Go Away. School spending tends to be eternal. If a program or position was funded once, it lingers on—even when it has become wasteful or unnecessary. Why? Every program has its enthusiasts, champions, or staff who will fight for it. Because it's the rare program that attracts heated opposition, the easy, popular move is usually to keep even ineffectual programs. (See, for example, "More PD: The Easy Answer.") Former Evansville, Indiana, superintendent Vince Bertram muses, "It's very difficult . . . to make things go away. We cut the things that appear to be easy to cut, we hang on to things that people like, but we don't spend as much time thinking about the things that are effective or the things that are advancing learning and helping students. What we did is, we took a step back and said, 'If this is not adding value, if kids aren't learning, then we're going to get rid of it and we're going to invest in things that work.'"

Heliodoro Sanchez, chief of staff in Texas's Ector County schools, was frustrated that, even when faced with sharp reductions in revenue, district staff seemed only to think in terms of new spending. Every push to cut outlays or end programs met with vocal opposition. Seeking to get staff to start weighing the value and cost of programs and services, Sanchez developed the "Strategic Abandonment Tool." With it, he was able to get the same passionate staff to make $11 million in cuts and to do so without tearing the district apart. Cathy Mincberg, CEO of the Houston-based Center for Reform of School Systems, says, "It is the best tool I have ever seen to help folks make cuts." (See appendix C for a copy of Sanchez's "Strategic Abandonment Tool.")

More PD: The Easy Answer

Given the premium on finding ways to ignore the mountain in favor of culture, coaching, and consensus, it's no surprise that professional development (PD) is every cage-dweller's favorite go-to. After all, if you're disinclined to rethink staffing or spending, replace employees, reward excellence, or root out mediocrity, hoping you can train staff to be better at their jobs is really all you've got left. The problem: most PD doesn't pay off.

Educational leaders like PD. It's genial. It's well received by teachers and experts and it doesn't provoke conflict. Indeed, when asked about their feelings toward various reforms, over 85 percent of school board members cite PD as "extremely" or "very" important.[25] It's no wonder that teachers are routinely subjected to fly-by consulting or enthusiastic workshops, without any sustained focus on particular problems or figuring how to use time, talent, and tools to solve them.

We spend a lot on professional development. Education Resource Strategies president Karen Hawley Miles studied five districts and found that, on average, they spent 3.6 percent of their budget, or $19 million apiece, on PD.[26] Knowledge Delivery Systems (KDS) reports, "The real cost of professional development at the district and state level is seldom known. While line items specifically listing staff development total $3,000–$5,000 annually per teacher . . . real costs consider items such as salaries, facilities, fees, substitutes, stipends, materials, travel, and equipment." KDS notes that, taking all this into account, staff development studies estimate costs of $8,000–$12,000 per year per teacher.[27]

Yet hardly any of this actually appears to make teachers better. A 2007 review of the research by the Institute of Education Sciences, the most authoritative analysis to date, found that only nine of 132 studies on PD met the evidentiary standards established by the Department of Education's What Works Clearinghouse. When it comes to school-based PD, the most common approach, researchers found no "valid" or "scientifically defensible evidence" of effectiveness. Indeed, they found that only the tiny sliver of PD involving thirty to one hundred hours of teacher time showed any evidence of correlating with student achievement gains.[28] Meanwhile, more than nine out of ten US teachers have participated in PD that consists primarily of short-term conferences or workshops.[29]

Perhaps the most damning indictment of PD is the fact that even teachers themselves regard it with contempt. Eric Hirsch, director of special projects with the New Teacher Center at the University of California, Santa Cruz, observes, "When you ask teachers what conditions matter most in terms of their future career plans and student learning, professional development has come in last on every survey we've done."[30]

Roxanna Elden, author of *See Me After Class*, wryly grouses that professional development is provided in sessions with names like, "Unlock the Sunshine! Shedding Light on the Opportunities Created by State Assessment 2.0." She explains, "Usually, these sessions use Power-Point presentations to [tell] teachers that rigor is important, suggest[ing] we've spent most of the year training our students to make different colored Play-Doh balls."[31]

The University of Maryland's Jennifer King Rice notes that states typically allow teachers to choose PD, and yet, "The incentive structure in most school systems does not explicitly reward teachers for making choices that promote effectiveness."[32] Stanford University's Linda Darling-Hammond, writing with several colleagues, terms professional development "poorly conceived and deeply flawed" and observes, "states and districts are spending millions of dollars on academic courses disconnected from the realities of classrooms." Darling-Hammond et al. further note the "support and training [educators] receive is episodic, myopic, and often meaningless."[33]

Once again, it's not either-or: you're not a cage-buster *or* a believer in PD. Rather, PD can be a boulder-rolling exercise until you're out of that cage and using it as a problem-solving tool.

Change the "Wish-Mode" Mentality. Spending requests can sometimes read like Christmas wish lists. There's a tendency to ask for things without paying attention to cost effectiveness or what else might be accomplished with those funds. Frederick County, Maryland, associate superintendent Ann Bonitatibus explains,

> Principals in general do not have a firm grasp of budgeting. And because they don't, they operate in a wish-mode mentality. So a department will say, "We really wish that we could have more kilns for our ceramics classes." And the principal will say, "Gosh, that's really expensive. I better call

central office and get them to help me out." They'll call me and say, "Hey, I have a tough situation. We need new kilns for art classes because one broke down." I'll pull up their budget and say to them, "You have $74,000 sitting in your budget, why are you calling me?" They try to bank their money for later wishes, hoping central office will ante up instead.

Changing this mind-set depends on changing incentives, so that leaders are recognized and rewarded when they manage resources wisely and held accountable when they do not.

An ROI Mind-Set Can Help Drive Cultural Change. Robert Sommers recalls that, as CEO of Butler Technology and Career Development Schools in Hamilton, Ohio, focusing on unit costs and performance helped move the culture. He says, "We implemented the Kalmus Ratio, or cost per successful student. Of course, the definition of a 'successful student' is the trick, right? We decided to use credit earning. A student completing math, science, and a career technical industry credential got three success points. We wanted to change the mind-set from 'spend your budget' to 'spend your budget in ways that result in improved performance.'" Sommers offers an example of the shift:

> Our custodial staff went to the local Marriott to learn how to better meet customer expectations and focus on customer service. They came back and implemented two things. They created the Strive for Five program, with cards for the teachers to rate them from 1 to 5 on how clean the room was and how supportive custodial staff were. They also decided their main responsibility was to keep bacterial counts down because that would affect attendance, and attendance was important for student performance . . . Custodians are usually kind of relegated to some corner office, but these folks were thinking about how they contribute to student learning.

RETHINK YOUR TEAM: BLOW UP THE SILOS

Odd as it sounds, a monomaniacal focus on instructional leadership has frequently made it harder to identify problems with how talent, tools, time, or money are used. Teaching and learning rest on the systems that procure talent, make wise use of time, harness technology, and support or enable that core work. A single-minded focus on instruction has meant that technology, HR, accounting, and other operational staff default to compliance or "more, better" reform—rather than less comfortable efforts to drive problem solving or free up resources.

The result: tech people provide and maintain technology. Whether new technology is cost-effective or used to rethink work routines is too often someone else's concern. Similarly, HR hires people, tracks employees, and processes checks. Whether employees are being used wisely or cost-effectively is treated as someone else's domain. Newark superintendent Cami Anderson saw this dysfunction firsthand when she came to New York's District 79: "In an old program designed to help kids get their GEDs, you would get a list of how many teachers are teaching in it from HR, and it would say fifty teachers. And then you'd go to the program and you'd see seventy-eight teachers listed. Then you'd go into the budget office and see sixty-three teachers budgeted. Then you'd go over to payroll and you see that eighty teachers are being paid. This was just because payroll, management, and human resources were so siloed." Nobody thought they were responsible for rectifying this or empowered to sort it out.

Staff ought to be relentlessly focused on using talent, technology, and resources to solve problems in smarter and better ways. Unfortunately, key operations staff are typically regarded as mere afterthoughts in terms of the instructional team. In cage-busting systems, these folks are treated as essential partners when it comes to instruction, staffing, and school improvement.

Human Resources

HR staff should be leading efforts to attract, retain, develop, and make smart use of talent. HR needs to know how much bang for the buck each recruiter is getting, which principals are doing a good job evaluating talent, and how much time new technology investments are saving. This requires working hand-in-hand with principals on supporting, evaluating, and managing teachers; with accounting to determine cost-effectiveness of personnel and programs; and with IT to ensure that new tools are saving staff time and improving faculty productivity.

"Most of the HR personnel in education have been there for years, make good money, and don't want to rock the boat," says Ranjit Nair, a veteran HR executive who has assisted K–12 systems. "When they are forced to fire people, they say, 'I'm so sorry, it'll never happen again,' instead of saying, 'They deserve to be fired because they aren't performing well and they are detriments to students.' That needs to be changed."

When she ran business services in Houston ISD, Cathy Mincberg, CEO of the Center for Reform of School Systems, recalls struggling to shift the culture of the human resources department:

> Every year, HISD opened school with over eight hundred vacancies for teachers. Finding a permanent teacher might take months. This had been going on as long as anyone could remember. We designed a comprehensive strategy to recruit earlier, with more carrots and more creativity. But this problem really belonged to the dozen or so HR generalists responsible for hiring. We brought them together, brainstormed, and asked how they could measure their success. They suggested tracking the vacancy fill rate. I had told them that, whatever metric they developed, we'd post weekly progress on a huge chart in the large open space where they all worked. They agreed. Now, when I took my plan to the superintendent's cabinet, there was outrage. How could I publicly post performance, even if staff had agreed the metric was fair and should be posted? I ignored the protests. To my surprise, a friendly rivalry emerged. There was no hostility. I watched the staff drag their principal-clients to the chart and explain how the principal's reluctance to make hiring decisions was hurting everyone's ability to get teachers in front of children. That fall, we filled all but 150 positions, many of which were special education specialist positions with particular challenges. The children had full-time committed teachers from day one, and the HR employees found camaraderie and purpose.

That's how to take HR seriously, and to engage HR as a full partner in improving instruction and righting the "culture of can't."

Information Technology

IT staff have a critical role to play in using new technologies to solve problems, making data systems user friendly, determining the cost-effectiveness of new devices, and designing smarter adoptions and implementations. IT ought not merely buy and maintain technology; it ought to serve as a hub for using tech to extend the reach of staff, save time, and streamline operations. IT needs to know how much data-entry time new software will save, how iPad adoption might allow schools to rethink attendance taking or homework or PD, and how to determine which support positions may be anachronistic due to new technology. IT needs to work hand-in-hand with instructional staff, HR, and accounting, to figure out how to ensure that technology is being used to rethink old routines and not just stapled atop them.

"It is difficult for people who are entrenched in the [school] culture to understand what technology can do," says Jerry Crisci, director of technology and codirector of the Center for Innovation at the Scarsdale Public Schools in New York. "One of the biggest mistakes schools make is they receive grants and put in a lot of equipment but they don't put the people resources in; they don't commit to having people embedded in the system to work with teachers and train them on how to really restructure their classrooms using technology . . . The most effective IT organizations are teams that have people with both technical and educational experience."

Accounting

Accounting has a lead role in making smart use of limited resources. This requires an appetite for collaboration and a willingness to calculate cost-benefit for a range of operational and instructional activities. Keeping track of dollars ought not be the job, it ought to be the minimal housekeeping obligation. The real work is gauging the bang for the buck of school A and school B, of this ELL program and that CTE program, or of ten minutes of teacher time spent entering student data. Accounting should operate like a giant funnel, since critical information will be scattered throughout various academic and operational units. Accounting staff need to work with all of them, to ask the hard questions and ensure that the answers inform tough decisions.

Breaking down barriers between departments enables staff members to become agents of problem solving rather than cogs in a wheel. This applies not just to "instructional" personnel. I'm talking about *every single member of your team*, even those who are often dismissed as "just" operations or support personnel.

TECHNOLOGY AS HAMBURGER HELPER

Technology has long been offered as the miraculous balm that will transform and improve teaching and learning. Enthusiasts have said this about iPads, laptops, the Internet, desktop computers, televisions, videotapes, well . . . you get the idea. And, in most sectors, technology has yielded huge savings and delivered massive increases in productivity. In education, though, it's been a different story. With each new advance, districts spend lots of money on nifty new gizmos, make grand promises, and get lots of enthusiastic press. And then, each time, nothing much changes. If anything, technology always seems to make schooling *more* costly. Here's the thing: technology *is* a powerful tool for driving productivity and quality, in schooling as elsewhere; the problem is not with the technology, but with *how we've used it.*

The key is to think of technology not as a *solution* but as *Hamburger Helper*™. Except for the occasional cash-strapped graduate student, Hamburger Helper isn't an alternative to ground beef; it's something that you stir into the pan so that the beef goes further. The key is to regard technology as the means to the end you'd like to achieve, rather than an end in itself.

Enthusiasm for "disruptive innovation" has sometimes blinded us to the fact that, 99 percent of the time, the biggest impact of technology is optimizing familiar tasks and routines—freeing up talent, time, and dollars for better uses. If teachers with one-to-one devices can, each day, spend ten minutes fewer entering data and grading quizzes, ten minutes fewer passing and collecting texts and papers, and ten minutes fewer walking students to the library or accessing student data, they will save eighty or ninety hours a year. That's like another *15 instructional days* that they can devote to teaching, mentoring, or lesson design.

Too often, rather than using new tools to free up time or make better use of talent or money, we've ladled them over what's already in place. Steve Hockett, principal of Colvin Run Elementary in Fairfax County,

Virginia, and former principal in residence at the US Department of Education, says, "People want the fastest, the best, the newest. I've gone into schools where they say, 'We have smart, interactive whiteboards in every classroom.' And then I'll go visit classrooms and they're basically using the whiteboard as an overhead projector where the print can't even be seen in the back of the room. So it's not interactive and it's not even a very good overhead projector, yet it costs $2,500."

Hockett explains, "School technology is really a vehicle and a tool. People are basically spending lots of money to own a Ferrari to drive a block to the store and back every day . . . They just felt that they had to jump and buy the next best iteration, but yet aren't even utilizing what they have." Ann Bonitatibus sounds a lot like Hockett, noting that principals will "spend a couple thousand dollars on SMART Boards and then there won't be a teacher in the building trained to use one. The high-tech board becomes nothing more than a glorified whiteboard, which is a waste of a resource and taxpayer money."

Technology can be a powerful lever for rethinking schooling. But it's the rethinking that matters, not the technology. Technology provides tools to help solve problems smarter, deliver knowledge, support students, extend and deepen instruction, and refashion cost structures. Unfortunately, too many educators, industry shills, and technology enthusiasts seem to imagine that the technology itself will be a difference maker.

Thinking this way offers another perk: it turns out that technology can help pay for itself in various ways. Ed tech consultant Rob Mancabelli explains that a little creativity allowed him to adopt new technology at almost no cost when he was CIO for Hunterdon, New Jersey. "People don't think about the revenue-generation side," Mancabelli says. "When I was CIO, I launched half a dozen revenue-generating programs in our district. We provided database services, allowed businesses and other districts to use our servers, and ran an annual conference on a subject our teachers were experts at. Overall, we were able to generate enough revenue to almost match the budget we were spending on nonhardware technology when I arrived." By leveraging the district's investments with an eye towards ROI, new technology became a breakeven proposition.

YEP, THIS EVEN APPLIES TO SPECIAL ED

When I talk about cage-busting, there's always skepticism about whether it can or should apply to special ed. It does. Nationally, special ed spending rose from four to 21 percent of total outlays between 1970 and 2005.[34] You can't rethink schools or systems without taking a look at those dollars and staff. Yet intimidating policies, deference to state and district special education coordinators, strong-willed parents, nervous school district attorneys, and claims that "maintenance of effort" makes it pointless to seek savings have led cage-dwellers to tiptoe around special ed. There are some real, and necessary, prohibitions in place when it comes to special education. But, as always, those are less absolute and less forbidding than most school and system leaders imagine.

Shying away from touching special ed is a losing proposition. As one principal explains,

> We spend about twice the money given to us by the [federal] government for special education students. That extra 100 percent comes directly from the general operating funds. For example, when a child enrolled in our school with a need for a one-on-one adult assistant, I had to cancel the after-school tutoring that served about sixty low-income students who were behind grade level in reading and math. Budgets are simple math. You get X dollars. If you have to spend $30,000 per year on an adult assistant for one child, you must cut $30,000 from other programs. I get about $8,000 to educate one child for an entire year. So this child is using up his money, and the money allotted for 3.5 additional children. When we have the annual meeting to discuss what support an individual special needs child should have, we are forbidden by law to discuss or take into account the cost of the services being discussed.[35]

The trick for cage-busters is to distort reality so that the "forbidden" becomes possible.

I recall talking to a roomful of district CFOs a few months after the 2008 financial crash. Worried about revenues, they were hungry for ways to cut spending and eager to share ideas . . . until special ed came up. The discussion promptly ground to a halt. I mentioned one small district that had three full-time teachers in a classroom with seven students, for no compelling reason. The superintendent took another look and figured out he could better utilize the third teacher, overruling the special ed coordinator's objection (with a thumb's up from outside counsel). In response, one CFO fired back, "You can't just move staff working with special ed populations. You're putting the system in the crosshairs." Another CFO countered, "I wouldn't be so sure. But the special ed folks will tell you that you can't." As with so much else, it comes back to asking questions and finding ways to get unstuck.

This isn't as hard as it sounds. Nate Levenson, author of *Smarter Budgets, Smarter Schools*, notes that special ed dollars generally fund teachers "who are trained in the law, know how to identify disabilities, and are steeped in theories of learning" but that "most students enter special education due to difficulty reading." Given this evident mismatch, Levenson thought it made sense to overhaul reading instruction—including for special education. When Levenson moved to revamp Arlington's reading program in accord with the research, however, his staff told him he was on a fool's errand. Levenson ended the district's collection of five remedial reading programs (Title I, special education, ELL, voluntary desegregation, and general education), and placed all reading staff under a single leader—despite the widespread assumption that any attempt to commingle special ed and general ed dollars is asking for trouble. Levenson recalls, "All teachers—classroom, remedial, and special education—used the same program and pacing." Principals were evaluated based on reading results, Arlington mandated thirty minutes of phonics each day, and teachers had input but weren't allowed to modify the plan. The results? Levenson writes, "The number of students K–2 not reading at grade level dropped by 52 percent. Two thirds of K–2 students who started the year behind in reading made more than one year's progress. Referral rates to special education dropped. Within three years, reading ceased to be a special education service for nearly all children."[36]

There are smarter ways to use teachers, whether in general or special education. Levenson captures this elegantly, recalling, "One day in a special education resource room in a secondary school I watched a bright, caring, passionate veteran teacher stand at the board and try to explain math to one student, English to another, biology to a third, and US history to a fourth." He mused that while general ed teachers hated teaching outside their specialty, this resource teacher was expected to teach everything. In response, he adopted a plan that opened math and English remediation to all general and special ed students. The classes were taught by general education teachers with subject matter expertise, they were 50 to 100 percent longer than regular classes, and the staff was handpicked in the same manner as Advanced Placement teachers. There was no additional cost. Levenson explains, "These programs were cost neutral in the short run because they only required shifting resources from special education to general education"—the thing that's supposedly impossible to do. "In the long run," he notes, "they will decrease costs by reducing the need for future services." High school test scores for students with special needs rose so dramatically that Arlington was profiled as one of the fastest-improving districts in the state, with proficiency rates for students in special education increasing 26 percent in English and 22 percent in math. Nonetheless, in a troubling but unsurprising development, special education teachers pushed back. Levenson recalls that they "felt devalued when their numbers decreased as we shifted to general education content–trained staff. In one school, both general education and special education staff were so fierce in their opposition that the changes weren't implemented at all, and they organized a parent revolt by suggesting that students wouldn't learn and laws would be broken."[37] This is why politics and pushback are an inevitable reality for cage-busters, as we'll discuss next chapter.

Maryland's Bonitatibus says,

> Principals think that they're obligated to provide certain services, particularly when we're talking about Title I or special education. Principals will say, "You need to buy me ten new iPads because I have autistic children with IEPs stating they need to have tactile kinds of interactions or visual cues." And then I'll challenge the request, saying, "But the law doesn't tell you that it has to be an iPad. What's another tool you could use?" Parents, of course, bring in advocates, and the [educators] are threatened with lawsuits and told, "You must provide this," when there's nothing in the law that said that's the tool we have to use. But many of our principals just don't take time to think about viable alternatives that provide equivalent service. Quite frankly, they get intimidated when they hear *law* and *attorney*.

Michael Casserly, executive director of the Council of the Great City Schools, says districts are held back by pinched notions of what they can do with IDEA dollars. "There's some confusion about whether or not the law allows you, as part of programmatic efforts, to hire staff," he says. "Under the law, there's absolutely no reason under either IDEA or Title III that you can't hire staff, but people are quite confused about it and are under the impression that you have to spend the money on either IEP development or instructional materials."

The key is to tackle special ed just like everything else. Ask the important questions: What problems are you solving? Are you solving them smart? Can you use talent, tools, time, or money more effectively? Then work with your consigliere to determine what the rules, regulations, and policies actually require and what might be possible.

THE COURAGE TO TAKE ON CAPONE

It's tempting to imagine that there's no way to do better without getting more. The truth is that, from the early 1930s until the start of the Great Recession in 2008, national per-pupil spending in the United States went up every single year. So leaders grew used to an environment where they could routinely count on getting more each year. This bred complacency and a lack of discipline. For better or worse, those days are gone. States are strapped after experiencing the biggest five-year decline in tax receipts on record. And states have competing priorities that were hit much harder than K–12 between 2008 and 2013. Meanwhile, the public supports schools, but has been much less willing to raise local taxes than in the past. In 2012, the Program on Education Policy and Governance at Harvard University reported based on a national survey that, when told how much their school district is currently spending, just 24 percent of the public supports raising taxes to fund schools.[38]

In her 2012 book *You Can't Do It Alone*, Public Agenda executive Jean Johnson explains that research shows: "Citizens and leaders in government, business, and higher education see sound K–12 education as an absolute necessity for the country to thrive . . . But the days of 'ask and you shall receive' are gone for a good long while. That means that school leaders need to make a solid case for why they need additional funds. They need to explain exactly what the money will do and assure stressed taxpayers that it will not be wasted."[39]

The silver lining is that tough times are rich with possibility. Yet a K–12 culture fascinated with consensus and buy-in has dissuaded leaders from embracing the opportunities that tight budgets provide.

After all, cost cutting is about much more than balancing budgets; it's about making sure limited resources are doing the most possible good for students. Taking a hard look at staffing and spending creates the opportunity to rethink the core work of teaching and learning. It can signal a commitment to tackling lethargic bureaucracies and operational units that otherwise hinder educators and alienate parents.

Such efforts inevitably lead into the realm of the political. Despite years as a school and system leader, Maryland state chief Lillian Lowery recalls that, when she served as secretary of education in Delaware, her initial sense of the role was "a little bit naive." She says, "I worked with a phenomenal governor. He was just a force and I thought, 'Great, he'll take care of the politics and I'll go in and do education.' I was wrong, wrong, wrong . . . When people come in to push aggressive reforms, it is politics because we need to move our agenda."

So, let's turn to politics.

7

The Chicago Way

MALONE: You said you wanted to get Capone. Do you really
wanna get him? You see, what I'm saying is, what are you
prepared to do?

NESS: Anything within the law.

MALONE: And then what are you prepared to do? If you open
the can on these worms, you must be prepared to go all
the way.

NESS: I want to get Capone! I don't know how to do it.

MALONE: You wanna know how to get Capone? They pull a
knife, you pull a gun. He sends one of yours to the hospital,
you send one of his to the morgue. That's the Chicago way.
And that's how you get Capone. Now, do you want to do
that? Are you ready to do that? I'm offering you a deal. Do
you want this deal?

—*The Untouchables*

BY THIS POINT, some readers are doubtless thinking, "This stuff has
been interesting in theory, but I'd like to see you try that in *my* school or
system. This is all way too political." Okay. Let's go there.

First, I'll repeat what I said in the preface: I'm betting you dramatically
underestimate how much you can do right now, today, in your current
situation. Second, it's true that reckless leadership is a loser—you can't do
much good if you're fired or wasting time on unwinnable fights. Third and

perhaps most important: cage-busters need to learn when to fight, how to fight, and how to maximize the odds that they'll win.

Too many school and system leaders think *politics* is a four-letter word—something unsavory and to be avoided whenever possible. News flash: when you're playing a leadership role in a public institution that spends public dollars to serve the public's children, you're right in the heart of the political beast, like it or not. The question is not *whether* you are engaged in politics, but *how well you use political levers* to serve your kids.

There's an obvious but oft-ignored subtlety here. Disputants in the world of education reform frequently talk as if there are only good guys and implacable, villainous enemies. The truth is that most people are neither with you nor against you. Most teachers and community members alike will be attached to the comfortable and skeptical of the unfamiliar. The savvy cage-buster anticipates these reactions and is prepared to educate the public, combat misinformation, and give supporters cause to rally around.

Some would-be reformers get that politics matters, but think it's beneath them. They think that they can run public institutions and spend public funds without securing public understanding and support. I've heard from more than one superintendent that they don't worry about "public relations" because they'll move student achievement and that will win over the public and silence critics. Nope. That's not the way it works. Your critics don't fold and go home just because you moved reading and math scores. More to the point, that's not the way things are *supposed* to work in a democracy. If you want to change public institutions, priorities, and policies, you need to convince the public that it's the right thing to do. It's not about public relations or forging consensus. It's about respecting and educating the public.

"EVERY BATTLE IS WON BEFORE IT IS EVER FOUGHT"

Sun Tzu, a Ch'i general who gained fame for his military exploits more than two thousand years ago, distilled his hard-won wisdom into *The Art of War*. Even today, the book remains a must-read for leaders. The wise cage-buster will pay special heed to Sun Tzu's caution: "Every battle is won before it is ever fought."

Indeed, Sun Tzu may well be the patron saint of cage-busting leadership. Massachusetts commissioner of education Mitchell Chester explains, "There's a distinction between being willing to take a risk and being reckless. Just being reckless can leave you out of a job pretty quickly, without having accomplished anything. You need to hold firm to what matters [but] when you're dogmatic and unwilling to bend, folks are going to abandon you or write you off. Eventually, you're going to end up in a situation where your authority or your agency is going to be diminished." That's why cage-busters make sure they're picking the "right fight." (See "Choosing the 'Right Fight.'")

While cage-busters work hard to avoid fighting, they don't duck necessary fights. But they do everything possible to stack the deck before it comes to that. That's why they work hard to be precise about the problem, determine what's possible, exploit existing authority, marshal evidence, gain leverage, and build a constituency for action.

In explaining how she worked to link teacher certification to demonstrated effectiveness, a move that one key state board member "adamantly opposed," Rhode Island chief Deborah Gist offers a primer on how the savvy cage-buster proceeds:

> [Make] sure that what you're proposing is as airtight as you can make it—that it's defensible, that it has a basis in research, that it's reasonable, so you don't give folks ammunition against you. And then engag[e] people . . . I think I called a million people to say, "Who can we talk to? Who would support this? How can we get letters from these people?" And I did that with help from national and local voices, making sure that the [Board of] Regents heard from those people; because I knew they were already going to hear from people who were opposed to it. You have to make sure they hear from supporters because oftentimes people who support it stay home, and it takes extra effort to get them there. It's about your relationships with your board, calling them, checking in, making sure they have all the information they need, asking if they have any questions and saying, "I'd really appreciate your support," and, "This is really important, and here's why."

Heather Zavadsky, author of *Bringing School Reform to Scale*, has suggested that sometimes, when it comes to convincing a board, "You can't get them to bite it off all the way, so a tiered approach can make sense. If

Choosing the "Right Fight"

Cage-busters fight only when it's necessary. They seek creative solutions, repurpose resources, and lean on their consiglieres precisely because they only want to fight when they have to. However, there are times when they've no choice but to fight. Figuring out when that is requires knowing how to pick the "right fights." On that score, business strategists Saj-Nicole Joni and Damon Beyer have penned a terrifically helpful book, titled (appropriately enough) *The Right Fight*.[1] They sketch three principles to follow when deciding whether to fight.

Focus on the future, not the past: Joni and Beyer report that "typically, leadership teams spend 85 percent of their time together sorting out the numbers, trying to figure out what went wrong or dissecting what went well, assigning blame or recognition—and *all* of these conversations are discussions centered in the past." This wastes valuable time that would be better spent addressing the future. "Right fights move beyond the blame game to focus on what is possible and to make what is possible actually happen," they write.

Make it material: "Right fights are about the big things, things that have the potential to change the performance and success of an organization and energize its people," Joni and Beyer write. There are three tests for determining whether an issue qualifies. One is *the value test*. Will a positive outcome "create significant value"? Second is *the thinking test*. If the problem has no routine answer but entails "exponential or out-of-the-box thinking," it's probably an answer worth fighting for. Finally, *the change test* dictates that "the result of a material fight should be a noticeable and sustainable difference in the way an organization works."

Spell out the noble purpose: "All great organizations are mission driven in the sense that they are focused on something bigger than who's in charge of what," argue Joni and Beyer. "In order for a fight to be a right fight, it needs to be connected with this noble purpose." Linking a spending decision, for instance, to the larger mission is critical to explaining why it's important and worth fighting about.

a board is freaked out about tying money and salary to value-add performance data, I would start with the value-add performance data and show them how that data can differentiate teaching and effective teachers. There's no risk there. You're just showing them the data and what that data can do for you. And if they're comfortable with that, then you can go to the next step."

I frequently encounter leaders frustrated that a pet project didn't get off the ground. Yet when I ask if they've done the spadework that Gist and Zavadsky describe here, they look at me as if I'm speaking in tongues. Are you thinking that you don't like having to worry about all this? That you just want to worry about curriculum and instruction? Then you shouldn't be leading a public school or school system. Like it or not, you're in the public square. You can't opt out. Your only choice is whether to engage effectively.

Poker players have an old saying, "If, after the first twenty minutes, you don't know who the sucker at the table is, it's you." Their advice: if it's you, get up from that table, fast. Same thing applies here. If you're a lead teacher walking into a meeting with your principal, a principal walking into a meeting with an associate superintendent, or a superintendent walking into a board meeting, and you're not confident how your request is going to be received, you've fallen down on the job.

THINK LIKE A POKER PLAYER, NOT A TOUGH GUY

Successful cage-busters think of themselves more as poker players than as tough guys. Tough guys will walk into a bar and fight just to prove how tough they are. They don't back down from a challenge, whatever the odds. Professional gamblers, on the other hand, work hard not to lose. They have no problem looking uncool if that helps them win. The cage-buster aims to educate kids and solve problems that'll help her do that; not to rack up style points or be outrageous. That said, none of this is an excuse to duck the hard fights. It simply means that cage-busters work diligently to stack the odds so that, when they do have to engage in a hard fight, *they expect to win.*

Poker players do everything they can to shave the odds. They bluff. They work every angle. One district was having trouble recruiting teachers in shortage areas. Its hands were tied by a CBA that did not permit it to offer bonuses, but the CBA said nothing about a private funder offering such bonuses. Once that option was on the table, recalls one district insider, the superintendent's discussion with the union "took on a very different complexion." The union wound up agreeing to a bonus provision that helped recruit much-needed math and science teachers.

Sun Tzu cautioned, "He who knows when he can fight and when he cannot, will be victorious." The time to win a fight or a debate is not when you're in it, but before you're in it. As Abigail Smith, an executive at the DC Public Education Fund, observes, "When it comes to the recipe for success, the willingness of political leaders to stand behind you is crucial. If you don't have that, you could have all your ducks in a row and be ready to move, but, if the political leadership is not willing to take the heat, that's where things fall apart." There are a number of things savvy leaders can do to increase the odds that they'll have the backing they need.

Prepare the Community. Being precise about the problem and your solution can make it easier to educate the public. (See "Find a Way to Share Your Truth" for another take on this.) Erie, Pennsylvania, superintendent Jay Badams was looking at a tough budget—so he put it out in November, about three months early, convening forums and commissioning a survey. Badams recalls,

> I went on a talk radio show we have in town where everyone calls in just to lob grenades. It's something my predecessor never would have done, because you don't know what people are going to say. But I just went out there saying, "Here's what it really is. It's this bad, and what are we going to do about it?" I was completely open with the press, laid out the magnitude of the problem, and didn't point fingers at my predecessor. I said, "Yes we spent more than we put in," but in the same breath said, "We spent it because we wanted to provide extra programming for kids, we hired extra teachers, we got smaller class sizes, but now the party's over."

Leverage External Support. There's great leverage in claiming that outside partners (like the business community or a funder) will help if and only if your school or system embraces X. When you're pursuing difficult changes, such partners can free you to tell skeptical employees or community members, "Hey, I understand the concerns, but we're only getting this money/leeway/support if we do X." This requires working with external partners to ensure that their conditions align with your aims. Former Washington, DC, public schools chancellor and current Students-First CEO Michelle Rhee did this elegantly in winning her path-breaking CBA in 2010. Rhee lined up $65 million in foundation support to implement big pay raises for DC teachers, but only if the new contract included dramatic changes to evaluation and tenure. Rhee could credibly tell the Washington Teachers Union, "Like it or not, we only get the money if you sign this deal." Even sympathetic union leaders can have trouble convincing members to accept hard changes, but doing so gets easier when it will unlock new funds.

Similarly, leaders who face stiff resistance on closing unneeded schools may find it easier if local business community leaders say, "We're ready to fight for that levy, but only if the system addresses half-empty facilities." For instance, Drew Scheberle, senior vice president for education at the Austin, Texas, Chamber of Commerce, says, "We had to have the moment when [Austin Independent School District] knew we were willing to walk away. We gave them a list of nonnegotiables [and] said, 'If you want [our support], then you have to do these things. If you don't, we're out.'" An alert cage-buster can turn this kind of "imposition" into a powerful asset.

Seek Opportunities to Split Your Opponents. In *The Art of War*, Sun Tzu advises, "If [your opponent's] forces are united, separate them." Far-sighted leaders craft proposals that can win new allies and fracture the opposition. For instance, veteran teachers are more likely than their more junior colleagues to insist that unions fight to preserve seniority when it comes to teacher compensation, job security, and school assignment. Given this, it may sometimes make sense to appease veterans by protecting them from the changes—or offering them a sweetener for going along. In particular, this use of "grandfathering" (e.g., protecting current employees from the changed rules) is how major changes to teacher contracts were obtained in Denver and Washington, DC, and it's how politicians pursue reforms to any number of policies—from Social Security to Medicare. (Moreover, these teachers have a valid point when they note they entered the profession under one set of expectations and now feel like states and school systems are suddenly, unilaterally reneging on their end of the deal.) Rather than denouncing or attacking your opposition en masse—whether the issue is school closings, adopting new instructional programs, or rethinking special education—find opportunities to woo some and assuage others.

Learn from Bre'r Rabbit. In K–12, we're used to hearing excuses that people can't act because there's no money or their hands are tied. Cage-busters turn that premise on its head. They use things like accountability, tight budgets, and contracts to explain, "Gosh, I hate to do this, but I have no choice." Think of it as the *Bre'r Rabbit strategy*. Remember how, in Joel Chandler Harris's *Uncle Remus* tales, Bre'r Rabbit was caught by the fox? Helpless and desperate, Bre'r Rabbit tricked the fox into throwing him in the one place that Bre'r Rabbit could escape—the briar patch. How'd Bre'r Rabbit manage it? By blubbering, insisting the briar patch was the one place he *didn't* want to be, and pleading, "Whatever you do, please, please don't throw me into the briar patch."

It's tough for any leader to zero out a popular but ineffective program or to cut a popular but ineffectual team member. It's much more manageable when a leader can argue that it's out of her hands, that she's got no choice but is being thrown into the briar patch. Smart superintendents and principals have done this for a decade with NCLB accountability, saying, "I hate to do this, but . . ." When they move to restructure schools, a time-tested tactic is to work arm-in-arm with third parties as they file lawsuits. It's a lot easier for superintendents or school boards to justify tough decisions on teacher evaluation or school zoning if they can say, "We have to do this because of that darned judge's ruling." When she'd determined that DCPS needed to close more schools, beyond those it had shuttered just a few years before, Washington, DC, chancellor Kaya Henderson knew the decision could spark outrage. So, instead of trying to sell it directly to the public, she spent months explaining the potential savings and the benefits to business, civic, and political leaders. "It got to the point," she says, "that every time I'd talk to a city council member, they'd be asking me when I was going to close those schools." Thus, rather than lead the charge, Henderson could say she was regretfully doing what a broad swath of civic leaders thought necessary. When Henderson finally announced the closures, there was remarkably little hoopla. That's winning the battle before it's fought.

Some Fights Aren't Worth Winning. Upon being appointed as superintendent of Arlington, Massachusetts, Nate Levenson set out to trim superfluous spending. What he learned, however, was that some fights aren't worth winning. "The poster child of old decisions carried forward was our crossing guards, a small army of lovely women helping kids cross the street on the way to school. Seems great, [but] a study conducted by the police department and two pro bono traffic experts concluded that a third of the crossing guards crossed no children or that no children crossed without a parent."[2] Levenson cut back the crossing guards' hours. "Yet," says Levenson, "these sweet little old ladies were all multigenerational Arlington residents. They protested the reduction . . . unionized . . . [and became] a rallying cry for Old Arlington to retake a number of seats on the school board. In the end, I saved a few bucks but lost two school board members—a very bad trade."[3]

Some Fights Are Worth Losing. Sometimes it's worth fighting a fight even when you lose, as you've signaled to your friends that you'll stand by them and to your opponents that you won't be bullied. A strategically selected battle can even frame the public debate in helpful ways. Former New York City chancellor Joel Klein put it this way, "When I was at the [US] Justice Department, I used to say, 'If we're winning every case we bring, we're not bringing enough cases.' And that's a guiding principle for me in the way I approach these challenges. If somebody says, 'Well, there's a 60 percent chance we'll lose this arbitration,' I'd say the value of winning is worth enough that if I have a 40 percent chance of winning, I'll do it."[4]

One superintendent recalls, "I had a situation where the county slashed the school board's proposed budget. The county supervisors were complaining that the district was refusing to tighten its belt and that results weren't improving. So I said to the employee groups, 'Hey, there's no new money for us.' I didn't communicate that privately; I made sure we leaked the letters to the unions and that I shared my thinking publicly." Thus, a public rejection by local officials helped set a marker and focus attention on the need to improve outcomes and budget discipline.

Sometimes, Cage-Busters Grind It Out. Sometimes, cage-busting is about mustering the patience and planning needed to make onerous, but necessary changes. That's when cage-busters do what it takes to wear down their opponents and get the work done. Houston superintendent Terry Grier's push to overhaul the district's teacher evaluation system is an instructive example. "There was a law on the books at the state level which said you cannot put into place a different evaluation system unless each of your school level committees actually generates that evaluation system and approves it," recalls TNTP honcho and Houston partner Ariela Rozman. She says it was probably put on the books precisely to make impossible the kind of reform Grier sought, as there were about three hundred school-level committees throughout the district. Rozman says Grier weighed the pros and cons and then decided, "This is not going to be easy, but we are going to comply with the requirements, get good input from our educators and get it done." Knowing the union was likely to fight the effort, no matter what, Grier partnered with TNTP to scrupulously follow the letter of the law. The process ultimately entailed over one thousand teachers in meetings at every school. That required a team of district and TNTP staff to make those meetings occur, ensure that notes were taken, and dot all the requisite *i*'s. The process yielded an ambitious overhaul of Houston's evaluation and termination policy, with a 7-2 board vote to adopt and strong testimonials from teachers.[5]

He's right. You can never communicate with teachers and parents enough. As Tennessee state chief Kevin Huffman says, "One of the things we've learned [in implementing ambitious changes to teacher evaluation] is that any time we've said something to teachers five or ten times, we should've said it twenty times."

Find a Way to Share Your Truth

Indiana state chief Tony Bennett used a piece of teacher-friendly legislation to gain the ability to communicate directly with teachers and ensure that his proposals would receive a fair hearing.

Bennett explains, "In 2009, we passed a law granting teachers qualified immunity from civil suits when a teacher is imposing reasonable discipline in the classroom. Under the law, we required districts to provide teacher e-mail addresses to the state. We just built a database from that. We're doing it to inform teachers of what's going on. Otherwise, far too many times, what they hear is being filtered through their organized representation."

He notes that he couldn't have done this as a district superintendent but can as a state chief. He explains, "Under Indiana's collective bargaining law, the union is the exclusive representative [for teachers]. This means that if you're a district superintendent, you have to communicate through the union. But [as state chief] I do not have a contractual relationship with teachers and so am not bound by those laws."

Bennett continues, "When we first started the legislative session in 2011 [when Indiana considered an extensive package of reforms], we communicated by e-mail about twice a week with teachers. The first one we sent, I think we got about eight hundred responses. Most of them were a 'You rotten SOB, never send me another one' kind of thing. I made our staff personally respond to every one, saying, 'We're sorry you feel this way, but we're going to continue to respond and inform you with factual information.' By the end of session, we were getting [fewer] than fifty responses. And most of those were, like, 'How come what you're telling me is so vastly different from what I'm getting from my union?'" Bennett's convinced that the ability to talk directly to teachers has been an invaluable tool.

PUBLIC DEBATES ARE ALL ABOUT LEVERAGE

Another, more prosaic, way to think about Sun Tzu's advice is to observe that public debates are all about leverage. Think of sumo wrestling. The vast majority of moves in a sumo match aren't intended to force your opponent out of the ring, but to get leverage that'll put him at a disadvantage.

When it comes to public debate, the same thing applies. Moreover, nature abhors a vacuum. If you're not pushing ideas and explanations into the public square, someone else will be. This means that *if you're not on offense, you're on defense*. Public debate is about pushing and pushing until you've backed your opponents into a position where they find it necessary to compromise, or backtrack.

When proposing uncomfortable policies, success depends on whether the public atmosphere makes it easier for your principal, superintendent, state chief, or legislators to say yes than to say no. The reality is that decision makers are responsive to what they hear from community leaders, editorial boards, advocates, donors, and the public. If key public voices are with you, you're working downhill. If they're not, well, if after twenty minutes you don't know who the sucker is . . .

While he was negotiating the 2005 contract with the United Federation of Teachers, New York City chancellor Joel Klein gained enormous leverage due to City Council hearings called by education chair Eva Moskowitz. Moskowitz's hearings filled the public square with examples of the inanities in the district's collective bargaining agreements and alerted the media, public, and civic movers and shakers to the problems. The public pressure that emerged put the United Federation of Teachers into a position where president Randi Weingarten opted to make concessions rather than defend now-radioactive contract provisions.

It also helps if a third party can help drive the debate. This is why it's vital for leaders to cultivate external allies. When advocacy groups like Democrats for Education Reform, 50CAN, or Stand for Children; civic groups; or business organizations are making the case for desired reforms, cage-busting superintendents or board members can play it cool and ride the wave. A cage-buster works with such groups to change the dynamics of public debate.

In Indianapolis, for instance, the school board was debating whether to modify the district's seniority-driven layoff policy. Such hearings are usually dominated by union members emphatically defending seniority. The debate inevitably gets framed as teachers against reformers. Well, today, there are a handful of organizations across the nation, like Educators 4 Excellence or Teach Plus, that can help even those odds. Teach Plus, for instance, engages accomplished early-career teachers in policy debates.

In Indianapolis, the local Teach Plus members had drafted an alternative proposal and showed up at a crucial board meeting to argue against strict seniority-based layoffs. They were outnumbered by union supporters, but their presence made it clear that there were teachers on both sides of the issue. This made it much harder for union leaders to claim an "attack" on teachers and much easier for board members to relax seniority-based layoffs and hand the union an unexpected defeat.

BUY-IN IS A TACTIC, NOT A CREDO

Cage-busters approach stakeholder buy-in *as a tactic, not a credo.* Cage-busters recognize the value of buy-in, but don't think elaborate efforts to pursue it are always worth the time and energy. The key is to strike a healthy balance, earning trust and commitment without being held hostage by naysayers or ungainly strategic plans. For instance, while new superintendents sometimes launch expensive citywide strategic planning efforts, these processes require enormous time and energy but rarely surface surprises (e.g., superintendents learn that parents want safer schools and business wants skilled graduates). And these processes can add less value than you'd hope. In San Diego, the board that selected superintendent Alan Bersin sponsored a months-long, community-based process, one it endorsed in three formal votes. Yet when Bersin was selected, board member Frances Zimmerman announced, "I am deeply troubled by the hurried, pressured, and secretive process the board experienced in making its final decision."[6] In other words, Zimmerman decided the process was illegitimate when she didn't like the outcome.

Former Charlotte-Mecklenburg superintendent Peter Gorman observes, "Gosh, one year we closed eleven schools. They were low-performing and underenrolled, and the kids went to higher-performing schools. But schools can be the core of a neighborhood, so something like that is devastating to the community. We did a whole series of public meetings and community meetings. We did dozens of meetings. But even in doing those, and through the entire process and when it was over, people said they felt like they didn't have a voice. In the end, they still picketed my home over the school closures. There is no good way to deal with such a bad situation."

Houston superintendent Terry Grier recalls that when he was superintendent in Sacramento, California, statute required the superintendent to recommend any new hires. When the board reneged on commitments it had made about process, Grier gave up on buy-in. He shifted gears and fully exploited this authority:

> When talking with the board about going [to Sacramento], I made sure I was going to control hiring. When I got there, we had a bunch of principal openings. We went through a thorough interview process with school-level input and came up with the candidates we felt would do the best job . . . At our post-year board meeting, I presented the board with the list of candidates for approval. There was hesitation. Finally, one board member said, "Where is the list of all the applicants?" I found out that the last superintendent would give them a list of everyone who had applied for open positions, ordered by seniority and race. I said, "What's that have to do with anything? My job is to identify the strongest applicants."
>
> They said, "Well, we usually are able to add applicants to the list." I said, "It's not going to be done that way anymore. If I'm going to be held accountable for school performance, I have to have control over HR and my staff. That's what I was told coming in." One board member laughed and said, "Yeah, that's what we said when we were recruiting you." Then the board asked, "What if we don't approve of a candidate?" I said, "I'll bring back the candidate the next month." They said, "What if we don't approve them the next month?" . . . It went on for months, until the board finally said, "School is coming up. What are you going to do when you have a bunch of schools with no principals?" I said, "I'm going to go to the press, I'm going to show them the list of candidates that you all have not approved, and you're going to have to explain why there are schools without principals."

The board folded.

Buy-in and consensus are good things. But they can also become a distraction, a time-suck, or an excuse for inaction. That's why cage-busters view them as tactics, not sacraments.

MAKE POLICY WORK FOR YOU

Policy has many shortcomings, but its signal strength is the ability to stack the odds before the battle is fought.

As we noted in chapter 4, policy is a simple tool. It can tell people what they *must* do and what they *must not* do. Policy can tell a teacher that she must use a formative assessment in every class, but it can't ensure that she actually uses it to guide instruction. This makes policy a lousy tool for governing complex behaviors. But it's a marvelous tool when it comes to steering simpler behaviors, allowing leaders to minimize distractions and focus on the things that matter most.

I recall teaching one principal who led a health sciences magnet school. Students were expected to wear scrubs and teachers to wear lab coats. One teacher consistently refused to wear the lab coat. When the principal brought it up, the teacher would half-heartedly wear the lab coat for a few hours or a few days, with it open and flopping around. The principal says, "For months we played this game. I got more and more frustrated." But he didn't want to make the lab coat a requirement, fearing it would undermine the school's culture. Finally, he decided he had it wrong. It was the cat-and-mouse game that was undermining a collaborative culture. He decided that formalizing the lab coat policy would remove the distraction. If the teacher refused to comply, the principal would no longer be the scold but the ally who could say, "Gosh, I'd hate to have to write you up, but I've got no choice." Either way, the principal could stop nagging and put that energy to more productive use. (The upshot was, the teacher stopped playing games, wore the lab coat, and then left the school at year's end.)

Used wisely, policy allows leaders to clarify minimal norms so that they can focus on what matters most. Policy may be unnecessary when culture is sufficiently strong or when there are so few weak performers that it's easy to deal with the occasional headache on a one-off basis. But few school or system leaders are that fortunate, meaning that policy can serve as a critical tool for strengthening culture and conserving time, resources, energy, and goodwill.

Use Policy to Create Leverage or Save Political Capital

Policy can be a terrific way to get the upper hand in a fight that might otherwise demand enormous time and energy. Rhode Island state superintendent Deborah Gist observes, "In Rhode Island law, a contract cannot be in violation of an existing law. So the law can't interrupt a contract, but once a contract expires, the contract has to change [to match the new law]. And so the regulation says evaluations have to be annual and they have to be based primarily on student growth and achievement. That means there's not an option in negotiations to not do it. So it gives the superintendents a starting place. They don't have to have conversations about *whether* it gets done, but can focus on *how* it gets done."

As noted in chapter 4, many Indiana superintendents opted to keep their old CBA language intact even after 2011 legislation narrowed the scope of bargaining. State superintendent Tony Bennett had to decide how to respond. Berating local districts could make enemies without having much practical impact. So he instead arranged for the Indiana Board of Accounts to start auditing district CBAs. He explains, "Each year, when a district is audited, the Board is going to audit the contract and issue an auditing exception against any district where the contract isn't in compliance. These audits are public documents. In Indiana, they're very public. The public, the media, and superintendents take them very seriously. No superintendent wants an audit exception—it's a black eye. So these audits have become a point of leverage. For all our competitive grants, we're also thinking about requiring on an application that the district's bargaining agreement comply with [Indiana Senate Bill 5755, which narrowed the permissible scope of bargaining]. We'd just disqualify districts that aren't in compliance."

One Ohio principal explains how the policies attached to a federal turnaround grant provided essential flexibility around the CBA's hiring language. She says, "When I came, the school was going through redesign. This meant all the staff members were surplused. Now, there are some contract policies around how we recruit and hire staff, but some of the provisions were waived because we were in redesign. We made sure that teachers were part of the hiring interview team to help hire colleagues that would best fit the needs of the school. So I hired the lead teachers first and built that foundation. They helped hire the remainder of the staff. The ability to look at new hires was huge because we had to redesign three schools at one time. So there were three displaced staffs out there looking for a job. If you hadn't been successful at your previous school, why would I want you in my school where I'm building a new culture? Out of thirty-five or forty surplused teachers, we ultimately hired about ten back." This kind of flexibility can too easily be taken for granted when explaining why a new school or program "worked." But it's the simple changes to policies or contracts that can help set leaders free to create stronger, more successful schools and cultures.

Climbing Through Policy Windows

Decades ago, in *Agendas, Alternatives, and Public Policies*, political scientist John Kingdon explained that the world sometimes arranges itself to make big policy changes possible. This occurs when problems, proposed solutions, and events conspire to create "policy windows."[7] Cage-busters are prepared for these opportunities and take advantage of them. Mitchell Chester, now Massachusetts commissioner of education but formerly associate state superintendent in Ohio, recalls, "When I first got to Ohio [in 2001], they had an accountability system that I thought was pretty crude and not very nuanced or effective. The system had been codified in law since shortly before I arrived. It was part of an omnibus package that had gone through some fierce legislative battles and no one wanted to reopen it. But [No Child Left Behind] gave us license to act, because we had to incorporate subgroup analysis and so forth. So NCLB gave us license to redo the system."

Popular or must-pass policies are great tools for creating policy windows. For instance, in Tennessee, one state official observed that the law creating the state's Achievement School District didn't provide enough flexibility when it came to procurement and hiring. There was concern, however, that a new bill narrowly focused on that issue wouldn't pass. So, the official explained, "We have to be smart and strategic about how we get it through, so we've attached it to the legislation that has to get written for the state's [NCLB] waiver request. Since every superintendent and school board in the state wants to get out from under AYP, everybody supports that. So, we stuck the legislation that we knew was going to be controversial in a bill that everybody wants to get done. It's just being crafty about how you find the loopholes and staying focused on what needs to get done."

Tight budgets offer another kind of policy window, making it possible to push changes that would be a tough sell in good times. When a dire fiscal situation forced Erie's Jay Badams to lay off hundreds of teachers, Pennsylvania law dictated that he proceed strictly based on seniority. Yet, rather than throw in the towel, Badams seized the chance to go to the board and win approval for a retirement incentive package. Teachers were offered $5,000 a year for five years and noninstructional staff would be given a one-time $7,500 payment. "We hoped to get forty retirements," Badams said. "We got 107. People saw the writing on the wall. It saved us money, because we were otherwise going to lose our youngest [and cheapest] teachers. We had some people who were on 'active retirement' anyway, and this pushed them out the door."

THESE AREN'T THE DROIDS YOU'RE LOOKING FOR

Cage-busters fight when they have to. But they don't go looking for fights. In fact, cage-busters prize the ability to escape the cage with brains rather than brawn. Cathy Mincberg, president of the Center for Reform of School Systems and a veteran board member, says, "The problem is when fighting is the leader's response to every disagreement. I have seen more great ideas die on the sword because fighting was the only strategy, whether it's the principal who tries to correct every injustice in the first month on the job or the superintendent who fights with everyone. A surprising number do that, only to be surprised when they never get support or sustainability."

Matt Candler, founder of 4.0 Schools and former CEO of New Schools for New Orleans, has spent as much time successfully sidestepping local political obstacles as anyone I know. When he talks to sitting or aspiring school leaders, Matt invariably plays one memorable *Star Wars* clip as a textbook example of how to win without fighting. You may remember the scene. Alec Guinness's Obi-Wan Kenobi and Mark Hamill's Luke are trying to smuggle two droids past Imperial storm troopers. Obi-Wan Kenobi, the old Jedi master, uses the "force" to bend the storm troopers to his will. Luke and Obi-Wan pull up to the storm trooper:

STORM TROOPER: Let me see your identification.
OBI-WAN (*makes small hand gesture*): You don't need to see his identification.
STORM TROOPER (*obediently*): We don't need to see his identification.

OBI-WAN: These aren't the droids you're looking for.

STORM TROOPER: These aren't the droids we're looking for.

OBI-WAN: He can go about his business.

STORM TROOPER: You can go about your business.

OBI-WAN: Move along.

STORM TROOPER (*waving them through*): Move along . . . move along.

Whenever possible, you want the force to work your will for you. When done right, it can look remarkably simple.

Mitchell Chester offers a terrific example of how to put the Jedi mindset to work:

> When I started in Massachusetts, I assumed I had license until I ran into a force that told me I didn't. Early in my tenure, it was important that I establish myself as the chief executive officer. I restructured the agency, dismissed some employees, brought in others, and decided not to ask for permission. By keeping the board informed of the direction, but not the details, I established this authority with the board. Most, although not all, of my board members expect me to exert leadership and be bold about the work to be done. As long as I keep them informed and provide opportunity for their input, they have largely embraced my leadership. My advice is to assume you have the license to act.

While serving as superintendent in Charlotte, North Carolina, Newscorp senior vice president Peter Gorman recalls, "We had to do layoffs due to financial shortfalls, and everyone had always done layoffs according to pure seniority. We asked why we weren't using the evaluations and performance to make layoff decisions. We started to do that and said, 'We're going to do this because it's the right thing to do and we're going to do it until we get told it's wrong and forced to stop.'" The district removed 883 teachers. It was never forced to stop.[8]

Education attorney Melissa Junge observes, "Ironically, my clients that ask, 'How far over the line can we get?' and are willing to take the consequences are the people that get left alone, because they have focus and purpose. There's so much you can do without asking the feds for a blessing if you just do it and own it." If you act professionally and purposefully, you may be surprised how often you'll just be told, "Move along . . . move along."

PREACH LESS, LISTEN MORE

Would-be school reformers are often impressed with their own righteous-ness, dismissing concerns and criticism as baseless or wrong-headed. As one impassioned district official told me, "We're doing the right thing and we're doing it for the right reasons—so [what's] the hold-up?" The prob-lem is that people can sometimes honestly disagree about "the right thing to do for kids." Failure to recognize this undercuts our ability to identify problems and design solutions.

Say you're in charge of your district's virtual school. You're working hard to ensure that all students can take advanced courses and specialized of-ferings, but find that principals aren't as supportive as you'd expect. As one district tech coordinator told me, "For some reason, our principals don't seem to understand how good this is for the kids." Well, try to empathize with the principals for a moment. Turns out, your district requires that on-line courses have a full-time teacher in the classroom, so a high school with students taking online classes is effectively devoting one full-time teaching position to supervising the virtual school. If only a half-dozen students are taking online classes during a given period, class sizes in traditional class-rooms have to increase. Even if it's good for the kids involved, principals might reasonably regard this as a bad deal for most students.

None of this means that the principals are "right," just that they're not being unreasonable. Listening may help us to ask what the problem is and how we might alter virtual school staffing, rules, or funding models to address the principals' concerns. It allows us to understand why critics might see things differently and helps identify strategies to solve problems. By finding opportunities for agreement, it reduces the number of right fights. Empathy is ultimately the difference between cage-busters who im-plode amidst endless battles and those who, studying their Sun-Tzu, win their battles *before they're fought.*

FOCUS ON SOLUTIONS

When talking to supervisors or to policymakers, it's easy for leaders to get caught up in what they want or think they need. Instead, try to lead with empathy by asking yourself, "What problem does this listener need my help to solve?" Whether you're talking to city council members, your superintendent, or your principal, don't tell them you need money or special treatment. That's what they hear from everyone, and it's exhausting. And, guess what? They probably can't offer much help. All you've done is identified yourself as part of the problem.

Principals, superintendents, and teacher leaders tend to pay remarkably little attention to "managing up." If you approach policy makers or bosses not as a claimant but as a fellow problem solver, I think you'll be pleasantly surprised at how often you'll get a green light. So help them understand how you can help solve the problems they're worried about. When you do so, it's in *their* interest to help provide the flexibility and backing that you need. Says Spring Branch ISD superintendent Duncan Klussmann, "A superintendent only knows 5 percent of what's happening on their campus. As a principal, if you're doing well, solving problems, and not asking for more resources, odds are I'll say yes to your request." (See "Working with Legislators" for one aspect of managing up.)

Working with Legislators

When it comes to winning policy fights, you need to know how to work with legislators.[9] A common mistake is to approach them with a lack of empathy for their needs and challenges. The wrong approach was crystallized for me by the big-district superintendent who found a legislator willing to carry his bill, only to walk away when the legislator wanted the bill to also promote charter schools. The superintendent's memorable quote? "We don't need to compromise. We're education. We always get what we need." Well, that's both inaccurate and destructive. Here are a few tips from the pros on dealing with legislators and winning a seat at the table in policy debates.

Don't Wait Until Budget Season to Meet with Legislators or Staff

Former Massachusetts Senate staffer Michele Shelton says, "At the start of a new session . . . set up appointments to do meet-and-greets. This is a better approach than waiting for the budget to come out. Setting up quick fifteen-minute meet-and-greets with new legislators,

(continued)

staffers, or chairs gets you on the radar screen in a way that's not asking anything." Shelton stresses the importance of developing and maintaining relationships with staff: "Coming in and sitting down with a legislator or staff [member] is more effective than hearings to communicate [your] message. If you can develop relationships with staff, that's the more effective way to advocate."

Prioritize, Prioritize, Prioritize

You can't win everything, so it's important to focus. Von Byer, director of the Texas Senate Education Committee, says, "Everything is a matter of priorities. You have a limited amount of time; you have to convince [staff] that whatever your particular issue is, it's so important that they have to make it a priority." Barry Mayer, a business executive deeply involved in Austin schooling, says the business community worked with local districts to identify top priorities. He explains, "We only have so many shots at the batter's box when we go to the legislator, but if we have two or three top issues, it's manageable."

Come In with Solutions, Not Wish Lists

Legislative staff say it's vital to show up with potential solutions. Of her experience crafting legislation in the Massachusetts Senate, Michele Shelton says, "When you're working on big reform bills, you want to work with people who are reasonable. Don't come in with a list of demands." Instead, show up with proposed solutions. Von Byer sounds a similar note, saying, "If you can convince a legislator that your issue is worth going after and [also] offer ideas for how to solve the problem, it makes it easier."

Say you're a principal who thinks that the district curriculum doesn't work for your kids. Fair enough. But consider this from the system perspective: can the superintendent do what you're asking for all her schools? If not, why should she do it for you? You need to have an answer in hand. Let's presume that the superintendent thinks you're a terrific leader and will make terrific choices. Still, why is it essential that you use a different curriculum? What's the evidence that this will help? How can the district avoid new costs for instructional materials and professional development if you're doing something different from everyone else? How will the superintendent justify to other school leaders and community members why she's giving this option to you but not to others? Show up with answers to these questions—and now the force is with you.

Cage-busters don't demand resources; they offer solutions. Former Virginia secretary of education Gerard Robinson admiringly says of Albemarle County, Virginia, superintendent Pam Moran,

> Pam never complained or asked about money. What she did was provide me successful examples and raise money to support her programs. In partnership with the Central Virginia Chapter of One Hundred Black Men, Inc., she created a program for black middle school boys having trouble with math and science. She raised the funds to work on a Saturday academy. She also has a broader program to help some of the black boys with at least a 3.0 [GPA] who would be first in their families to go to college. Rather than say, "If I had more money from the state I could do more," what she is saying is, "I wanted a program so I went and raised money, and I produced results." As a result, when I was out and would identify possible funders, I made sure they would get [connected] to chiefs like Pam . . . But, really, I am putting Pam in contact with funders because I know what she is doing. If all you tell me is what you do not have, I cannot support you. But if you tell me what you are doing, and I see that need, then I can help.

THERE WILL BE FIGHTING

Sometimes there's no choice except to fight the "right fight." As public institutions, schools and school systems are sometimes subject to fierce fights between people who have real, honest disagreements. When you try to modify benefits or close schools, there are going to be losers and they will be angry. You can try to split the opposition, mollify them, empathize, and the rest, but there will be times when a cage-buster has to fight.

In a bookend to the Peter Gorman story at the start of this chapter, here's one from Abigail Smith, former chief of Washington, DC's Transformation Management Office. Smith recalls the community response to chancellor Michelle Rhee's push to close nearly two dozen half-empty, dilapidated schools:

> We got attacked for not involving the community, but there was a ton of community engagement around the school closures. There were dozens of meetings. Literally, the chancellor took every single meeting request that

came from the community. So in addition to a dozen large community meetings around the city, and then individual closure meetings at every single one of the schools [recommended for closure], there were dozens of small group meetings with the chancellor and staff. Anyone who wanted to get a direct audience got it. Through that process it still ended up being twenty-three schools, [though] there were some changes made as to which schools, and there were changes in terms of providing transportation and other things that would address community concerns. But at the end of the day, if you close people's schools they're not going to be happy about it. . . What it takes to get through those barriers, on the political side, is really just someone who has the spine to do it.

It's frustrating. A cage-buster can stack every deck and play every card, and sometimes it'll still come down to butting heads. There's no science to this. Sometimes public persuasion will quiet skeptics; sometimes it won't. Some leaders seem to draw less vitriol, due to their manner, skin color, local relationships, pace, or because they're following someone who started excavating the mountain. All you can do is stack the deck and then play the hand you're dealt.

When it does come to butting heads, you want to know you've done everything possible to shape the outcome. But you also want to be willing to stand tall. Former Nogales, Arizona, superintendent Shawn McCollough, now the president of the American Board for Certification of Teacher Excellence, notes, "Ultimately, you need leaders who are willing to stand in the fire and fight for what they know is morally right for kids, families, and communities . . . At the core of all successful leaders that I've ever worked with, there has been an undeniable willingness to stand and fight the hard fight when it's necessary."

WHEN YOU'RE READY TO RUMBLE

You can't always play nice. When a cage-buster has identified a problem, decided it's important, and settled on a solution, he may feel obliged to move, now. When they think it's time, cage-busters act. They do it smart, with an eye to the long-term. But they fight hard, and they'll fight dirty if the situation calls for it.

In Charlotte-Mecklenburg, superintendent Peter Gorman had trouble getting principals to rigorously evaluate their teachers. So, he says, "We started to take our teachers who had been bumped and send them to the schools where everyone had a positive evaluation. I said to principals, 'If everyone's already doing well, you can take this displaced teacher.' And the principal would say, 'Hey, well, that person's a lemon.' I'd say, 'Now clearly, you can handle it because everyone at your school's got a great evaluation. You've got time to work with them.' So principals realized, 'Oh my God, taking the lazy way out impacts my school negatively. I've got to start jumping on this.'" Consequences for irresponsible behavior send a stark message.

Robert Sommers says proposing contract language that strikes fear into the union leadership is a powerful lever for wringing concessions at the bargaining table. He recalls an episode when he was superintendent of Butler Tech school district in Hamilton, Ohio:

> One mistake I made was thinking that if you treated teachers really well that the union would be happy. This wasn't the case. So we thought, well, we'll make the union earn their members by proposing to do away with fair share. [*Fair share* provisions require non-union employees to pay a fee to the union to cover costs of collective bargaining. Eliminating it would have hit the union in the wallet, hard.] We entered negotiations with forty-some changes we wanted and the union came with twenty-five or thirty language items. All through negotiations we wouldn't take fair share off the table. And [the union] kept giving us more and more of our language items . . . Going into the fall we had pretty much gotten everything that we wanted out of the contract language and we had given them three items.

In Houston, the district's new evaluation system flagged 169 out of about 11,000 teachers as ineffective. The district offered to buy out these teachers, mostly veterans, with a year's worth of salary, in order to get them off the payroll; 150 accepted the offer. The 19 who didn't were put into substitute teaching roles—but not just casual sub duty. The district prohibited them from teaching in the same school more than two days in a row. "These are teachers who either cannot or will not meet our expectations for kids," says superintendent Terry Grier. "Kids are only going to be exposed to them for one day. As a result," Grier drily notes, "teachers found themselves wearing the rubber off their tires." All 19 teachers accepted the buyout offer the following year.

Washington, DC, chancellor Kaya Henderson was determined to give principals a hefty pay raise, averaging close to $30,000 a year. However, the bargaining unit that represented the principals also represented other administrative personnel (like school business managers) and insisted that any raise be granted across the board. Henderson says, "I know how valuable our sitting principals are and I know where we needed to get their pay. But I was not going to give out an across-the-board increase in the aftermath of a massive recession. That wasn't happening." Stymied, Henderson took a hard look at the CBA. She says, "I found a provision that allows me to increase pay for any member of the bargaining unit by up to $20,000 a year. It's intended for recruitment or to keep us from losing principals to Fairfax or Montgomery County. But the contract didn't say that. So I told the bargaining unit that we were going to go ahead and boost pay for all of our principals by $20,000. The next year, we'd boost it again until they were where we thought they should be. The union said, 'You can't do that.' I said, 'Yes, I can.' And I did. I told them they could claim credit for the raise if they wanted. Or not. It was their call."

Henderson notes, "Districts just take things as gospel truth. Most people are not rule-breakers. That translates to a reluctance to challenge the status quo. But once you do, you get a sense of possibility."

Justin Cohen, president of the School Turnaround Group at Mass Insight Education, tells of one Boston principal: "For years, he was trying to remove a teacher, and both the district and the union were blocking him . . . Finally, it came to the point where the union president's daughter was about to be in the grade level this teacher taught. So the principal shifted things around to put the union president's daughter into that teacher's classroom. The union president came into the principal's office the next day and said, 'All right, I give [in]. What do you want?'"

THE VIRTUOUS CYCLE

Cage-busters benefit from a virtuous cycle. Each win helps blast away impediments and norms that stifle problem solving; forge a can-do culture;

and make possible deep changes in pedagogy, instruction, and learning. Victories create new possibilities, breed the confidence that comes with success, and mark you as a valuable ally. Sun Tzu said it best: "Opportunities multiply as they are seized."

Getting the politics and policy right creates room for a positive culture, while convincing community members and even national observers that you've got things moving in the right direction. As Rhode Island state chief Deborah Gist says, "It's like a flywheel. You get that momentum going and people get energized."

Fortune has a way of favoring the bold. Let's close with a word from Brockton, Massachusetts, superintendent Matt Malone, who recalls,

> I took a vote of no confidence from my union. It was a big public ugly thing. Want to know why? We had two teachers in tech education and one had to be eliminated. One had been there longer than the other, but they both were essentially tied for seniority based on when they were certified. The union wanted me to pick the person who had been there longer. I picked the better teacher . . . The consequence was that vote of no confidence, which could be a career killer. But it helped me to lay the gauntlet down. Sometimes you need to see beyond your situation. I went from being a superintendent of a tiny school system to the fourth-largest school system in the state. I got there because I had to handle a lot of hard situations and handled them boldly.

Not a bad motto, that, for a cage-buster.

8

A World Without Borders
and Boundaries

"Some men see things as they are and say why?
I dream things that never were and say, why not?"

—ROBERT F. KENNEDY

"I don't know the future. I didn't come here to tell you how
this is going to end, I came here to tell you how this is going
to begin . . . I'm going to show these people what you don't
want them to see. I'm going to show them a world without
you, a world without rules and controls, without borders or
boundaries. A world where anything is possible. Where we go
from there is a choice I leave to you."

—NEO, *The Matrix*

CAGE-BUSTING MAKES IT EASIER for school and system leaders to
tackle problems, drive improvement, and forge strong cultures. Whether
one does any of that is an open question, and *that's* where instructional
leadership comes into play. Remember, there are *two halves* to the leadership equation; one that makes it possible to lead, and one that involves
the ins and outs of leading. Just as it's foolish to imagine that structural reforms will yield great teaching and learning, it's naive to think that

instructional leadership and good intentions can overcome dysfunctional rules, regulations, and routines. We ignore this truth at our peril. And yet it's routinely ignored.

The result is a curious malady. Instructional leadership's emphasis on coaching and culture shaping has too often blinded us to the effects of stifling strictures or paralyzing bureaucracy, seemingly in the belief that kindness can conquer all. As former Canton City, Ohio, superintendent Michele Evans observes, "The biggest mistake I see leaders make is thinking that everybody's going to love them. If you're going to move student achievement and everyone's happy, you're probably not ruffling enough feathers. If the status quo hasn't worked to this point, there's no reason to believe it's going to work going forward. It's not that I don't want people to like me, but what I really want is my kids to get a good education."

Michelle Rhee, former chancellor of Washington, DC's schools, frequently told one tale of her time there. In her first year, she sat down with all her principals. One led a school where just a quarter of the kids were reading at grade level. She asked the principal what percentage of his teachers he judged effective. "All of them," he told her. As Rhee tells it, she said, "That can't be right. Only a quarter of your kids are reading at grade level. Are you blaming them?" He said no, but again insisted that all his teachers were effective. Knowing the principal had a granddaughter, Rhee asked, "Okay, well, how many of those teachers would you feel comfortable teaching your granddaughter?" As Rhee tells it, the principal looked at her and said, "Well, gosh, if *that's* the bar, then none."

That answer reflected a deeply rooted mind-set, one that pervaded the district's culture, norms, and practices. Such things do not change quickly or easily. They run deep. They're intertwined with policies, contract provisions, and the confidence that there's no consequence for mediocrity. Such habits may resist even the most skillful coaching. Insisting that leaders can overturn all this through coaching and consensus is a recipe for ensuring that only preternaturally charismatic and persuasive superheroes will succeed.

The power of cage-busting is that it allows leaders to succeed even absent heroic personal gifts or boulder-rolling techniques.

CAGED LEADERSHIP LEADS TO
ONE-SIZE-FITS-ALL POLICY

Caged leadership frustrates policy makers and advocates, leading them to propose new rules and policies as they scramble to force leaders to, well, lead. In this way, caged leadership creates a perverse cycle and actually makes the mountain steeper.

When school and system leaders fail to rigorously evaluate staff, spend dollars cost-effectively, or push the boundaries of the possible, reformers may decide they have to compel leaders to do these things. The problem: because the solutions are intended to force leaders to act, they are written into policy. And, as we discussed in chapter 4, policy is not nimble. It's a crude lever to force the hand of laggards. And it often creates new headaches or burdens for others.

But the inaction of cage-dwelling leaders invites efforts to use just such a lever. By blithely labeling nearly all of their teachers as satisfactory, school and system leaders have convinced reformers that they can't be trusted to rigorously gauge quality. After all, in the influential 2009 report *The Widget Effect*, The New Teacher Project reported that, in districts using binary teacher evaluations, *over 99 percent* of teachers were rated as satisfactory.[1] In fact, notes TNTP President Tim Daly, "In Chicago, we learned that the state law said that you have three evaluation ratings that you can assign to a teacher: unsatisfactory, satisfactory, and excellent. While researching their system, we found that Chicago had applied for a waiver to put an additional rating on top of that system. It's called 'superior,' and we could not find any official definition that explained the difference between superior and excellent. It was just better than excellent. So, we kept asking people, 'Why do, like, 65 percent of your teachers get this rating? Can anyone even tell us what it means?'" In another district, an underperforming principal remained in place because, as one observer explains, "The Post-it Note on the person's desk that said 'Fire the principal' never made it to the right place. There wasn't an internal system for ensuring that happened."

Such destructive behaviors can't be blamed on unions. This is a leadership failure. Even for teachers with tenure, principals could, at the very least, take stronger steps to evaluate them. Faced with inaction, would-be reformers feel they have no recourse but to champion inflexible state or federal policies that will finally force school and district leaders to act.

Absent cage-busting leadership, reformers will feel compelled to push top-down, one-size-fits-all state policies. Cage-busting, on the other hand, can help reassure reformers that leaders will lead on their own and temper the appetite for heavy-handed policies. While school and system leaders frequently demand "autonomy" and "flexibility," too rarely do they explain precisely what they need flexibility *from* or what problems it'll permit them to solve. In identifying particular impediments and making clear why they matter, cage-busting helps pinpoint ways in which reform-minded advocates and federal, state, and district officials can operate as allies rather than antagonists.

CAGE-BUSTERS GET A SEAT AT THE TABLE

Frustrated with cage-dwelling leadership, would-be reformers frequently wind up championing poorly designed proposals. The ensuing problems are well-documented in the case of No Child Left Behind (NCLB), where well-intentioned policy makers managed to create a slew of perverse incentives, while tarnishing sensible ideas. Though NCLB has some real virtues, many school and system leaders are justifiably frustrated by its crude level-based measures of Adequate Yearly Progress, the paper-heavy measures of teacher quality, and the one-size-fits-all nature of the mandated remedies. Educational leaders had only themselves to blame, however, for the minimal role they played in addressing the law's design defects.

They'd have had a much bigger voice if key members of Congress hadn't come to regard the education community with suspicion prior to 2001. After their fierce opposition to even the modest voluntary testing proposed by President Bill Clinton in the 1994 reauthorization of the Elementary and Secondary Education Act, educators were viewed as naysayers and foot-draggers unwilling to help craft workable accountability systems. Cage-busting leaders could have assured themselves a seat at the table, along with key organizations—like the Education Trust or the Council of the Great City Schools—that were welcomed by Congressional leaders as credible, constructive voices.

Foundations, advocacy groups, and policy makers are similarly dismissive of cage-dwellers, but enthusiastically inclined to support and engage cage-busters. They're eager to work with and listen to those they view as no-excuses problem solvers. Cage-busters, by showing that schooling can be improved and refashioned by practitioners, also temper the sense that reformers need to "fix" schools through policy. All of this requires, however, that leaders seize opportunities when policy makers present them. (See "Don't Blow Your Chance at a Clean Slate.")

JOHN HENRY IS *NOT* A ROLE MODEL

Readers will recall the tale of mighty John Henry, who swore he could shovel through a mountain faster than a steam-powered hammer. Big John had a unique approach to navigating the mountain, all right, but the

Don't Blow Your Chance at a Clean Slate

Sometimes life does you a favor. The question is whether you'll seize it. As we noted in chapter 4, cage-dwelling leaders show a disheartening tendency to let even do-overs pass them by. In 2011, Indiana and Wisconsin changed state laws to narrow the scope of collective bargaining for public employees. The new laws specified that unions could bargain only over wages and wage-related benefits, not the raft of minutiae— from school start times to professional development—that dot so many CBAs and fuel the "culture of can't."

In most sectors, union demands are kept in check by industry competition. Firms that make unaffordable concessions either win changes or eventually fall by the wayside. Overly aggressive unions recalibrate demands or risk pushing an employer into bankruptcy. When it comes to public employees, though, these restraints don't exist. After all, public agencies don't have to worry about market share, and they know that tax dollars will keep on coming. Indeed, public employee unions help elect the school boards with whom they negotiate. Factor in timid general counsels and conflict-averse communities, and it all adds up to district negotiators who have too often rolled over.

(continued)

Lawmakers in Indiana and Wisconsin offered district leaders a clean slate. Suddenly, school boards and superintendents were freed from decades of concessions. They were told they were no longer allowed to bargain away their operating authority, making it easy to resist union demands.

It's on the districts, though, to seize those opportunities. Too many have whiffed when given the opportunity. As Tennessee state superintendent Kevin Huffman observes, even after Tennessee reduced the scope of collective bargaining, "Honestly, districts didn't know what to do differently." As noted in chapter 4, Indiana superintendents who had previously complained they needed more flexibility signed CBAs retaining restrictive provisions, even after the legislature made them illegal.

Meanwhile, a few Wisconsin districts took advantage of the opportunity to narrow the scope of collective bargaining—and benefited handsomely. Wisconsin allowed districts to competitively bid on health insurance, and required employees to contribute to health and pension plans. Wisconsin's Legislative Fiscal Bureau estimated the pension provision alone would save schools $600 million over its first two years, and that competitive health bidding was saving $220 per student per year in 2012. The forty-seven-hundred-student New Berlin district reduced health-care costs by $2.3 million, retirement costs by over $1 million, and other liabilities by $15 million, then used the savings to hire new staff and add programs. Other Wisconsin districts, like Milwaukee, Kenosha, and Janesville, had rushed to extend their old agreements prior to the reforms. In 2012, squeezed by the commitments they had locked in, the three districts accounted for 40 percent of Wisconsin's teacher firings, though they educate only 13 percent of the state's students. Unable to save on benefits, these districts had to slash positions even as they demanded more funds.[2]

When you get a do-over, be sure to proceed as a professional gambler, and not as a tough guy. William Hughes, former superintendent in Greendale, Wisconsin, cautions, "Don't turn the flamethrower on. One group of Wisconsin districts was looking at firing or pushing out union leaders when they got the chance. The law created a gray period where you could use administrative review, with no more arbitration." That kind of retribution sows bitterness and calls motives into question. You're leading a public enterprise. Take a deep breath and remember your Sun Tzu.

effort killed him. Johnny Cash memorialized the tale in "The Legend of John Henry's Hammer," singing: "If you bring that steam drill 'round, I'll beat it fair and honest, I'll die with my hammer in my hand."

Leaders need to look to John Henry as a cautionary tale—not a role model. Something that strikes me again and again when talking to school and system leaders is the degree to which they've internalized the notion that leaders demonstrate their commitment by the number of hours they work and the number of meetings they take. If you kill yourself hammering through that mountain, you're not much good to anyone.

Cage-busters believe leaders should work hard and lead by example. But way too many K–12 leaders work ridiculous hours, slogging through breaks and weekends. That's self-defeating. Transformative leadership entails setting a vision, seeing clearly, asking questions, managing relationships, clearing obstacles, ensuring accountability, and creating a culture. This requires energy and engagement; it suffers when leaders are scattered adrenaline junkies or exhausted husks. A few tips for striking a healthy balance:

Remember that your time has value: It's crazy for cage-busters to stop thinking "more, better" and then to treat their own time as disposable. Yet too many leaders allow their schedules to be stuffed with a hodgepodge of meetings, handholding sessions, and ceremonial obligations. This burns them out and leaves little time to learn, read, reflect, or strategize. I'll lay money that almost any leader can slim down the hours they work without sacrificing anything of import. If you're not sure what can go, get in the habit of asking, "Is this the best use of my time?" (See "Do the 10 Percent, Not the 90 Percent.")

Cage-bust your calendar: Can't figure out where to save time? Bring your cage-buster's sensibility to bear. If you're a principal and can't find enough time for observations or coaching new teachers, the problem isn't lack of time—it's how you're *using* your time. How much time do you spend refereeing spats someone else can resolve? How much dotting *i*'s on evaluation paperwork that a careful deputy or employee relations staffer could handle?

Delegate, delegate, delegate: If you've got staff you trust, you need to hand off decisions and responsibilities. And if you don't have staff you trust,

Do the 10 Percent, Not the 90 Percent

A great tip for prioritizing comes from Michael Halberstam's 1970s best-seller, *The Wanting of Levine*.[3] A.L. Levine is a rich, chubby political operative and retired real estate developer who accidentally winds up running for president. Early on, he spends a long night planning his primary schedule with his campaign manager, Philip Bell, and high-level staff. After hours of painstaking labor, Levine turns with satisfaction to Bell:

LEVINE: We got a lot done.

BELL (*half-heartedly*): I suppose so.

LEVINE: How do you mean, "suppose"?

BELL: I guess I think your time is too important to be used working out scheduling and all that crap.

LEVINE: Look, I know scheduling.

BELL: I know that. You were scheduling when I was in law school. It's different now. You're not a technician, you're the candidate.

LEVINE: And so I'm supposed to give up everything I know, become some kind of puppet? No thanks, mister. I know something, I'm going to use it.

BELL: Sure, sure, but don't use it the way you did tonight. Stay away from the fine print. Let them sweat over the schedule. They bring it to you, you check it out, add, subtract, change it around. Let's face it, ninety percent of it is mechanical: how many days you can spend in one part of the country, how to connect with the big local events, what the fuel allotment is going to be. Have them work out the ninety percent, you save yourself for the other ten.

LEVINE: You make sense. I was foolish.

BELL (*smiling*): No, you weren't. It's just that you've never run for president before.

This is critical advice for any leader taking on a new role. It's easy to slip into familiar 90 percent routines and not focus on the 10 percent. Enthusiastic turnaround directors can find themselves spending hours each week working as one more coach aiding struggling teachers, instead of tackling their 10 percent.

Leaders must focus on the 10 percent—because they're the only ones in the organization empowered to do so. If the leader doesn't bust the cage, provide vision, challenge familiar assumptions, or embrace accountability, no one else has the authority to do it. There are a lot of people charged with tackling the 90 percent. The 90 percent is a vast sea, and cage-dwellers can pointlessly exhaust themselves trying to help bail it out with one more bucket.

you're not going to get real far anyway. Leaders who try to do it all by their lonesome are in for a long stretch of boulder rolling. If you're using your *whole* team wisely—not just instructional staff—there's a wealth of important work that others ought to be handling.

It's a marathon, not a sprint: Remember the cage-busting credo and work smarter, not harder. No matter how noble John Henry's effort, he wasn't there the next day. Success built on an insane schedule and personal charm will prove fleeting. Educational leadership isn't a mad dash, it's a marathon.

DON'T BE CONSUMED BY ROLLING THE BOULDER

However many hours they work, it's easy for school, state, or system leaders to spend 70 or 80 percent of their time rolling the boulder. It's a natural phenomenon. You take a leadership job full of hope and big-picture vision, and then are suddenly swamped wooing community players, stamping out fires, answering e-mails, dealing with irate parents, or running from meeting to meeting. Before you know it, you're working long days, every day, just to keep things from blowing up. The result: a loss of focus, a tendency to fall back on "more, better" strategies, and a lack of time or energy for precise, creative, empathetic problem-solving.

As former San Diego superintendent and California secretary of education Alan Bersin says, "Leadership requires imagining a future state, thinking through the steps to get there, and then executing on those. The challenge is that events rarely play out entirely as imagined. Kicking off change, then, is like playing chess. The trick is that strategic thinking is given short shrift in education. Instead, new leaders let themselves get bogged down in day-to-day decisions."[4] There are tactics that can help you avoid just rolling the boulder:

Challenge Your Assumptions. It's incredibly easy for any leader to develop tunnel vision. In fact, I'd say this is the norm, especially for passionate, hard-charging leaders eager to make a difference. Yet, cage-busting demands beginner's mind, seeing clearly, asking questions, and exploring possibilities. This requires reaching out to people who may not agree with your assumptions or expectations. It requires cultivating trusted friends who may disagree about strategy or tactics. It requires being open to bad news and fair-minded criticism, and reaching out to those who will deliver it. It's easy for leaders, their staff, their hired consultants, and well-wishers to tune out the "noise"; the successful cage-buster does everything possible to combat that temptation.

Manage Up. Take care to manage your boss, or bosses, sensibly and strategically. Harvard professor and former superintendent Tom Payzant says superintendents need to actively manage the relationship with their board:

> Get clarity with the board about roles right up-front, because there are a number of boards out there that just expect the superintendent to be spending all of his or her time with them. You've got to put your stake in the ground early. There are superintendents that every Friday, for example, that's their "call day"—to call each of their board members and spend anywhere from a half an hour to an hour on the phone with them. You can lose a whole day doing that. That doesn't mean you don't connect with your board members, but you meet with the board chair and maybe the vice chair. In San Diego, when I was there, we had board meetings every week. In the first few weeks, I had one-on-ones with the board as the new superintendent. Then I would always take and return their calls, but they did not get into the habit of expecting they were going to regularly have an hour of my time.

The lesson holds equally for principals and grade-level leaders; be sure to work with your boss(es), but in a manner that respects both their responsibilities and your time.

Find a Trusted Partner. Find a colleague, collaborator, or consigliere who can anticipate challenges, identify opportunities, and help you think about smarter and better ways to solve problems. You need someone you trust to challenge you, cultivate your beginner's mind, and battle the habits of "sucks less" thinking. Such an ally can help combat the tendency to let day-to-day demands narrow your vision.

Make Policy Work for You. A cage-buster sees policy not as an alternative to culture building, but as a way to police performance, minimize personal friction, and redirect time and energy toward what matters most. Cage-busters create smart policies and processes so that they don't get stuck in countless meetings every time someone has a neat idea or wants to expand a popular program. For instance, insisting that all proposals itemize costs and document anticipated benefits, and then having accounting score these projections before anything moves forward, can deter half-baked proposals and clarify expectations. This can save time, energy, and political capital.

Stack the Deck for a Common Culture. The big advantage of organizations that agree on aims, mission, and norms is that they minimize distractions. School choice, for instance, makes it easier for educators and families to select schools aligned to their values and notions of good schooling. Creating "houses" or academies within a high school can serve a similar role. These all offer the chance to create coherent cultures where leaders can spend more time leading for achievement and less time pleading for agreement.

YOU CAN'T DO IT ALONE

Finding the talent and support to drive improvement is a crucial part of the cage-buster's job. The plain truth is that few schools or systems have the tools or the muscle to succeed all by themselves. You need to seek out and cultivate allies and partners. In this work, national networks, the local business community, and philanthropy can all play invaluable roles.

Tap Your Network. Aggressively work your external networks. When Lillian Lowery took the helm of the Delaware Department of Education, she sought talent from all over the country: "I was a Broad Academy affiliate, and one of the first calls I made was to the Broad Foundation. They helped me select people who could help with the work and challenges here. [Delaware's] Rodel Foundation also knew people from all over the country, in nonprofit and entrepreneurial environments." In a model worth exploring, Washington, DC, has created a competitive summer internship program that brings dozens of graduate students to the district, giving leaders a chance to check them out and creating a deep bench of talent.

Look to Community Resources. Find ways to connect with resources in your community, whether those are attorneys in local law firms or professionals willing to mentor and tutor kids. Veteran HR executive Ranjit Nair, who has worked with school systems on personnel issues, says, "Superintendents who are genuinely willing to embed selected, qualified business leaders in their systems can benefit immensely. One-off meetings with them every three months aren't going to cut it. You're not going to move the dial if these people aren't embedded in the process. They have to be there in heart and soul and dedicated to helping with sleeves rolled up." Another type of support is the kind available from Citizen Schools, mentioned in chapter 6, which uses adult volunteers to deliver extended learning time to middle school students. Citizen Schools offers apprenticeship and academic support programs for three hours in the afternoon, four days a week in schools in more than a dozen cities by engaging forty-two hundred volunteers.[5]

Engage Nimble Partners. In Nashville, Tennessee, the business community helped secure the district's top candidate for associate superintendent. "We brought Jay Steele in for a speech on his work with [small learning communities]," says Ralph Schultz, president of the Nashville Chamber of Commerce. "[Superintendent] Jesse Register stands up and says, 'I'm convinced of the idea, and that's our guy. How are we going to get him?'" One of the local CEOs in attendance offered to lend the use of this private plane. Schultz recalls, "So a delegation got in the plane a couple of weeks later, flew down [to Florida], and met with Steele. And he saw the commitment of the business community, and thought Nashville was the place to be." Nashville mayor Karl Dean notes the value of that kind of support. "You know how complicated it is for government workers to get plane tickets," Mayor Dean says. "Business can say, 'Let's get in the plane and go down there.'" When they so desire, business and philanthropy can move with an alacrity that public systems cannot.

Embrace the Unique Capabilities of Outsiders. In Austin, Texas, business support proved crucial when it came to a community-wide effort to boost college enrollment. "Your mama's always going to tell you you're pretty, and your counselor's always going to tell you that you should go to college," says Roy Larson, a college enrollment manager at Manor Independent School District outside Austin, but "when business is saying it, it makes it the community's voice, not just the school's." By 2010, the Austin Chamber of Commerce was helping to host thirty-three "Financial Aid Saturdays" in fifteen local districts. Program staff called all graduating seniors, and ensured that notices were sent home in every senior's report card. The campaign ran in English and Spanish, featured more than 1,300 radio spots, nearly 3,000 public service announcements on cable, more than 17,000 ads in five cinemas, and a twelve-page insert in *The Statesman*, Austin's major newspaper. Austin superintendent Meria Carstarphen says, "The Chamber has put community muscle to [work] to help students and families navigate the red tape."[6]

Leverage Outside Political Muscle. In Nashville, associate superintendent Jay Steele says that local businesses are "organizing their lobbyists around things we have asked. They can get a lot of things done . . . that I can't." The Nashville Chamber of Commerce established a political action committee (PAC) to endorse reform-minded candidates for the school board. Marc Hill, the Chamber's chief education officer, notes that "none of the other nonprofits get involved in politics."[7] In a given four-year cycle, the Chamber donated more than $25,000 to each of its chosen candidates. That may not sound like a lot, but a 2011 national study found that three-quarters of board members spent less than $1,000 on their most recent campaign.[8] As of 2011, seven of the nine board members had been endorsed by the Chamber's PAC. Advocacy groups and the business community can provide the support and muscle needed to drive transformation.

Tap Philanthropy for Crucial Funds . . . and Enthusiasm. Don McAdams, founder of the Center for Reform of School Systems, says that philanthropy typically involves modest dollars but can have an outsized influence because of its agility and public impact. Since most districts spend 80 percent or more of all funds on salaries and benefits, they've little ability to repurpose funds. This is where philanthropy can provide crucial fuel. McAdams and Lynn Jenkins have written, "Philanthropic dollars are especially valuable because they can be invested in activities that have no political constituency but are high priorities for reform leaders."[9] Philanthropy can also build local enthusiasm, inspire other funders, and garner national interest—attracting additional talent and support, and getting that flywheel spinning.

Marshal Legal Resources. Another place philanthropy and community allies can offer crucial support is by connecting attorneys and law students with schools and districts in need of assistance. When Michelle Rhee was chancellor in DC, she'd invariably tell me about meeting local attorneys or visiting some DC law firm, where attorneys would enthusiastically ask, "What can we do to help?" She didn't have a good answer to give them. There's huge potential value in networks that can connect supportive pro bono attorneys with interested districts, recruit young lawyers to work in districts, or find ways to tap the research capabilities of law students.

EIGHT CAGE-BUSTING TIPS TO REMEMBER

I've thrown a lot of stuff at you, I know. For convenience's sake, let's take a moment to review a few practical tips that are especially helpful to keep in mind. (For a bit more of that, check out appendix D.)

Don't just punch the feather bed: Changing cultures without addressing the underlying policies and rules doesn't yield lasting change. As President Franklin Roosevelt once said of the US Navy, "To change anything in the Na-a-vy is like punching a feather bed. You punch it with your right and you punch it with your left until you are finally exhausted, and then you find the damn bed just as it was before you started punching."[10] Trying to do instructional leadership alone often amounts to an energetic bout of feather bed punching.

Act as if ye have faith: In the 1982 movie *The Verdict,* Paul Newman's drunken attorney Frank Galvin offered a bit of wisdom that really ought to be Biblical: "Act as if ye have faith, and faith shall be given to you." That's terrific advice. Take a few bold but smart initial steps, show some success, and then take larger and longer steps. Don't jump off the cliff on your first day, but don't move so hesitantly that you're asking permission every time you move.

Measure progress right: Would-be cage-busters often do a poor job of measuring or justifying progress. Cage-busters spend a lot of time and energy addressing things that are important and measurable but unlikely to show up in short-term reading and math scores. This makes it a mistake when they report their progress almost entirely in terms of test scores, understating key accomplishments and diminishing real victories. Things like fixing special education assignment, shuttering underutilized schools, overhauling broken textbook distribution, improving teacher hiring, or creating a top-shelf, performance-based evaluation system are important, and they equip educators and students to succeed. Such wins won't make kids learn more today, but they sure put them in a position to learn more tomorrow.

Carry a pocket constitution: You know how some politicians always carry a pocket-sized copy of the Declaration of Independence and the US Constitution in their jacket pocket? Well, take a page from the Cami Anderson, Kaya Henderson, and Adrian Manuel playbook, and do just that with your CBA and board policies. If your copy of the CBA isn't dog-eared, you're not fully prepared to lead. Period.

Know that "innovation" is a four-letter word: Most "innovations" are overhyped miracle cures or new wrinkles on familiar practices, dressed up with fancy jargon. Cage-busters don't do "innovation." They solve problems. This yields innovation when talent, tools, time, and money are used in smarter ways—but the focus is on problem solving and not innovation. If the problem is a need for high-quality tutoring, cage-busting leaders explore how to do that—via virtual instruction, community volunteers, computer-assisted instruction, and the like. When you use digital tools, it'll probably be called "innovative." When you just use local tutors, it generally won't be. But all a cage-buster cares about is which approach is cheapest, fastest, most effective, most feasible, and, ultimately, best for kids—not about labels.

Don't imagine that best practices alone will get it done: Much of what passes as today's "reform" rests on the premise that improving schools and systems is primarily a technical matter of learning "what works" and transferring it to new schools. Yet, these well-intentioned efforts have consistently disappointed, with the results inevitably chalked up to flawed implementation or a lack of buy-in. The problem is that they amount to a series of boulder-rolling techniques, which is all well and good—except that they ignore that inconvenient mountain. Transformative improvement requires flattening the mountain.

Remember that money is only the easiest way to solve a problem: Money is the lazy man's way to procure time or talent. Ultimately, it's just a shortcut for those who can't marshal the skill or will to free up talent, time, and dollars in other ways.

Use incentives to complement cultural change: Rewards and recognition can help changes get going downhill. For instance, it can be tough to reduce teacher absences. Few principals actually know how many absences their teachers rack up a year or how much those cost, and even fewer are held accountable for such things. This is true, even though teacher absences hurt learning and even though many systems spend perhaps $1,000 per teacher on subs each year. Incentives can complement more personal efforts to change norms. The first step is ensuring that principals know how their school stacks up. The second is working with principals and teachers to clarify expectations. The third is recognizing and rewarding schools and teachers that are serving kids and saving money. How? Perhaps pay a share of unused sub funds out to faculty, or publicly report school-by-school breakouts of faculty absentee rates. There's no "right" solution; there are various approaches that might work for you. And the specific solution matters less than the fact that you're getting unstuck. Aligning rewards and recognition with culture is how you get going downhill.

PICK A GOOD FIT

Cage-busters will fail where they have no support and no way to build it. After all, every battle is won before it's fought. Three keys to keep in mind on this count. First, know the circumstances that will allow you to be effective. Second, you're always in your strongest position before you take a job, so know what to ask for before you say yes. Third, take care not to get so intrigued by a new role that you fail to make sure the situation is workable.

There's often a destructive dance in which boards offer platitudes and promises and would-be leaders say what they think the interviewers want to hear. Shawn McCollough, who's served as superintendent in Nogales, Arizona, and Greene County, Georgia, says,

> One of the big problems is being able to evaluate whether a board is telling you what they want you to hear. All boards say the same things. They say, "We want change." They say, "We want to improve." The real issue is if that's what they really want. If they are just saying they want change, and you go in trying to create the change, you won't last very long. Meanwhile, superintendents are often so desperate to get a job that they'll say whatever it takes to make the board happy, thinking they'll later be able to maneuver. In reality, they get broken and bend to the school board or get run out of town.

McCollough recalls turning down a job because it wasn't the right match:

> You have to be honest with the school board. I walked out of an interview in Phoenix a couple years ago where the school board said very clearly, "We're going to need you to work with our people." I mean, what does that mean? That means, "You're not going to be able to fire any of our people; you're going to have to work with who we've got." I pushed back from the table and I said, "Look folks, I don't need to waste your time. You might have other people that are a good fit for this, but I'm going to leave now

because there is no way this is going to be a good working relationship." But most superintendents are unwilling to do that.

You may disagree with McCollough on the particulars here. That's fine. But his clarity about what he needs to succeed is something every cage-buster should emulate.

Think this advice just applies to superintendents? Hardly. Almost any principal, assistant principal, or system official has likely experienced a version of this same ambiguous dance. As always, precision is your friend. Before you accept a job, while you still have leverage, get crystal clear on what's expected of you, and what you can expect.

Former Charlotte-Mecklenburg superintendent Peter Gorman recalls, "I interviewed [my board] as much as they interviewed me. I walked into a situation where the board had just adopted core beliefs and commitments and a theory of action, and it was fine. Then, anytime I went and did something, I connected it back to that. If they got angry or upset, I said, 'Look, I'm doing exactly what you said wanted to be done.' And sometimes it gave me a bully pulpit and sometimes it gave me kind of that entrée to do things that would have been more difficult."

Harvard's Tom Payzant muses, "You know, your best day on the job is your first day on the job. As I coach first-time urban superintendents, the most critical variable is the extent to which the board-superintendent relationship does or does not work. Getting results is a question of having a good match between a board and a superintendent. You won't have all of the information you need, but you've got to do as much due diligence as possible, to get some indication of what the board is like, what the history has been, and why the superintendent that preceded you left." Aspiring school leaders and system staffers need to ask exactly these same kinds of questions.

Ivy Prep Academy founder Nina Gilbert advises potential charter school leaders, in particular, "Research your territory very carefully. Make sure that you're not going into a community where the [charter school] authorizer is hostile. If you're going to have a hostile authorizer, make sure you have political allies to help wage war against them—because this is totally David and Goliath . . . As a charter school leader, every day is like a house of cards. If anything goes wrong, at any moment, it all falls down. So go in fully prepared."

Honesty, self-awareness, information, preparation. These are the watchwords that can help ensure a good fit.

TAKE YOUR TALENTS TO SOUTH BEACH?

Basketball superstar LeBron James announced in a summer 2010 ESPN special modestly titled *The Decision*, "I'm taking my talents to South Beach." With that, he departed the Cleveland Cavaliers for the Miami Heat, to team up with fellow all-stars Dwayne Wade and Chris Bosh. While James's TV announcement may have been tone-deaf, his instincts were plenty sensible. If you're in a setting where you don't think you can make the best use of your talents, it may be time to look for *your* South Beach.

Shawn McCollough explains: "I have left a couple of places because I've realized I can't further develop this board. We can't get the right people on this board to make the right changes, so I've had to bow out. Sometimes selfless leadership is giving way for someone who may have a better chance of moving the district. Maybe you are not the answer." Whereas we usually hear that educators have an obligation to stay put, McCollough suggests that maybe it's *selfish* to stay "when you know you can't move the system."

Heather Zavadsky, author of *Bringing School Reform to Scale*, echoes McCollough's advice: "At the point where you know what needs to happen and you know what's good for kids, but you're not able to do that because you do not have the support of the board, it's time to go elsewhere."

A willingness to look elsewhere if your best efforts are unwelcome can keep you from getting stuck. Vince Bertram, former Evansville superintendent and current CEO of Project Lead the Way, says, "Some superintendents say, 'You know I can't push on that because I'll lose my job.' I've always taken the approach that, if I lose my job for doing what's right, I'll find another one."

At this point, you may be thinking, "Well, that's easy for them to say. For me, there's no way I can walk away from my students or community." Fair enough. These are choices you have to make. If you're so committed to a school or community that it's worth staying in place, even if it means your best efforts are frustrated, that's fair—just make sure that you're doing the best for yourself and the kids, and not rationalizing inertia.

LOOK BEYOND THE SCHOOLHOUSE

Few of today's school and system leaders are prepared to make hard choices about personnel, budgets, and programs. They've been socialized, trained, and prepared in a bubble that has insulated them from how most of the world thinks about the challenges of leadership.

For instance, management icon Jack Welch encourages leaders to routinely identify and remove mediocre performers. Indeed, while CEO at General Electric, Welch worked to trim the weakest tenth of his employees every year, explaining, "Making these judgments is not easy . . . but . . . this is how great organizations are built. Year after year, differentiation raises the bar higher and higher."[11] Jim Collins argued in his best-selling *Built to Last* that visionary companies "are not exactly comfortable places . . . visionary companies thrive on discontent. They understand that contentment leads to complacency, which inevitably leads to decline."[12]

Welch and Collins sound remarkably different from the thinkers typically read by aspiring K–12 leaders. Their more sharp-edged stance clashes with the gentler take of the champions of instructional leadership. Now, I'm not arguing that Welch and Collins are obviously right, and it's certainly possible to reconcile their views with those more familiar in schooling. The point of looking outside is not to find some new orthodoxy or silver bullet, but to see that leadership is an imperfect art that draws on a range of skills, benefits from considering diverse views, and can be practiced successfully in different ways.

Leaders ought to take pains to broaden the spectrum of ideas they're encountering, and to insist that instruction and professional development help do so. Below are a few suggestions.

Explore thinking from the contemporary management canon, such as *Good to Great*, by Jim Collins; *The Innovator's Dilemma*, by Clay Christensen; *Working with Emotional Intelligence*, by Daniel Goleman; and *In-*

novation and Entrepreneurship, by Peter Drucker.[13] The goal isn't to find new silver bullets, but to explore how other ways of seeing and thinking might help identify problems and suggest smart solutions. Rice University's Educational Entrepreneurship Program (REEP), for instance, prepares educators to be school leaders, but does so within the "professional" MBA track at its elite business school. This offers exposure to a broad swath of thinking on leadership and management. Bill Glick, dean of Rice's Jones School of Management, notes, "We don't train technicians—we train leaders. We don't know anything about engineering, drilling, or how to save patients. But we do know a lot about management, leadership, and entrepreneurship."

Professional training should address subjects like compensation, staffing, and budgeting—not with the customary emphasis on compliance—but with an eye to cage-busting. Leaders ought to learn how to wield the law as a tool of reform and to work with tough-minded employment litigators and operational pros who can help them think differently about personnel management, information technology, data management, or HR.

School and system leaders should seek advisers and team members who can infuse their efforts with thinking and experience from outside of K–12, especially when it comes to crucial functions like hiring, personnel evaluation, information technology, budgeting, operations, and legal support.

Meanwhile, schools, systems, and preparation programs should cultivate internships and exchanges that can introduce leaders to dynamic management outside of K–12. This might entail partnering with the military, four-week paid externships at local tech firms, or mentoring programs. The point is not for leaders to stumble upon new best practices, but to ask hard questions, consider bold new solutions, and emerge less willing to take K–12 conventions for granted.

FROM PG TO R

My friend Matt Candler, founder of 4.0 Schools, has a nice riff he uses when talking to aspiring leaders. It's a take-off on Vince Vaughn's "be R-rated" monologue in *Swingers*. You don't remember it? Well, come to think of it, it's the perfect note for us to close on.

If you've seen the film, you'll remember Trent (played by Vaughn) as *Swingers'* self-assured ladies man, constantly bucking up his self-doubting pal Mike. In a memorable scene, Trent tells Mike to go approach a girl. But, cautions Trent, "I don't want you to be the guy in the PG-13 movie everyone's *really* hoping makes it happen. I want you to be like the guy in the rated-R movie, you know, the guy you're not sure whether or not you like yet. You're not sure where he's coming from. Okay? You're a bad man. You're a bad man, Mikey. You're a bad, bad man."[14]

At the end of day, Candler tells aspiring leaders that they need to decide whether they're really, truly serious about great teaching and learning. Because, if so, they won't be content to roll the boulder. They won't settle for being cuddly, PG-13 naifs, full of good intentions. Instead, they're going to be bad, bad leaders. Bad, bad leaders who are deadly serious about doing what needs to be done for their kids.

Cage-busting leaders are ready to be R-rated. They're poker players—not tough guys—but they know this is tough work. They're not worried about whether everyone is going to like them. They avoid unnecessary fights, remember that every battle is won *before* it's fought, and constantly seek the smartest way to solve a problem—and they're in this for keeps.

The reward? The chance to create schools and systems equal to your aspirations; to spend time and energy supporting great teaching and learning, not complaining about rules and pleading for permission to act. To create schools and systems that can unlock the talents of teachers, leaders, and students, and start to realize the new possibilities of twenty-first-century schooling. To forge cultures among passionate colleagues united by common purpose. To coach, mentor, and support educators eager to benefit from your guidance. Cage-busters believe that's a deal worth taking.

APPENDIX A

Cage-Busting for Beginners

CHAPTER 1: IT DOESN'T HAVE TO BE THIS HARD

The mountain is the accumulated rules and regulations, policies and practices, contracts, and cultures that exhaust educators and leaders. The mountain means that leaders are constantly sweating their way uphill, spending most their time asking permission or battling to change old routines. This leaves them little time or energy to tackle the things that matter most. Cage-busters don't do these things *instead* of mentoring, coaching, and inspiring, but so that they can do these things *better*.

Caged Leadership

Rather than think about school and district leaders pushing that boulder up a mountain, think of them living in a cage that restricts what they can do and how they can do it. *Cage-dwellers* spend most of their energy trying to stamp out fires, woo recalcitrant staff, or beg for resources. *Cage-busters*, on the other hand, wake up every morning putting their heart and soul into identifying big challenges, dreaming up solutions, and blasting their way forward.

Cage-Busting Is Not About Picking Fights

Cage-busting is not about picking fights, attacking unions, or firing people, and it does not give license to wantonly alienate educators or community members. It is nothing more (or less) than thinking ambitiously about how to create great schools and then doing what is necessary to make those ambitions real.

How Experts Have Encouraged Caged Leadership

Most ed leadership authorities devote the whole of their attention to culture, coaching, and collaboration, while implicitly (or explicitly) dismissing challenges like contracts and policy. But cage-busters know there are *two halves* to the leadership equation: one that makes it possible to lead, and one that involves the ins and outs of leading. Cage-busting is not a program or pedagogy. It's a mind-set. It's not a substitute for coaching, instructional rounds, mentoring, culture-building, or instructional leadership—it makes it possible to do these things better.

How We Got Here

Progressive reformers worked hard to import the best practices of private industry to American education. Since that era, though, K–12's rhythms have been preserved as if in amber. Today, few school or system leaders have much experience outside the confines of K–12. Leaders typically start as teachers and receive all of their leadership training in schools of education. This means that most leaders have little opportunity to see how budgeting, accountability, personnel evaluation, or compensation are tackled in other sectors.

Is Cage-Busting Just for Martyrs?

Even when they're successful, cage-busting principals, superintendents, school board members, teacher leaders, and state chiefs can encounter brutal blowback. But cage-busters can boost the odds they'll be more than martyrs by taking full advantage of existing laws and regulations, tapping all their resources, reducing friction, framing the public debate, mobilizing allies, and fortifying their political positions.

CHAPTER 2: SEEING DIFFERENTLY

Cage-busting requires seeing the world in fresh ways and setting aside shopworn assumptions. This is critical because, when we listen to convention, we hear a lot about what educational leaders *can't* do.

Excuses Found in the "Culture of Can't"

- *The collective bargaining agreement:* But, as Price, Hess and Loup, and Ballou have noted, many contracts are much more flexible than widely believed.[1]
- *State and federal regulations:* But when given the opportunity, few leaders take advantage of waivers or exemptions from these regulations.
- *Lack of money:* Yet districts rarely prune staff or programs, even when a new product or service might enable nine employees to accomplish what once took ten. Managing this way means that reform proceeds only as fast as new resources are layered atop the old.

Four Traps That Ensnare Leaders

- *The platitudes trap:* Vapid generalities and pleasant-sounding banalities can obscure the cage and allow leaders to duck the tough decisions about how to use limited talent, tools, and resources in smarter, better ways.
- *The "sucks less" trap:* Cage-busters resist the temptation to define excellence solely in terms of increasing reading and math scores and graduation rates. They ask what excellence looks like, and don't settle for doing well by today's minimalist yardsticks.
- *The "more, better" trap:* Perhaps the signature mark of cage-dwelling leadership is the belief that improvement is only possible with additional dollars. All too often, extra dollars inspire false confidence and allow schools or systems to avoid seeking a new path.
- *The MacGyver trap:* Like MacGyver, today's successful leaders tend to use an ingenious bag of tricks to circumvent the cage. That's good as far as it goes, but it understates the value of addressing the cage and frequently fails to pioneer system-wide solutions.

Ways to Avoid the Traps

- *Bring a beginner's mind:* Approach subjects with curiosity and a lack of preconceptions, even when you think you already know it all.
- *Get help from outsiders:* Veteran educators can tap fresh perspectives by seeking advisers, mentors, or team members from outside the confines of K–12. Those from outside may find it easier to recognize

when the emperor has no clothes and to challenge orthodoxy by asking, "Why do we do it this way?"

- *Get going downhill:* A useful rule of thumb is that, in any organization,
  20 percent of the employees are responsible for 80 percent of the work.
  An equally useful rule is that leaders typically spend 80 percent of
  their time monitoring, mentoring, and dealing with the least effective
  20 percent of their team. Cage-busters craft policies and routines that
  reduce the time they have to spend addressing mediocrity and support
  the kind of culture they aspire to see.

Cage-busting doesn't tell leaders *what they should do*, but begins by
helping them see with fresh eyes so that they *can determine what they
need to do.*

CHAPTER 3: WHAT'S YOUR PROBLEM?

Cage-busting leadership requires clarity and honesty. Ask yourself: What
is *your* vision of a terrific school or system? *That's* the school or system you
want to lead.

Getting from Here to There

- *Own your beliefs:* What are you trying to do? What are your goals?
  What do you think a great school or system looks like? Answers like
  "Raise test scores" or "Make AYP" are bad answers. That's because
  they're secondhand goals, defined for you by policymakers and test
  developers. A good answer identifies the destination and lights a path
  forward.
- *Precision is your friend:* A cage-buster can't settle for ambiguity, banalities, or imprecision. These things provide dark corners where excuse
  making can hide. Thus, cage-busters strive to see things clearly and
  discuss them precisely.
- *Calling problems by their given name:* There's great value in setting
  concrete, granular goals for students, teachers, schools, programs, offices, or systems. Once you've set targets, gauge where you are. If you'd
  like to be at 50 percent of students mastering a second language and

you're currently at 40 percent, that's a *problem*. And this is great! It helps generate clear, concrete goals and flag precise solutions.

- *The "Curly rule"*: The value of identifying all of these problems and possibilities is *not* because you necessarily need to address them all right now. Cage-busting doesn't tell you what your priorities are supposed to be. It's about helping you figure out how to do better at those things *you* deem important.
- *Think talent, tools, time, and money*: Cage-busters focus not on "more, better" education but on finding ways to improve teaching and schooling. And this is largely a question of finding smarter ways to employ *talent*, *tools*, *time*, and *money*.
- *It's not reform if it costs more*: It's not reform if it costs more. *Reform* is finding ways to improve teaching, learning, and schooling with the resources you've got.
- *Use data like a problem solver*: Cage-busters need to be sure they're collecting data with an eye to solving problems. A simple mantra is to *always be sure that you're not working for your metrics and measurements, but that they're working for you.*
- *The power of creative problem-solving*: You don't have to solve every problem head-on. That can be exhausting. Tackling what you can with shortcuts or creative solutions can make it easier to isolate and focus on the real impediments.

Always Ask, "What Problem Are You Solving?"

Cage-busters try to begin every conversation by talking about the problems they've identified and how they might solve them. Ultimately, six questions should guide every action you take:

1. Is X *important*?
2. If so, how well *should* we be doing when it comes to X?
3. How well *are* we doing with X?
4. If we're not doing as well as we should, how can we *improve* X?
5. What's *stopping* us from improving X?
6. And, finally: How do we *remove, blast through, or tunnel under the bars* stopping us from improving X?

CHAPTER 4: SEEING THROUGH THE SHADOWS

Is That Bar Really There?

Whether dealing with contracts or policy, cage-busters need to aggressively gauge the bars that stand in their way. There are certainly plenty of *solid bars* out there. But other bars are *illusory and self-imposed*. Distinguishing the things you can do from those you can't also makes it easier to tell allies and supporters how they can help.

Making Sense of Policy

- *Policy deals with the floor, not the ceiling:* Policy makers don't gear policies to the needs or strengths of all-stars; rather, they work with an eye to what bad actors might do wrong. Except in the rarest of cases, policy is not a tool for promoting excellence.
- *Policy can make you do things, but it can't make you do them well:* Policy makers can require schools or systems to comply with punch lists, but they can't require them to do these things *well*. The trouble is that most of what we care about when it comes to teaching and learning is about *how* you do things, rather than *whether* you do them.
- *Policy makers possess a limited toolbox:* Policy makers really only have three crude tools at their disposal. They can *give away money* for particular purposes, tell you *what you must do*, and tell you *what you can't do*. Yet, with just these three blunt instruments, they are under immense pressure to make the world a better place.
- *The difference between* big P *and* little p *policy:* Big P policies are formal statutes and contractual provisions that present stubborn and hard-to-change barriers. *Little p* policies, on the other hand, are local policies, accepted practices, or district conventions that can be more readily altered.

Making Sense of Collective Bargaining

- Before venturing near the bargaining table, cage-busters understand what they're obliged and *not* obliged to do. In states with collective bargaining, state statutes almost always spell out three categories of bargaining subjects: mandatory, permissible, and prohibited.

- Case law is the body of judicial opinions that have been issued by your state courts and by federal courts. Arbiters, mediators, and courts ruling on cases that touch on similar issues are typically bound to follow these precedents.

- Understanding the strength of your hand requires distinguishing between mandatory subjects of bargaining and those that may be bargained. In Massachusetts, for instance, local districts are free to establish layoff procedures. However, two-thirds of districts have bargained CBAs that make seniority (not performance) the dominant factor used in determining layoffs.

BE CAREFUL OF WHAT GETS INTO THE CONTRACT

Leaders unnecessarily give away provisions they're not even empowered to. Districts across the land have agreed to CBAs that address things the legislature has made it illegal to collectively bargain. Even when legislators have changed statute to recapture management prerogative, cage-dwelling district leaders have proven only too willing to give away their newfound autonomy. If the law says you can't give the language away, you can just shrug and tell union negotiators, "Sorry, my hands are tied."

The Evergreen Problem

District leaders often agree to certain provisions in the spirit of cooperation, trusting they can later remove the provision if they need to. Unfortunately, it's never that easy. For those district leaders operating under a contract or state statute that contains an "evergreen clause," this way of thinking becomes even more dangerous. Evergreen provisions stipulate that contract terms remain in force until a new contract is put in place, making it nearly impossible to get something out of a CBA if the union wants to keep it. Serious leaders have an *obligation* to start removing the obstacles in their way. Otherwise, they compromise ends and means in order to accommodate those obstacles.

CHAPTER 5: SWINGING THAT LOUISVILLE SLUGGER

Ambiguity Doesn't Mean You Can't

We can readily identify five kinds of situations leaders face. There are those things:

You can already do

You might be able to do

You can do if you're a little creative

You can do if you alter little p *policies*

You can only do if you change big P *policies*

Getting the Law on Your Side

- *Stop getting bullied:* There's a professional inclination for lawyers, *unless you tell them otherwise*, to focus on avoiding unpleasantness. If you want them to help you solve problems, you need to say so.

- *Hire a consigliere:* When things get rough, you need an aggressive, wily, and intrepid consigliere who can help you figure out what's possible. Once you find your consigliere, how do you use them? What do you ask them? There are four key rules to guide you:
  - Always start with "What problem are you solving?"
  - Find a consigliere aligned to your values and priorities.
  - Work closely with your legal team.
  - Prepare to make tough choices.

GET THE RIGHT PEOPLE IN PLACE

- *Rewarding your stars:* Almost any would-be cage-buster can list her "stars": people whose motivation, skill, effort, and performance is unquestioned. If you could only have more people like them, you'd be able to really go places. What can you do to attract more of those folks and try to ensure that they stick around?

- *It's not okay to be bad at your job:* For reasons that are never quite clear, folks in K–12 sometimes have trouble saying, "It's not okay to be bad at your job." Culture, coaching, and inspiration are all terrific things. But there will be staff who don't share your vision, are undermining your efforts to build a coherent culture, or lack critical skills. Cage-busters believe that it's sometimes necessary and healthy to cut people loose.

Seeing the Law as It Is

Cage-dwellers have come to see laws, rules, regulations, and contracts as immutable, inviolate things. That's how we've built the "culture of can't." Cage-busters know better. The law is a tool. Lawyers are allies who can wield it. Cage-busters don't need to be legal experts, they just need to know enough about the law so they can use it to ask the right questions.

CHAPTER 6: EVERYONE KNOWS WHERE THE BOOZE IS

Stretching the School Dollar

- *Think unit cost:* Breaking down costs to per school or per pupil is a useful way to help make sense of spending. Breaking out unit costs can make clear that "cheap" program has an exorbitant per pupil cost, or that an "expensive" data system will actually cost $10 per student per year over its lifespan.
- *Optimizing the familiar things:* One way to get more bang for the buck involves straightforward efforts to improve the operational efficiency of today's schools and districts. This includes taking steps like using buses more efficiently or constructing class schedules in more cost-effective ways.
- *Rethinking schooling:* Another tack is to not merely do the same things better, but to figure how we might use new tools and designs to deliver instruction in profoundly better, smarter, cheaper, faster ways.

You Can *Create* Resources

- *Use time wisely:* More than 80 percent of school spending is on salary and benefits. You're paying these folks for their time. An easy place to start is to ensure that you're making smart use of the time you've bought.
- *Get more time . . . for free:* The rules, regulations, and policies that restrict time are permeable. Take full advantage. For instance, many

districts have the ability to waive policies or CBA provisions for "innovative programs" or turnaround schools.

- *Leverage community resources:* Communities throughout America boast adult populations with a historic wealth of talent, expertise, and energy. There is much that teachers do—whether supervising study hall, coaching debate teams, counseling alienated teens—that others in the community may be able to help with, and may even do as well as the pros.
- *Use people smarter:* If you've got employees with scarce skills, it's ludicrous to do anything except take the fullest possible advantage of their talent.
- *Tap your team's skills:* When schools or districts want to do something new, the impulse is to pay someone to do it. That's classic lazy man's lobster. Another option is to do a better job of surfacing and taking advantage of the talents of those you already employ.

It's Not Just About the Money

- *The truth shall set you free:* Truth-telling makes it possible to get serious about pinpointing challenges, chasing away excuses, and solving problems.
- *Sometimes programs and policies should go away:* If a program or position was funded once, it tends to linger on—even when it has become wasteful or unnecessary. If a program isn't adding value, put those dollars to better use.
- *Change the "wish-mode" mentality:* Leaders have a tendency to ask for things without paying attention to cost effectiveness or what else might be accomplished with those funds. Changing this mind-set depends on changing expectations, accountability, and culture.
- *An ROI mind-set can help drive cultural change:* Focusing on unit costs and performance can help move the school culture. This can change the mind-set from "spend your budget" to "spend your budget in ways that result in improved performance."

Technology as Hamburger Helper

Technology can help solve our problems in better, smarter, faster, cheaper ways. The key is to regard technology as a tool, not an answer.

CHAPTER 7: THE CHICAGO WAY

"Every Battle Is Won Before It Is Ever Fought"

One reason cage-busters work so hard to clarify aims, take advantage of what they are already permitted to do, isolate barriers, and draw on a talented team is precisely so that they can find a path forward without relying on brutal public combat. This doesn't mean cage-busters can avoid fights, and they certainly don't duck necessary ones. But they do everything possible to shape and stack the deck before they have to fight.

Think Like a Poker Player, Not a Tough Guy

Cage-busters work extra hard to stack the odds so that, when it is time to fight, *they expect to win even the hard fights.* There are seven keys to doing this well:

- *Prepare the community:* Being precise about the problem and your solution can make it easier to educate the public.
- *Leverage external support:* When you're pursuing difficult changes, outside partners can free you to tell skeptical employees or community members, "Hey, I understand the concerns, but we're only getting this money/leeway/support if we do X."
- *Seek opportunities to split your opponents:* Rather than denouncing or attacking your opposition en masse, find opportunities to woo some and assuage others.
- *Learn from Bre'r Rabbit:* It's much more manageable for a leader to make tough decisions if she can argue that she's got no choice but is being thrown into the briar patch.
- *Know that some fights aren't worth winning:* Some victories are so costly that they're ultimately not worth it. Those are the fights not worth fighting.
- *Know that some fights are worth losing:* Sometimes it's worth fighting a fight even when you lose, as you've signaled to your friends that you'll stand by them and to your opponents that you won't be bullied.
- *Sometimes, cage-busters grind it out:* Cage-busters do what it takes to wear down their opponents and get the work done.

Make Policy Work for You

Policy is a marvelous tool when it comes to steering simpler behaviors, allowing leaders to minimize distractions and focus on the things that matter most.

- *Use policy to create leverage or save political capital:* Policy can be a way to get the upper hand in fights that could otherwise demand enormous time and energy. Policy can free leaders from having to nudge and nag, and depersonalize otherwise spirit-sapping interactions.
- *Take advantage of policy windows:* Popular or must-pass policies can create policy windows. Tight budgets offer another kind of policy window, making it possible to push changes that would be a tough sell in good times.

Preach Less, Listen More

Failure to recognize that people can sometimes honestly disagree about "the right thing to do for kids" undercuts our ability to identify problems and design solutions. Empathy is ultimately the difference between cage-busters who implode amidst endless battles and those who, studying their Sun-Tzu, win their battles *before they're fought.*

Focus on Solutions

When talking to your superiors or to policy makers, it's easy for leaders to get caught up in what they want or think they need. Instead, try to lead with empathy by asking yourself, "What problem does this listener need my help to solve?" Savvy cage-busters don't demand resources; they offer up solutions.

There Will Be Fighting

Schools and school systems are public institutions, and that means they sometimes involve fierce fights between people who disagree. It's frustrating, but a cage-buster can stack every deck and play every card, and sometimes it'll still come down to butting heads. When it does, you want to know that you've done everything in your power to shape the outcome. But you also need to be willing to stand in the fire.

The Virtuous Cycle

Cage-busters benefit from a virtuous cycle. Each win helps blast away impediments that stifle problem solving; forge a can-do culture; and make possible deep changes in pedagogy, instruction, and learning. Having won a victory creates new possibilities, breeds the confidence that comes with success, and marks you as a valuable ally.

CHAPTER 8: A WORLD WITHOUT BORDERS AND BOUNDARIES

Caged Leadership Leads to One-Size-Fits-All Policy

Cage-dwelling leadership frustrates policy makers and advocates, leading them to propose rules and policies in a scramble to force leaders' hands. The problem: because these solutions are intended to make reluctant leaders take action, they tend to be blunt and prescriptive. Policy is not designed to cater to top performers. It's a way to force minimal norms on laggards.

Cage-Busters Get a Seat at the Table

Cage-busters can help correct for policy overreach. By showing that schooling can be improved and refashioned by practitioners, cage-busters can temper the sense that reformers need to "fix" schools through policy.

John Henry Is *Not* a Role Model

- *Remember that your time has value:* It's crazy for cage-busters to stop thinking "more, better" and then to treat their own time as disposable.
- *Ask "How important is this?":* If you're not sure what can go, get in the habit of asking, "Is this the best use of my time?"
- *Cage-bust your calendar:* If you're a principal and can't find enough time for things you deem important, the problem isn't lack of time— it's how you're *using* your time.

- *It's a marathon, not a sprint:* Remember the cage-busting credo and work smarter, not harder.

Don't Be Consumed by Rolling the Boulder

Leadership is even more exhausting when your personality and charm are the main drivers of improvement; when everything rests on your ability to woo people and win them over. Yet, there are tricks that can help you manage these burdens.

- *Challenge your assumptions:* It's easy for leaders, their staff, their hired consultants, and well-wishers to tune out the "noise" and only talk to those who agree with them. The successful cage-buster does everything possible to combat that temptation.
- *Manage up:* Be sure to work with your boss(es) in a manner that respects both their responsibilities and your time.
- *Find a trusted partner:* Find a colleague, collaborator, or consigliere who can anticipate challenges, identify opportunities, and help you think about smarter and better ways to solve problems.
- *Make policy work for you:* A cage-buster sees policy not as an alternative to culture building but as a way to police performance, minimize personal friction, and redirect time and energy toward what matters most.
- *Stack the deck for a common culture:* The big advantage of agreeing on aims, mission, and norms is that leaders can spend more time leading for achievement and less time pleading for agreement.

You Can't Do It Alone

Few schools or systems have the tools or the muscle to succeed all by themselves. You need to seek out and cultivate allies and partners.

- *Tap your network:* Aggressively work your external networks to create a deep bench of talent.
- *Look to community resources:* Find ways to connect with resources in your community, whether those are attorneys in local law firms or professionals willing to mentor and tutor kids.
- *Engage nimble partners:* When they so desire, business and philanthropy can move with an alacrity that public systems cannot.

- *Embrace the unique capabilities of outsiders:* Business and community groups, for instance, can launch initiatives or say things that system leaders cannot.
- *Leverage outside political muscle:* Advocacy groups and the business community can provide the support and muscle needed to drive transformation.
- *Tap philanthropy for crucial funds:* In addition to dollars, philanthropic support can bring glamour and glitz, build local enthusiasm, inspire other funders, and garner national interest.
- *Marshal legal resources:* Philanthropy and community allies can offer crucial support by connecting attorneys and law students with schools and districts in need of assistance.

Eight Cage-Busting Tips to Remember

- *Don't just punch the pillow:* Changing cultures without addressing the underlying policies and rules doesn't yield lasting change.
- *Act as if ye have faith:* Take a few bold but smart initial steps, show some success, and then take larger and larger steps. Don't move so hesitantly that you're asking permission every time you move.
- *Measure progress right:* Track useful markers of progress—not just test scores.
- *Carry a pocket constitution:* If you're a principal or superintendent or you work with one and your copy of the CBA isn't dog-eared, you're not fully prepared to lead.
- *"Innovation" is a four-letter word:* Cage-busters don't do "innovation." They solve problems.
- *Don't imagine that best practices alone will get it done:* "Best practice" reform only addresses boulder-rolling techniques. Transformative improvement requires flattening the mountain.
- *Remember that money is only the easiest way to solve a problem:* Money is just a shortcut for those unable to marshal the skill or will to free up the time and dollars they need in other ways.
- *Use incentives to complement cultural change:* Rewards and recognition can help changes get going downhill.

APPENDIX B

In Every Problem Lies an Opportunity

Cage-busters relentlessly search for problems because they illuminate opportunities for improvement. Trouble is, many leaders have been so bombarded with platitudes that they can have difficulty deciding where to start. Here's a warm-up drill that can help get ideas flowing.

As you read the questions below, don't worry about your priorities. For the moment, just start throwing out possibilities. This is just a chance to start thinking differently about problem solving.

- What percentage of your fourth-graders should be proficient at reading? What percentage really are? Is there a gap? If so, that's a problem.
- How many minutes a day should your best fourth-grade teacher be teaching reading? How many minutes a day is that person teaching reading? If those aren't the same number, that's a problem.
- Is there any reading intervention that you've seen, heard of, or read about that you think would improve student learning? Are you using it? If not, we've just identified a problem.
- What percentage of your kids should be enrolled in AP classes? What percentage are? Is there a gap?
- What percentage of your kids should be getting college credit on AP exams? What percent are? Is there a gap?

- What percentage of your students would you like to see mastering a second language? What percentage are doing so? Is there a gap?
- What percentage of instructional time do you think should be spent on student discipline? What percentage is actually being spent on discipline? Is there a gap? (A precious few folks have any idea of how to answer this one—and that points to a pretty gaping problem in its own right.)
- What percentage of your parents do you think should be in the school each month talking to teachers? What percentage actually are?
- How much time each day do faculty and administrators spend on data entry? How much time should they be spending?
- How fast does HR interview and make an offer to attractive candidates? How long should that process take?
- What percentage of kids are getting 5s on the AP Biology or AP Calculus BC exams?
- What percentage of parents are volunteering on campus?

Keep in mind, the disparities are *failures*. This is true no matter how well you are doing. This is *you* declaring that you have *failed to meet your own aims*. Cage-busting can help with that.

APPENDIX C

When to Keep Programs— or Cut 'Em

One of the trickiest things for any leader is to cut loose an existing program. Doing something about the potpourri of questionably effective programs requires the will to act and the conviction that limited resources need to be spent as wisely as possible. Fortunately, in moving forward on that count, Heliodoro Sanchez, the chief of staff in Texas's Ector County School District, has devised a simple "Strategic Abandonment Tool" that can help staff determine which programs are worth maintaining, of questionable value, or ought to be discontinued.

Criteria	Founded (3)	Questionable (2)	Unacceptable (1)
1. The program maintains a clear metric for measurement.	The program's outcome or service rendered is defined, and a clear metric exists to measure the program on a frequent basis.	The program's outcome or service rendered is defined, but no metric to measure the program is available.	The program's outcome or service rendered is unclear and undefined.
2. The program's outcome or service rendered is measured frequently and without undue bias.	The program's outcome or service rendered is measured in an impartial manner on a regular (weekly or monthly) basis or better.	The program's outcome or service rendered is measured regularly (weekly or monthly), but bias cannot be eliminated from the evaluation.	The program's outcome or service rendered is not measured regularly or no documentation exists to verify accountability.

Criteria	Founded (3)	Questionable (2)	Unacceptable (1)
3. The program supports teaching and learning.	The program directly supports teaching and learning through enhancing the educational setting, and faculty and staff can directly identify the tie between the program and instruction.	The tie between teaching and learning and the program is related upon evaluation. However, faculty and staff are not aware of the program's direct impact on instruction.	There is no close tie or a very limited tie between the program and teaching and learning.
4. The program's service cannot be replicated otherwise.	The program's service is specialized and must be provided by specially trained personnel to ensure effectiveness, efficiency, and safety to all the program serves.	The program's service can be provided by alternative personnel, but training and specialized supervision are necessary for the service to be conducted in an efficient, effective, and safe manner.	The program's service can be provided by alternative personnel with little to minimal training within the scope of the workday or workweek.
5. The program's cost-to-service ratio is defensible.	The program's total cost divided by those it serves is better than what is found in similar districts without compromising the service it provides.	The program's total cost divided by those it serves is within normal estimations of districts with similar programs.	The program's total cost divided by those it serves is beyond the norm for similar programs in similar districts or industries.
6. The program is operated by the best personnel.	The program is administered by personnel who are familiar with the program and who stay within timelines and budget the vast majority of the budget year.	The program is administered by personnel who are familiar with the program, yet personnel struggle to meet timelines or stay within budget.	The program is administered by personnel who are unfamiliar with the program or unable to execute the program's intent within acceptable timelines and costs.

Criteria	Founded (3)	Questionable (2)	Unacceptable (1)
7. The program is necessary for the successful functioning of the district.	Should the program not operate, the district would feel an immediate impact and the service would have to begin immediately for the district to maintain successful operation.	Should the program not operate, the district would function at a less-than-acceptable level, and the service would have to begin anew within a month of its discontinuance.	Should the program not operate, the district would continue to function with minimal disruption within a semester or an academic year.
8. The loss of the program would cause a problem with a significant stakeholder group.	A significant stakeholder group depends on this program, and loss would create a loss of faith.	A significant stakeholder group is interested in this program but loss would not create a loss of faith.	No significant stakeholder group is invested in this program.
Total Score = _____	19–24 = Founded	15–18 = Questionable	14 or below = Unacceptable
Program Evaluator:	Program Evaluated:	Date:	

1. Heliodoro Sanchez, *Strategic Abandonment Tool* (Houston: Center for Reform of School Systems, 2012), http://www.crss.org/tl_files/Documents/Strategic%20Abandonment%20Tool.pdf.

Six Acronyms to Help Keep Things Straight

We've covered a lot of ground, I know. So, it can be useful to remember a half-dozen key acronyms just to help keep everything straight.

RTB: Remember, the whole point of cage-busting is to let you lead so that you're not spending all your time *rolling the boulder.* Leaders have higher and better uses for their time, and the point of cage-busting is to free you up to focus on what's most important.

INMM: One of the most common complaints by caged leaders who are busy rolling the boulder is *I need more money.* The assumption that only more money can drive improvement is a hallmark of caged leadership.

TMT: The belief that, because some immensely talented principal can deliver results, the bars of the cage don't matter, is *the MacGyver Trap.* Just because MacGyver can build a chainsaw from scotch tape and Q-tips doesn't mean that we should expect that everyone can. This is a case where optimism can eventually become a pathology.

OMTOMP: Too much activity in schooling amounts to one more burden that people are supposed to obligingly take on, out of the sheer goodness of their heart. It means the reward for good work and long hours is often . . . more work. This leads to *one more thing on my plate* syndrome and it's a recipe for alienated staff and exhausted leaders who spend all their time RTB.

GGD: Escaping OMTOMP syndrome requires that leaders *get going downhill.* Rather than struggling uphill behind that boulder, the aim is to alter rules and policies so that you're working your way downhill.

WPAYS: The key to everything a cage-buster does is the mantra *"What problem are you solving?"* When you stay focused on identifying problems and finding smart ways to solve them, improvement happens. The amazing thing is that, if you solve enough problems, you're an innovator and a transformer without ever intending to be.

Notes

Preface

1. R. Dale Ballou, *Teacher Contracts in Massachusetts* (Boston: Pioneer Institute for Public Policy Research, 2000), viii.
2. Mitch Price, *Are Charter School Unions Worth the Bargain?* (Seattle: University of Washington, Center on Reinventing Public Education, 2011), 3.
3. Arthur Levine, *Educating School Leaders* (Washington, DC: The Education Schools Project, 2005), 12.

Chapter 1

1. Mike Judge [director], *Office Space* (Los Angeles: Twentieth Century Fox Film Corporation, 1999).
2. Elissa Gootman and David M. Herszenhorn, "Getting Smaller to Improve the Big Picture," *New York Times*, May 3, 2005, http://www.nytimes.com/2005/05/03/nyregion/03small.html.
3. Frederick M. Hess, *Common Sense School Reform* (New York: Palgrave Macmillan, 2004); Frederick M. Hess, *Education Unbound: The Promise and Practice of Greenfield Schooling* (Alexandria, VA: ASCD, 2010).
4. Unless otherwise noted, quotations in this book are from interviews conducted by the author and/or research assistant Whitney Downs between September 2011 and June 2012.
5. Walter Isaacson, *Steve Jobs* (New York: Simon & Schuster, 2012), 118.
6. Ibid, 565.
7. Kyle Wind, "New Kingston High Principal Coming Home to Challenge," *Daily Freeman*, July 22, 2011, http://www.dailyfreeman.com/articles/2011/07/22/news/doc4e28d9c654c30734105534.txt.
8. Thomas J. Sergiovanni, *Leadership for the Schoolhouse* (San Francisco: Jossey-Bass, 1996), xiv.
9. Ibid.
10. Richard F. Elmore, *School Reform from the Inside Out: Policy, Practice, and Performance* (Cambridge, MA: Harvard Education Press, 2004), 43.
11. Donald G. Hackmann and Martha M. McCarthy, *At a Crossroads: The Educational Leadership Professoriate in the 21st Century* (Charlotte: Information Age Publishing, 2011), 99.
12. Elmore, *School Reform from the Inside Out*, 47.13. Ibid., 58.

247

14. Wayne K. Hoy and Cecil G. Miskel, *Educational Administration: Theory, Research, and Practice*, 7th ed. (New York: McGraw-Hill, 2005), 206–207.

15. Ibid.

16. Andy Hargreaves and Dean Fink, *Sustainable Leadership* (San Francisco: Jossey-Bass, 2006), 27.

17. Ibid., 19.

18. Elizabeth A. City, *Resourceful Leadership: Tradeoffs and Tough Decisions on the Road to School Improvement* (Cambridge, MA: Harvard Education Press, 2008), 3.

19. Michael Fullan, *What's Worth Fighting for in the Principalship?* 2nd ed. (New York: Teachers College Press; Ontario, Ontario Principals' Council, 2008), vii.

20. Ibid., 18.

21. Ibid., 51.

22. Ibid., 54–55.

23. Searches in this section were performed in May 2012 using the in-text search feature on Amazon.com.

24. Ben Levin, *How to Change 5000 Schools: A Practical and Positive Approach for Leading Change at Every Level* (Cambridge, MA: Harvard Education Press, 2008), 119–120.

25. Ibid., 120.

26. Ibid., 130.

27. Jean Johnson, "The Principal's Priority 1," *Educational Leadership* 66, no. 1 (September 2008), http://www.ascd.org/publications/educational-leadership/sept08/vol66/num01/The-Principal's-Priority-1.aspx.

28. Eileen Lai Horng, Daniel Klasik, and Susanna Loeb, *Principal Time-Use and School Effectiveness* (Washington, DC: Urban Institute, 2009).

29. Thelbert L. Drake and William H. Roe, *The Principalship*, 6th ed. (Upper Saddle River, NJ: Merrill Prentice Hall, 2003), 185.

30. Michael Fullan and Andy Hargreaves, *What's Worth Fighting for in Your School?* (New York: Teachers College Press, 1996), 87.

31. David F. Labaree, *The Trouble with Ed Schools* (New Haven, CT: Yale University Press, 2006), 146–147.

32. Ellwood P. Cubberley, *Public School Administration: A Statement of the Fundamental Principles Underlying the Organization and Administration of Public Schools* (Boston: Houghton Mifflin Company, 1916), 338.

33. Frederick M. Hess, *The Same Thing Over and Over: How School Reformers Get Stuck in Yesterday's Ideas* (Cambridge, MA: Harvard University Press, 2010), chapter 5.

34. Diane Ravitch, *The Death and Life of the Great American School System* (New York: Basic Books, 2011), 47; Fenwick W. English, "The 10 Most Wanted Enemies of American Public Education's School Leadership," *UCEA Review* 51, no. 3 (Fall 2010).

35. Hess, *The Same Thing Over and Over*, xiii.

36. Kowalski et al., *The American School Superintendent Survey: 2010 Decennial Study* (Lanham, MD: Rowman & Littlefield Education; Arlington, VA: The American Association of School Administrators, 2011), 24.

37. Arthur Levine estimates that 88 percent of principals have studied in education schools. Arthur Levine, *Educating School Leaders* (Washington, DC: The Education Schools Project, 2005), 12.

38. See Kowalski et al., *The American School Superintendent Survey*, 31.

39. Kowalski et al., *The American School Superintendent Survey*.

40. Steve Farkas, Jean Johnson, and Ann Duffet, *Rolling Up Their Sleeves: Superintendents and Principals Talk About What's Needed to Fix Public Schools* (New York: Public Agenda, 2003), 39.

41. Frederick M. Hess and Andrew P. Kelly, "Learning to Lead? What Gets Taught in Principal Preparation Programs," *Teachers College Record* 109, no. 1 (January 2007): 244–274.

42. Frederick M. Hess, "Cages of Their Own Design," *Educational Leadership* 67, no. 2 (October 2009): 28–33.

43. Hess and Kelly, "Learning to Lead?"

44. Donald G. Hackmann and Martha M. McCarthy, *At a Crossroads: The Educational Leadership Professoriate in the 21st Century* (Charlotte, NC: Information Age Publishing, 2011), 205, 290.

45. Jean Johnson, Ana Maria Arumi, and Amber Ott, *Reality Check 2006*, Issue No. 4 (New York: Public Agenda, 2006), 18.

46. Ibid.

47. Frederick M. Hess and Olivia Meeks, *School Boards Circa 2010: Governance in the Accountability Era* (Washington, DC: National School Boards Association, Thomas B. Fordham Institute, and Iowa School Boards Foundation, 2010), http://www.asbj.com/MainMenu Category/Archive/2011/March/0311pdfs/School-Boards-in-the-Accountability-Era.aspx.

48. Noelle M. Ellerson, *Surviving a Thousand Cuts: America's Public Schools and the Recession* (Arlington, VA: American Association of School Administrators, 2010).

49. Rick Ginsberg and Karen D. Multon, "Leading Through a Fiscal Nightmare: The Impact on Principals and Superintendents," *Phi Delta Kappan* 92, no. 8 (May 2011): 42–47.

50. 2011 Association of School Business Officials Membership Survey, made available by ASBO in May 2010.

51. Kowalski et al., *The American School Superintendent Survey*, 127.

52. Ibid., 80.

53. New Leaders for New Schools, *Evaluating Principals: Balancing Accountability with Professional Growth* (New York: New Leaders for New Schools, 2010), 11.

Chapter 2

1. Frederick M. Hess, "Cages of Their Own Design," *Educational Leadership* 67, no. 2 (October 2009): 28–33.

2. Corinne Gregory, comment on "The Culture of 'Can't' in American Schools, *Rick Hess Straight Up Blog*, entry May 11, 2012, http://blogs.edweek.org/edweek/rick_hess_straight_up/2012/05/the_culture_of_cant_in_american_schools.html.

3. Frederick M. Hess and Coby Loup, *The Leadership Limbo: Teacher Labor Agreements in America's Fifty Largest School Districts* (Washington, DC: The Thomas B. Fordham Institute, 2008).

4. R. Dale Ballou, *Teacher Contracts in Massachusetts* (Boston: Pioneer Institute for Public Policy Research, 2000), vii.

5. Mitch Price, *Teacher Union Contracts and High School Reform* (Seattle: University of Washington, Center for Reinventing Public Education, 2009), 7, 24.

6. Henry M. Levin, "Why Is This So Difficult?" in *Educational Entrepreneurship: Realities, Challenges, Possibilities*, ed. Frederick M. Hess (Cambridge, MA: Harvard Education Press, 2006).

7. Ibid., 173.

8. Ibid., 174.

9. Xiu Cravens, Ellen Goldring, and Roberto V. Penaloza, *Research Brief: Leadership Practices and School Choice*, (Nashville, TN: National Center on School Choice, 2011), 3, http://www.vanderbilt.edu/schoolchoice/documents/briefs/brief_leadership_practices.pdf.

10. Ibid., 1.

11. The foreword to the report, written by the Thomas B. Fordham Institute's Chester E. Finn, Jr., and Amber M. Winkler, reads, "The typical charter school in America today lacks the autonomy it needs to succeed—a degree of freedom we equate with a grade *no better* than a C+—once federal, state, and authorizer impositions are considered. Dana Brinson and Jacob Rosch, *Charter School Autonomy: A Half-Broken Promise* (Washington, DC: The Thomas B. Fordham Institute, 2010), 5.

12. Kathleen Porter-Magee, *The Xerox Effect: Why Replication in Education Falls Short*, Thomas B. Fordham Institute, September 7, 2012, http://www.edexcellence.net/commentary/education-gadfly-daily/common-core-watch/2012/the-xerox-effect.html.

13. Ben Levin, *How to Change 5000 Schools* (Cambridge, MA: Harvard Education Press, 2008), 133.

14. Steven Brill, *Class Warfare: Inside the Fight to Fix America's Schools* (New York: Simon & Schuster, 2011), 100.

15. Tim Waters, Robert J. Marzano, and Brian McNulty, "Balanced Leadership: What 30 Years of Research Tells Us About the Effect of Leadership on Student Achievement" (working paper, Mid-continent Research for Education and Learning, Denver, CO, 2003), http://www.mcrel.org/pdf/.LeadershipOrganizationDevelopment/5031RR_BalancedLeadership.pdf.

16. Shunryu Suzuki and Trudy Dixon, *Zen Mind, Beginner's Mind* (New York: Walker/Weatherhill, 1970), 1.

17. Robert Pirsig, *Zen and the Art of Motorcycle Maintenance* (New York: Bantam, 1975), 250–258.

18. Hess, "Cages of Their Own Design," 28–33.

19. Barbara Davison, "Management Span of Control: How Wide Is Too Wide?" *Journal of Business Strategy* 24, no. 4 (2003): 22–29.

20. Ibid.

21. Frederick M. Hess and Whitney Downs, *Partnership Is a Two-Way Street: What It Takes for Business to Help Drive School Reform* (Washington, DC: U.S. Chamber of Commerce, Institute for a Competitive Workforce: 2011), 15.

22. Steven R. Weisman, ed., *Daniel Patrick Moynihan: A Portrait in Letters of an American Visionary* (New York: Public Affairs, 2010), 3.

23. Brill, *Class Warfare*.

Chapter 3

1. Nathan Levenson, "First-Person Tale of Cost-Cutting Success," in *Stretching the School Dollar: How Schools and Districts Can Save Money While Serving Students Best*, ed. Frederick M. Hess and Eric Osberg (Cambridge, MA: Harvard Education Press, 2010), 256–257.

2. Ibid., 257.

3. Arthur M. Schlesinger, *The Coming of the New Deal, 1933-1935* (New York: First Mariner Books, 2003), 131.

4. Warren Bennis, Daniel Goleman, and James O'Toole, *Transparency: How Leaders Create a Culture of Candor* (San Francisco: Jossey-Bass, 2008), 28.

5. Ron Underwood [director], *City Slickers* (Los Angeles: New Line Home Video, 1991).

6. For further discussion of these shifting trends, see Frederick M. Hess, *The Same Thing Over and Over: How School Reformers Get Stuck in Yesterday's Ideas* (Cambridge, MA: Harvard Education Press, 2012), 15–26.

7. Organization for Economic Co-operation and Development, *Education at a Glance 2011: Highlights* (Paris: OECD Publishing, 2011), 77.

8. See "Redesigning Schools to Reach Every Student with Excellent Teachers: Summary of Teacher Career Paths," available at http://opportunityculture.org/wp-content/uploads/2012/05/Summary_of_Teacher_Career_Paths-Public_Impact.pdf.

9. Jean Johnson, *You Can't Do It Alone: A Communications and Engagement Manual for School Leaders Committed to Reform* (Lanham, MD: Rowman & Littlefield Education, 2012), 46.

10. Bennett Miller [director], *Moneyball* (Culver City, CA: Columbia Pictures, 2011.)

11. Ibid.

12. Frederick M. Hess, "The New Stupid," *Educational Leadership* 66, no. 4 (December 2008/January 2009).

13. George W. Bohrnstedt and Brian M. Stecher, Class Size Reduction in California: Early Evaluation Findings, 1996–1998. (Palo Alto, CA: American Institutes for Research, 1999.)

14. Jason Reid, "'Moneyball' is Compelling, but Leaves Out Much of the Real Story," *Washington Post*, October 11, 2011, http://www.washingtonpost.com/sports/nationals/moneyball-is-compelling-but-leaves-out-much-of-the-real-story/2011/10/11/gIQAMA1cdL_story.html.

15. You might think it was the FBI that got Capone. But, for those of you interested in history, turns out it was the Internal Revenue Service.

16. James H. Lytle, *Working For Kids: Education Leadership as Inquiry and Invention* (Lanham, MD: Rowman & Littlefield, 2010), 52–53.

Chapter 4

1. Layoff procedures for public school districts are governed by the Pennsylvania Public School Code of 1949. Section 1125.1 of the Pennsylvania Public School Code of 1949, entitled "Persons to be suspended," states: "Professional employees shall be suspended under section 1124 (related to causes for suspension) in inverse order of seniority within the school entity of current employment." West Virginia Code Chapter 18A, Article 4 (j), "School Personnel," reads, "Whenever a county board is required to reduce the number of professional personnel in its employment, the employee with the least amount of seniority shall be properly notified and released from employment pursuant to the provisions of section two, article two of this chapter," available online at http://www.legis.state.wv.us/WV-CODE/Code.cfm?chap=18a&art=4#04.

2. Mitch Price, *Teacher Union Contracts and High School Reform* (Seattle: University of Washington, Center on Reinventing Public Education, 2009).

3. Agreement between Board of Directors Little Rock School District and the Little Rock Classroom Teachers Association: 2009-2012, Article 29, Section M, http://www.nctq.org/docs/Little_Rock_CBA_09-12_searchable.pdf.

4. Montana Board of Public Education, *Montana School Accreditation Standards and Procedures Manual*, section 10.55.712, http://opi.mt.gov/pdf/Accred/05AccredManual.pdf.

5. Yatsko, et al., *Tinkering Toward Transformation: A Look at Federal School Improvement Grant Implementation* (Seattle: University of Washington, Center on Reinventing Public Education, 2012), http://www.crpe.org/cs/crpe/view/csr_pubs/495.

6. Melissa Junge and Sheara Krvaric, *Federal Compliance Works Against Education Policy Goals* (Washington, DC: American Enterprise Institute, 2011), 4, available online at http://www. aei.org/article/education/k-12/federal-compliance-works-against-education-policy-goals/.

7. For more, see the Single Audit Act, OMB Circular A-133, and its accompanying annual Compliance Supplement at OMB, "Circulars," www.whitehouse.gov/omb/circulars_default.

8. Melissa Junge and Sheara Krvaric, "The Supplement Not Supplant Conundrum," *Rick Hess Straight Up Blog*, October 25, 2011, http://blogs.edweek.org/edweek/rick_hess_straight_ up/2011/10/the_supplement_not_supplant_conundrum.html.

9. U.S. Department of Education, Office of Inspector General, *Philadelphia School District's Controls Over Federal Expenditures: Final Audit Report* (Philadelphia: U.S. Department of Education, Office of Inspector General, 2010), http://www2.ed.gov/about/offices/list/oig/ auditreports/fy2010/a03h0010.pdf.

10. Melissa Junge and Sheara Krvaric, "The Compliance Culture in Education," *Rick Hess Straight Up Blog*, October 24, 2011, http://blogs.edweek.org/edweek/rick_hess_straight_ up/2011/10/the_compliance_culture_in_education.html.

11. Ibid.

12. Cynthia G. Brown, et al., *State Education Agencies as Agents of Change* (Washington, DC: Center for American Progress; American Enterprise Institute, 2011), 7.

13. Center on Education Policy, "Educational Architects: Do State Education Agencies Have the Tools Necessary to Implement NCLB?" (Washington, DC: Center on Education Policy, 2007).

14. Brown, et al., *State Education Agencies as Agents of Change*.

15. Center on Education Policy, "Educational Architects," 7.

16. Ibid.

17. Elizabeth Shaw, "Implementing Teacher Quality 2.0 in States and Districts" (working paper presented at the American Enterprise Institute, Washington, DC, 2012), 8.

18. Michael Fullan, *What's Worth Fighting For in the Principalship?* (New York: Teachers College Press, 1997); Michael Fullan, *Change Leader: Learning to Do What Matters Most* (San Francisco: Jossey-Bass/Wiley, 2011); Richard Dufour and Robert J. Marzano, *Leaders of Learning: How District, School, and Classroom Leaders Improve Student Achievement* (Bloomington, IN: Solution Tree Press, 2011); Robert J. Marzano, Timothy Waters, and Brian A. McNulty, *School Leadership That Works: From Research to Results* (Alexandria, VA: Association for Supervision and Curriculum Development, 2005); Todd Whitaker, *What Great Principals Do Differently: Fifteen Things That Matter Most* (Larchmont, NY: Eye on Education, 2003); Thomas J. Sergiovanni, *Strengthening the Heartbeat: Leading and Learning Together in Schools* (San Francisco: Jossey-Bass, 2005); Terrence E. Deal and Kent D. Peterson, *Shaping School Culture: The Heart of Leadership* (San Francisco: Jossey-Bass Publishers, 1999); Lee G. Bolman and Terrence E. Deal, *Leading with Soul: An Uncommon Journey of Spirit* (San Francisco: Jossey-Bass Publishers, 1995); Lee G. Bolman and Terrence E. Deal, *Reframing the Path to School Leadership: A Guide for Teachers and Principals* (Thousand Oaks, CA: Corwin Press, 2002). Searches in this section were performed in September 2012 using the in-text search feature on Amazon.com and Google books.

19. For more, see Terry M. Moe, *Special Interest: Teachers Unions and America's Public Schools* (Washington, DC: Brookings Institution Press, 2011).

20. As University of Minnesota law professor Stephen F. Befort notes, "Clearly, public employers in jurisdictions that do not permit collective bargaining have full unilateral authority to set and alter terms and conditions of employment." See Befort, "Unilateral Alteration of Public

Sector Collective Bargaining Agreements and the Contract Clause," *Buffalo Law Review* 59, no. 1 (January 2011).

21. Emily Cohen, Kate Walsh, and RiShawn Biddle, *Invisible Ink in Collective Bargaining: Why Key Issues Are Not Addressed* (Washington, DC: National Council on Teacher Quality, 2008), 4.

22. Author tabulations of data available from National Council on Teacher Quality's Teacher Rules, Roles and Rights (TR3) Database, "State Bargaining Rules Interactive Map," http://www.nctq.org/tr3/scope/#interactiveMap.

23. Data compiled from ibid.

24. Data compiled from ibid.

25. Howard L. Fuller, George A. Mitchell, and Michael E. Hartmann, "The Milwaukee Public Schools' Teacher Union Contract: Its History, Content, and Impact on Education," Report 97-1 (Milwaukee, WI: Institute for the Transformation of Learning, Marquette University, October 1997), 4.

26. *OKCPS American Federation of Teachers Collective Bargaining Agreement: 2011–2012*, "Section 2: Bulletin Boards," 11, available online at http://www.nctq.org/docs/Oklahoma_City_CBA_Teachers_FY_2011_2012.pdf.

27. *Contract Between Eau Claire Area School District Board of Education and Eau Claire Association of Educators, July 1, 2009–June 30, 2011*, Article V, Section B (1), 27, http://www.ecasd.k12.wi.us/central_office/HR_/ECAE%20Contract%202009-2011%20Signed.PDF.

28. *Agreement Between the Board of Education of the City of Chicago and the Chicago Teachers Union, Local No. 1, American Federation of Teachers, AFL-CIO July 1, 2007–July 30, 2012*, Section 44-17, http://www.nctq.org/docs/4.pdf.

29. *Contract Between The School Board of Orange County, Florida and the Orange County Classroom Teachers Association 2010-2011*, Article VI, Section V, p. 28–29, http://www.nctq.org/docs/CTA_Contract_2010-11_FINAL_updated.pdf.

30. Price, *Teacher Union Contracts and High School Reform*, 6.

31. Ibid., 20.

32. Frederick M. Hess and Coby Loup, *The Leadership Limbo: Teacher Labor Agreements in America's Fifty Largest School Districts* (Washington, DC: The Thomas B. Fordham Institute, 2008), 21.

33. Price, *Teacher Union Contracts and High School Reform*, 6.

34. *Negotiated Agreement Between the Clark County School District and the Clark County Education Association 2011–2012*, Article 40-1, http://www.nctq.org/docs/Clark_County_10_11_CCEA_Agreement_updated.pdf.

35. Author's calculations based on the National Council on Teacher Quality's Teacher Rules, Roles, and Rights (TR3) database as of September 2012. Board policy–type agreements were excluded from the count. Database available online at http://www.nctq.org/tr3/home.jsp.

36. For example, Missouri Revised Statute 295.090 reads, "Such [collective bargaining] agreement shall be presumed to continue in force and effect from year to year after the date fixed for its original termination unless either or both parties thereto inform the other, in writing, of the specific changes desired to be made therein," http://www.moga.mo.gov/statutes/C200-299/2950000090.HTM. The Revised Code of Washington [State] (41.56.123) states, "After the termination date of a collective bargaining agreement, all of the terms and conditions specified in the collective bargaining agreement shall remain in effect until the effective date of a subsequent agreement, not to exceed one year from the termination date stated in the agreement."

37. Jordan Weissmann, "Why Does Buffalo Pay for Its Teachers to Have Plastic Surgery?" *The Atlantic*, January 18, 2012, http://www.theatlantic.com/business/archive/2012/01/why-does-buffalo-pay-for-its-teachers-to-have-plastic-surgery/251533/.

38. Ibid.

39. Frederick M. Hess and Andrew P. Kelly, "Scapegoat, Albatross, or What?" in *Collective Bargaining in Education: Negotiating Change in Today's Schools*, ed. Jane Hannaway and Andrew J. Rotherham (Cambridge, MA: Harvard Education Press, 2006), 85–86.

40. Data based on contracts and board policies available on the National Council on Teacher Quality's Teacher Rules, Roles and Rights (TR3) Database in September 2012. Alert readers will notice that NCTQ reports on ninety districts here, but only eighty a few pages back when we discussed evergreen provisions. That is because this tally also includes ten districts that do not have formal collective bargaining agreements.

41. In 2012, Massachusetts passed SB 2197, An Act Promoting Excellence in Public Schools, which requires the selection criteria for layoffs to be based on certifications, merit, and ability, including results from educator evaluations. However, this law will not go into effect until the 2016–2017 school year.

42. Stand for Children Massachusetts, *2011 End of Year Report* (Waltham, MA: Stand for Children, 2012), 13, http://stand.org/sites/default/files/Massachusetts/SFC_MA_EOY_2011_122811_final.pdf?j=2610&e=mperfetuo@hotmail.com&l=54_HTML&u=51384&mid=1064472&jb=0.

43. Michigan Compiled Law 423.215 reads: "(3) Collective bargaining between a public school employer and a bargaining representative of its employees shall not include any of the following subjects . . . (f) The decision of whether or not to contract with a third party for 1 or more noninstructional support services." http://www.legislature.mi.gov/(S(1drp2e55ueqepobzks4csh55))/mileg.aspx?page=GetObject&objectname=mcl-423-215.

44. Mackinac Center Legal Foundation, *Jurrians v. Kent ISD*, http://www.mackinac.org/14187.

45. Ibid.

46. Ibid.

47. Michigan Compiled Laws 423.215(3)(b).

48. "School District of the City of Detroit Settlement Proposal to the Detroit Federation of Teachers, Local 231," p. 28, http://www.nctq.org/docs/Detroit_09-12_7626.PDF.

49. Kansas Statutes Annotated (2009), chapter 72: Schools, Article 54: Teachers' Contracts. K.S.A. 72-5413(I)(3) reads: "Matters which relate to the duration of the school term, and specifically to consideration and determination by a board of education of the question of the development and adoption of a policy to provide for a school term consisting of school hours, are not included within the meaning of terms and conditions of professional service and are not subject to professional negotiation," available online at http://kansasstatutes.lesterama.org/Chapter_72/Article_54/72-5413.html.

50. *Wichita Public Schools Teachers Employment Agreement 2011–2012*, pp. 4–5, http://www.nctq.org/docs/Wichita_CBA_TEA-Final_2011-2012.pdf.

51. *Negotiated Agreement Between the Teachers Association of Anne Arundel County and Board of Education of Anne Arundel County*, July 1, 2009-June 30, 2013, p. 46, http://www.nctq.org/docs/Anne_Arundel_agreement_TAAAC.pdf.

52. *Negotiated Agreement Between Prince George's County Educators' Association and the Board of Education of Prince George's County*, July 1, 2007 to June 30, 2009, p. 7, http://www.nctq.org/docs/PG_County_updated.pdf. NCTQ confirms that the contract is still valid for 2012.

53. For example, subsection A of section 25 of the collective bargaining agreement between the Silver Falls School District and the Silver Falls Education Association reads: "Savings Clause. Should any Article, Clause or Provision of this Agreement be declared illegal by final judgment of a court of competent jurisdiction, such invalidation of such Article, Clause or Provision shall not invalidate the remaining portions thereof, and such remaining portions shall remain in force and effect for the duration of this Agreement. Should any Article, Clause or Provision of this Agreement be declared illegal, the parties may enter into discussion for a replacement Article, Clause or Provision upon written request by either party." See *Silver Falls School District and Silver Falls Education Association/Mid-Valley Bargaining Council Collective Bargaining Agreement July 1, 2007–June 30, 2013*, p. 40, http://silverfalls. orvsd.org/content/sfea-licensed-collective-bargaining-agreement-20072013.

54. Theodore J. Kowalski, et al., *The American School Superintendent: 2010 Decennial Study* (Lanham, MD: Rowman & Littlefield Education; The American Association of School Administrators, 2011), 48.

Chapter 5

1. Robert Penn Warren, *All the King's Men*, 2nd ed. (New York: Mariner Books, 1996), 137.

2. Frederick M. Hess and Lance D. Fusarelli, "Superintendents and the Law: Cages of Their Own Design?" in *From Schoolhouse to Courthouse: The Judiciary's Role in American Education*, ed. Joshua M. Dunn and Martin R. West (Washington, DC: Brookings Institution Press, 2009), 52.

3. All searches in this paragraph were conducted in September 2012, using the in-text search function of the magazine archives, available by subscription from the SAGE journals database.

4. Hess and Fusarelli, "Superintendents and the Law," 64.

5. National School Boards Association, "Council of School Attorneys," http://www.nsba.org/cosa.

6. Perry Zirkel, "The Myth of Teacher Tenure," *The Answer Sheet*, Washington Post, July 13, 2010, http://voices.washingtonpost.com/answer-sheet/teachers/the-myth-of-teacher-tenure.html.

7. Author's calculation based on data drawn from Maryland Negotiation Service's state board opinions database, "Scope of Bargaining Cases," http://www.mnsmd.org/state-board-opinions/scope-of-bargaining-cases/.

8. Author's calculation drawn from Minnesota's Bureau of Mediation Services' database of representation decisions, http://www.bms.state.mn.us/representation_decisions.html. Representation decisions determine whether an individual or class of workers are covered by collective bargaining agreements or which bargaining unit individuals/groups shall be placed into. Decisions resulting in a split finding or no finding were excluded ($n = 8$).

9. Author's calculations based on Iowa Public Employment Relations Board's database of decisions, http://www.iowaperb.org/search.aspx?db=iowa-state-arbs&sm=c_d. The decisions analyzed were limited to grievances by K–12 professional staff as of June 1, 2012. Decisions resulting in a split finding or no finding were excluded ($n = 3$).

10. Author's calculation drawn from Washington state's Public Employment Relations Commission's database of decisions from January 2000–May 2012, http://www.perc.wa.gov/hearings-decisions.asp. Decisions that resulted in a remand or split were not included. Actions arising out of a single incident (appeals, etc.) were counted individually. The decisions were found by performing a search of all decisions that contained the phrase *school district*, then double-checked against a numerical list of all PERC decisions.

11. The ABA Standing Committee on Pro Bono and Public Service, *Supporting Justice II: A Report on the Pro Bono Work of America's Lawyers* (Chicago: American Bar Association, 2009).

12. Data compiled from *U.S. News and World Report* Law School Rankings, 2009.

13. Peter D. Hart Research Associates, Inc., *Teaching as a Second Career* (Princeton, NJ: The Woodrow Wilson National Fellowship Foundation, 2008), http://www.woodrow.org/images/pdf/policy/Teaching2ndCareer_0908.pdf.

14. All content in this sidebar adapted from Mitch Price, *Teacher Union Contracts and High School Reform* (Seattle: University of Washington, Center on Reinventing Public Education, 2009), 13–20.

15. A.C.A. [Arkansas Code] § 6-17-1502, "Teacher Fair Dismissal Act" (2011), http://law.justia.com/codes/arkansas/2010/title-6/subtitle-2/chapter-17/subchapter-15/6-17-1502/.

16. Kyle Zinth, *Maximum P–12 Class-Size Policies* (Denver, CO: Education Commission of the States, 2009), http://www.ecs.org/clearinghouse/82/91/8291.pdf.

17. See Standard 2.1, "Class Size/Assigned Enrollments," Missouri Department of Elementary and Secondary Education, *Standards and Indicators Manual: Accreditation Standards for Public School Districts in Missouri*, 9, http://dese.mo.gov/divimprove/sia/msip/Fourth%20Cycle%20Standards%20and%20Indicators.pdf.

18. N.M.S.A. [New Mexico Statutes] 10-7E-6(c), "Public Employee Bargaining Act," http://www.pelrb.state.nm.us/pdf/statutes/10-7E-6_Rights%20of%20public%20employers.pdf.

19. Author's calculations based on the National Council on Teacher Quality's Teacher Rules, Roles, and Rights (TR3) database as of September 2012. Board policy–type agreements were excluded from the count. Database available online at http://www.nctq.org/tr3/home.jsp.

20. Maine Statute Title 20-A, pt. 6, ch. 502, 13016, 1, http://www.mainelegislature.org/legis/statutes/20-a/title20-Asec13012.html.

21. Nebraska Revised Statutes, 79-824 (3), http://nebraskalegislature.gov/laws/statutes.php?statute=79-824.

22. Ohio Revised Code 118.06(f), "Local Fiscal Emergencies," http://codes.ohio.gov/orc/118.

23. Jonathon V. Holtzman, K. Scott Dickey, and Steve Cikes, "Declarations of Fiscal Emergency: A Resurging Option for Public Entities Attempting to Deal with the Current Economic Climate," *Public Law Journal* 34, no. 1 (Winter 2011): 11–13.

24. Brian Meyer, "Buffalo Teachers, Workers Lose Bid for Pay Step Hikes During Wage Freeze," *Buffalo News*, March 29, 2011, http://www.buffalonews.com/city/schools/article379261.ece.

25. Jim Collins, *Good to Great: Why Some Companies Make the Leap . . . and Others Don't* (New York: HarperBusiness, 2001), 13.

26. TNTP, *The Irreplaceables: Understanding the Real Retention Crisis in America's Urban Schools*, 2012, p. 5.

27. Frederick M. Hess and Andrew P. Kelly, "Learning to Lead: What Gets Taught in Principal-Preparation Programs," *Teachers College Record* 109, no. 1 (2007): 259.

28. Michael Fullan and Andy Hargreaves, *What's Worth Fighting for in Your School?* (New York: Teachers College Press, 1996), 87.

29. Daniel Weisberg, et al., *The Widget Effect: Our National Failure to Acknowledge and Act on Differences in Teacher Effectiveness* (Brooklyn, NY: The New Teacher Project, 2009).

30. Frederick M. Hess and Whitney Downs, *Partnership Is a Two Way Street: What It Takes for Business to Help Drive School Reform* (Washington, DC: The US Chamber of Commerce, Institute for a Competitive Workforce, 2011), 29.

31. Elena Silva, et al., *Waiting to Be Won Over: Teachers Speak on the Profession, Unions, and Reform* (Washington, DC: Education Sector, 2008), http://www.educationsector.org/publications/waiting-be-won-over.

32. Warren, *All the King's Men*, 136.

Chapter 6

1. Nathan Levenson, *Smarter Budgets, Smarter Schools: How to Survive and Thrive in Tight Times* (Cambridge, MA: Harvard Education Press, 2012).

2. Salary and benefit data compiled from National Center for Education Statistics, Common Core of Data "Build a Table," column "Finance Distribution Ratios [District]," El-Sec expenditures 2008–2009. Across all districts, salary comprises 57 percent of expenditures, while benefits make up 19 percent. See http://nces.ed.gov/ccd/bat/selectcolumns.asp; Michael Podgursky, "Teacher Compensation and Collective Bargaining," in *Handbook of the Economics of Education* 3 (2011): 279–313.

3. Rick Ginsberg and Karen D. Multon, "Leading Through a Fiscal Nightmare: The Impact on Principals and Superintendents," *Phi Delta Kappan* 92, no. 8 (May 2011): 42–47.

4. "In Crisis, Opportunity for Obama," *Wall Street Journal*, November 21, 2008, http://online.wsj.com/article/SB122721278056345271.html.

5. Ulrich Boser, *Return on Educational Investment: A District-by-District Evaluation of U.S. Educational Productivity* (Washington, DC: Center for American Progress, 2011), 26.

6. Ibid.

7. For more on unit costs, see Marguerite Roza, "Now Is a Great Time to Consider the Per-Unit Cost of Everything in Education," in *Stretching the School Dollar: How Schools and Districts Can Save Money While Serving Students Best*, ed. Frederick M. Hess and Eric Osberg (Cambridge, MA: Harvard Education Press, 2010).

8. June Kronholz, "What's Happening in the States," in Hess and Osberg, *Stretching the School Dollar*, 53.

9. Jill Corcoran et al., "Large-Scale Cost Cutting and Reorganizing," in Hess and Osberg, *Stretching the School Dollar*, 200.

10. Michael Casserly, "Managing for Results in America's Great City Schools," in Hess and Osberg, *Stretching the School Dollar*, 105.

11. Ibid., 107.

12. Steven F. Wilson, "The Efficient Use of Teachers," in Hess and Osberg, *Stretching the School Dollar*, 134–135.

13. John E. Chubb, "More Productive Schools Through Online Learning," in Hess and Osberg, *Stretching the School Dollar*, 174–175.

14. Heather Staker and Michael B. Horn, *Classifying K–12 Blended Learning* (Mountain View, CA: Innosight Institute, 2012), http://www.innosightinstitute.org/innosight/wp-content/uploads/2012/05/Classifying-K-12-blended-learning2.pdf.

15. All information in sidebar excerpted from John Fensterwald, "Inside Rocketship, One of the Best-Known Blended Learning Initiatives in the Country," *Scholastic Administrator* (Spring 2012).

16. Theodore R. Sizer, *Horace's School: Redesigning the American High School* (New York: Mariner Books, 1997).

17. Albert Shanker, "The Revolution That Is Overdue," speech delivered at Herbert H. Lehman College, City University of New York, 1987, https://www.reuther.wayne.edu/files/64.28.pdf.

18. Dan Goldhaber, Michael DeArmond, and Scott DeBurgomaster. "Teacher Attitudes about Compensation Reform." *Urban Institute* Working Paper 50. June 2012.

19. Doug Lemov, *Teach Like a Champion* (San Francisco: Jossey-Bass, 2010), 186.

20. *2009–2011 Terms and Conditions of Professional Employment Agreement Between the Saint Paul Board of Education and the Saint Paul Federation of Teachers*, Section 7, "Experimental Programs," p. 45, http://www.nctq.org/docs/St_Paul_Agreement_teacher.pdf.

21. Author calculation based on data available on NCTQ's Teacher Rules, Roles and Rights (TR3) Database as of June 2012. For more, see http://www.nctq.org/tr3/search.jsp.

22. Peter D. Hart Research Associates, Inc., *Teaching as a Second Career* (Princeton, NJ: The Woodrow Wilson National Fellowship Foundation, 2008), http://www.woodrow.org/images/pdf/policy/Teaching2ndCareer_0908.pdf.

23. James H. Lytle, *Working For Kids: Education Leadership as Inquiry and Invention* (Lanham, MD: Rowman & Littlefield, 2010), 51.

24. Ibid., 49.

25. Frederick M. Hess and Olivia Meeks, *School Boards Circa 2010* (Alexandria, VA: National School Boards Association; Thomas B. Fordham Institute; Iowa School Boards Foundation, 2010), http://www.asbj.com/MainMenuCategory/Archive/2011/March/0311pdfs/School-Boards-in-the-Accountability-Era.aspx.

26. Karen Hawley Miles et al., "Inside the Black Box of School District Spending on Professional Development: Lessons from Comparing Five Urban Districts," *Journal of Education Finance* 30, no. 1 (Summer 2004): 1–24.

27. Knowledge Delivery Systems, *Professional Development: Quality, Impact and Outcomes: What is your Professional Development Return on Investment (ROI)?* (New York: KDS, n.d.), 6.

28. K.S. Yoon et al., *Reviewing the Evidence on How Teacher Professional Development Affects Student Achievement* (Washington, DC: US Department of Education, Institute of Education Science, National Center for Education Evaluation and Regional Assistance, Regional Laboratory Southwest, 2007), http://ies.ed.gov/ncee/edlabs/regions/southwest/pdf/REL_2007033.pdf.

29. Linda Darling-Hammond et al., *Professional Learning in the Learning Profession: A Status Report on Teacher Development in the United States and Abroad* (Palo Alto, CA: Stanford University, National Staff Development Council, 2009), 5.

30. Anthony Rebora, "Empowering Teachers," *Education Week*, March 1, 2008, 32–33, http://www.edweek.org/tsb/articles/2008/03/01/02hirsch.h01.html.

31. Roxanna Elden, "Five Words and Phrases that Sound Different to Teachers," *Rick Hess Straight Up blog*, http://blogs.edweek.org/edweek/rick_hess_straight_up/2011/01/five_words_and_phrases_that_sound_different_to_teachers.html.

32. Jennifer King Rice, "Investing in Human Capital through Teacher Professional Development," in *Creating a New Teaching Profession*, ed. Daniel D. Goldhaber and Jane Hannaway (Washington, DC: Urban Institute, 2009), 240.

33. Darling-Hammond et al., *Professional Learning in the Learning Profession*, 2.

34. Nathan Levenson, *Something Has Got to Change: Rethinking Special Education* (Washington, DC: The American Enterprise Institute, 2011), 1.

35. The Individuals with Disabilities Education Act (IDEA) reads, "(F) Assurance of a Free Appropriate Public Education—Nothing in this paragraph shall be construed . . . (i) to authorize a State educational agency or local educational agency to establish a limit on what may be spent on the education of a child with a disability" (118 Stat. 2670).

36. Nathan Levenson, "First-Person Tale of Cost-Cutting Success," in Hess and Osberg, *Stretching the School Dollar*, 253–254.

37. Ibid., 255–256.

38. William Howell, Martin West, and Paul E. Peterson, "Reform Agenda Gains Strength," *Education Next* 13, no. 1 (2013).

39. Jean Johnson, *You Can't Do It Alone: A Communications and Engagement Manual for School Leaders Committed to Reform* (Lanham, MD: Rowman & Littlefield Education, 2012), 86.

Chapter 7

1. All material in sidebar adapted from Saj-Nicole Joni and Damon Beyer, *The Right Fight: How Great Leaders Use Healthy Conflict to Drive Performance, Innovation, and Value* (New York: HarperBusiness, 2010), 75–107.

2. Nathan Levenson, "First-Person Tale of Cost-Cutting Success," in *Stretching the School Dollar: How Schools and Districts Can Save Money While Serving Students Best*, ed. Frederick M. Hess and Eric Osberg (Cambridge, MA: Harvard Education Press, 2010), 240.

3. Ibid., 241.

4. Frederick M. Hess and Lance D. Fusarelli, "Superintendents and the Law: Cages of Their Own Design?" in *From Schoolhouse to Courthouse: The Judiciary's Role in American Education*, ed. Joshua M. Dunn and Martin R. West (Washington, DC: Brookings Institution Press, 2009), 60.

5. Ericka Mellon, "HISD Toughens Teacher Evaluations," *Houston Chronicle*, May 12, 2011, http://www.chron.com/news/houston-texas/article/HISD-toughens-teacher-evaluations-1690576.php.

6. Richard Lee Colvin, *Tilting at Windmills: San Diego, Education Reform, and America's Future* (Cambridge, MA: Harvard Education Press, 2013).

7. John W. Kingdon, *Agendas, Alternatives, and Public Policies*, 2nd ed. (London: Longman, 2002), 88.

8. Ann Doss Helms, "School Layoff Report Confounds," *Charlotte Observer*, September 4, 2011, http://www.charlotteobserver.com/2011/09/04/2577941/school-layoffs-report-confounds.html; Math and reading reports are available at National Assessment of Educational Progress, "The Nation's Report Card," http://nationsreportcard.gov/.

9. Material in this sidebar adapted from Frederick M. Hess and Whitney Downs, *Partnership Is a Two-Way Street: What It Takes for Business to Help Drive School Reform* (Washington, DC: U.S. Chamber of Commerce, Institute for a Competitive Workforce, 2011), 45.

Chapter 8

1. Daniel Weisberg, et al., *The Widget Effect: Our National Failure to Acknowledge and Act on Differences in Teacher Effectiveness* (Brooklyn, NY: The New Teacher Project, 2009).

2. Kimberly Strassel, "Scott Walker's Education Victory," *Wall Street Journal*, A13, June 7, 2012, http://online.wsj.com/article/SB10001424052702303753904577452862561051838.html.

3. Michael Halberstam, *The Wanting of Levine* (New York: Berkley Publishing Group, 1979), 198–199.

4. Alan D. Bersin and Richard Lee Colvin, *Tilting the Windmills: Politics, Urban School Reform and America's Race to Improve Public Education.* (Washington, DC: Rowman and Littlefield, forthcoming).

5. Citizen Schools, "About," n.d., http://www.citizenschools.org/about/.

6. Frederick M. Hess and Whitney Downs, *Partnership Is a Two-Way Street: What it Takes for Business to Help Drive School Reform* (Washington, DC: US Chamber of Commerce, Institute for a Competitive Workforce: 2011), 18.

7. Ibid., 27.

8. Frederick M. Hess and Olivia Meeks, *School Boards Circa 2010: Governance in the Accountability Era* (Washington, DC: National School Boards Association, Thomas B. Fordham Institute, and Iowa School Boards Foundation, 2010), 67, http://www.asbj.com/MainMenu Category/Archive/2011/March/0311pdfs/School-Boards-in-the-Accountability-Era.aspx.

9. Lynn Jenkins and Donald R. McAdams, "Philanthropy and Urban School District Reform: Lessons from Charlotte, Houston, and San Diego," in *With the Best of Intentions: How Philanthropy Is Reshaping K–12 Education*, ed. Frederick M. Hess (Cambridge, MA: Harvard Education Press, 2005), 153–154.

10. Richard E. Neustadt, *Presidential Power and the Modern Presidents* (1960; rept. New York: Free Press, 1991), 37.

11. Anthony McDonnell and Patrick Gunnigle, "Performance Management," in *Human Resource Management: A Critical Approach*, ed. David G. Collings and Geoffrey Wood (New York: Routledge, 2009), 189.

12. Jim Collins and Jerry I. Porras, *Built to Last: Successful Habits of Visionary Companies* (New York: HarperCollins, 1994), 186–187.

13. Jim Collins, *Good to Great: Why Some Companies Make the Leap . . . and Others Don't* (New York: Harper Business, 2001); Clayton Christensen, *The Innovator's Dilemma* (Boston: Harvard Business School Press, 1997); Daniel Goleman, *Working with Emotional Intelligence* (New York: Bantam Books, 2000); Peter Drucker, *Innovation and Entrepreneurship* (New York: Harper Business, 2006).

14. Doug Liman [director], *Swingers* (Los Angeles: Miramax Films, 1996).

Appendix A

1. Mitch Price, "Teacher Union Contracts and High School Reform" (Seattle: University of Washington, Center for Reinventing Public Education, 2009); R. Dale Ballou, *Teacher Contracts in Massachusetts* (Boston: Pioneer Institute for Public Policy Research, 2000), vii; Frederick M. Hess and Coby Loup, *The Leadership Limbo: Teacher Labor Agreements in America's Fifty Largest School Districts* (Washington, DC: The Thomas B. Fordham Institute, 2008).

Acknowledgments

I owe an enormous debt of gratitude to those who provided the advice, insight, and support that made this volume possible. First and foremost, I'd like to offer my heartfelt thanks to the marvelously talented and übercompetent Whitney Downs for her essential role in researching and crafting this book. Whitney was more collaborator than research assistant, as she conducted interviews, plowed through statutes and collective bargaining agreements, tallied anything you could imagine, and offered incisive feedback and whip-smart editing. After Whitney departed for the rigors of law school, I was fortunate to be able to rely on the remarkable talents of her successor, Allie Kimmel. Allie played a crucial role in editing, updating, and improving the manuscript you hold in your hands. I also want to thank their colleagues Lauren Aronson, KC Deane, Taryn Hochleitner, Daniel Lautzenheiser, Michael McShane, and Jenna Talbot for their invaluable support. I also owe a vote of thanks to interns Sarah Baran, Rebecca Chubb, Luke Sullivan, and Eric Eagon.

This is a book informed by the wisdom of those doing the work in the field. Whitney and I spoke with well over a hundred school and system leaders, attorneys, reformers, and observers in the course of this project. Those extended conversations complemented and built on thousands of discussions I've had over the years, with a wealth of smart and busy educators, advocates, and civic leaders. I owe a special thanks to all those who made time to talk to us or to help us along the way. I want to offer a special

261

word of appreciation to LeAnn Buntrock, Jim Guthrie, Kaya Henderson, Melissa Junge, Sheara Krvaric, Don McAdams, Cathy Mincberg, Mitch Price, Carolyn Sattin-Bajaj, and Heather Zavadsky for their gracious willingness to peruse the manuscript and provide insights, suggestions, and valuable feedback.

As ever, I owe the deepest appreciation to the American Enterprise Institute and its president, Arthur Brooks, for the remarkable support and backing that allow me to pursue this work. I also want to thank the terrific team at Harvard Education Press, especially HEP publisher Douglas Clayton for his faith in this project and his unwavering friendship, as well as Chris Leonesio, Laura Madden, Rose Ann Miller, and Sumita Mukherji. I've had the privilege of publishing with HEP for nearly a decade, and it's a relationship that just keeps getting better.

Once again, I'm indebted to my wife, Joleen, for her love, understanding, and droll editorial support, things that helped carry me through this project as they have through so many others. And I owe big thanks to my loving dad, Milton Hess, for years of insights and anecdotes that helped me better understand organizations, leadership, and management.

Finally, it goes without saying that any mistakes, flaws, or inanities are mine and mine alone, while most of the good stuff was inevitably cribbed from one of the aforementioned. But such is life.

About the Author

An educator, political scientist and author, Frederick M. Hess studies K–12 and higher education issues. His books include *The Same Thing Over and Over, Education Unbound, Common Sense School Reform, Revolution at the Margins*, and *Spinning Wheels*. He is also the host of the popular *Education Week* blog, *Rick Hess Straight Up*. Rick's work has appeared in scholarly and popular outlets such as *Teachers College Record, Harvard Education Review, Social Science Quarterly, Urban Affairs Review, American Politics Quarterly, The Chronicle of Higher Education, Phi Delta Kappan, Educational Leadership, U.S. News & World Report, National Affairs, National Review,* the *Atlantic,* the *Washington Post,* and the *New York Times.* He has edited widely cited volumes on education philanthropy, school costs and productivity, and the impact of education research and No Child Left Behind. Rick serves as executive editor of *Education Next,* as lead faculty member for the Rice Education Entrepreneurship Program, and on the review boards for the Broad Prize in Urban Education and the Broad Prize for Public School Charters, as well as on the boards of directors of the National Association of Charter School Authorizers, 4.0 SCHOOLS, and the American Board for the Certification of Teaching Excellence. A former high school social studies teacher, Rick has taught at the University of Virginia, the University of Pennsylvania, Georgetown University, Rice University, and Harvard University. He holds an MA and PhD in government from Harvard University as well as an MEd in teaching and curriculum.

Index